You Are a Priority, Not an Option:

Processing grief, understanding love, and staying kind – especially to yourself – unconventional yet warm wisdom from a therapist who has been through it all

Soledad Jewell

Copyright © 2025 Soledad Jewell

Dedication

I would like to dedicate this book to my mum and dad, my children, Jordan, Amy, and Daniella.

About the Author

My name is Soledad Jewell. I am Spanish and originally from the beautiful island of Gran Canaria. My journey into becoming a therapist began in 2007, but the story behind why I chose this path is deeply personal and rooted in my own struggles. At the age of 40, I found myself questioning everything about my life. Why was I repeatedly making mistakes? Why was I attracting the wrong people? Why was I facing difficulties that seemed never-ending? These questions haunted me, and I knew I needed answers—not just for my clients, but for myself.

When I first started my counselling course, I clearly remember a moment that made a lasting impression on me. My teacher asked why I had chosen to take this course. I wasn't ready to admit that it was for my own healing, so I joked, "I like to tell people what to do." Everyone laughed, including my teacher. Then he gently corrected me, saying that counselling wasn't about telling people what to do, but about truly listening. At that moment, I thought, "Oh dear, that's going to be difficult for me." But despite my doubts, I pushed forward. My marriage had recently broken down, and I was left to care for three young children. I was determined not to repeat the mistakes of my parents and to create a better life for myself and my family.

This book was born out of a period of profound change and loss. My father passed away on September 5th, and the grief brought with it a flood of emotions and thoughts. Over the years, I had supported many people through my work, but I realized I hadn't truly cared for myself. It was time to turn the attention inward and to find my own direction. Around that time, I reconnected with a friend back in Gran Canaria, a teacher who shared his own struggles and a passion for books. His encouragement inspired me to start writing—to channel my experiences, my pain, and the lessons I've learned into words.

Writing became my refuge. It was like water slowly breaking against rocks, each article and piece helping me to release some of the pain and fears I had carried for so long. I poured my heart into these writings, hoping that if someone else read them, they might find comfort and guidance, especially those who cannot afford therapy or don't know where to turn.

As the anniversary of my father's passing approaches, I find myself still shedding tears—not just for him, but for the father I never truly had. Through this process, I have found moments of laughter, healing, and hope. I want to share these with you. Life is incredibly difficult at times, and many of us want to give up. But I want you to know that it's possible to keep going, to find light in the darkness, and to create your own path to healing.

This book is for you—whether you are struggling right now or simply looking for a reminder that you are not alone. I hope you read it, laugh, reflect, and find a little hope along the way. And if you can, share it with others who might be going through their own battles.

Thank you for taking the time to read my story. I will continue writing because this has become a powerful way for me to release my pain and fears, and to transform them into something meaningful. Writing has given me a new voice and a new purpose, and I hope it can do the same for you.

Table of Contents

Chapter 1: Understanding Yourself 1

    Self-Acceptance 4

    Building Self-Esteem: Finding Beauty Within 10

    Shame 14

    Self-Criticism and the Impact of Others' Words 17

    Wearing a Mask? 20

    Be Yourself: The Key to Building Genuine Relationships 23

    Impostor Syndrome 26

Chapter 2: Setting Boundaries and Finding Your Voice 29

    There It Is 29

    You Don't Have to Change Who You Are to Protect Yourself 31

    You are a Priority, Not an Option 34

    What Truly Belongs to You 35

    Living Beyond Expectations 38

Chapter 3: Personal Growth and Life Lessons 41

    Overcoming Fear 41

    Have You Achieved Your Dreams 44

    Do You Think People Can Change 45

    Life Teaches Us – And It's Never a Waste 46

    You Matter - And That's Not Up for Debate 48

    The Past – and How It Can Hold Us Back from Moving Forward 50

    Let It Go: Embracing Change and Moving Forward 52

Living with Hope 55

Ego Stages 57

Chapter 4: Health and Wellness 59

You Are What You Eat 59

The Major Illnesses of the 21st Century 61

Why Do We Drink or Use Substances That Harm Us 64

What Is Anxiety 68

Understanding Cancer and Its Impact 70

Chapter 5: Social Awareness and Kindness 74

Why Are We So Cruel—to Others and to Ourselves 74

Supporting Neurodivergent Students - Understanding Their Challenges 77

Why Animals Hold a Special Place in Our Hearts 80

Chapter 6: Understanding Love 84

Understanding What is Love 86

Can You Love Yourself This Way? 88

Quality in the Relationship versus Material Things in Life 89

Getting the Love You Deserve – Why Some Relationships Work and Others Don't 90

When the Romance Fades: Remembering Love and Choosing It Again 92

Love Doesn't Stop—But Effort Often Does 94

To the Ones Who Feel Invisible 94

Chapter 7: Finding and Building Healthy Relationships 96

Finding the Right Person 96

v

Recognising True Character 98
Building Healthy Relationships 101
The Power of Communication 104
Healing and Self-Awareness 106
Love at Every Stage of Life 109

Chapter 8: Relationship Challenges **112**
Power Dynamics and Control 112
Jealousy and Its Destructive Power 114
The Reality of Infidelity 117
When Relationships End: The Pain of Divorce 120
Rebuilding Trust 123
The Complexity of Truth and Lies 125

Chapter 9: Dating and Modern Romance **129**
The Reality of Mature Dating 129
Beyond Physical Appearance: Learning from Film 132
Confronting Gender Double Standards 134
Understanding Love Beyond Commercial Traditions 136

Chapter 10: Family Dynamics **140**
Dreams of Parenthood and Life's Deepest Desires 140
The Delicate Balance of Partnership and Parenthood 142
The Strength of Single Parents 145
Children Come First... Or Do They? 148
Understanding Our Earliest Bonds 150
Celebrating Motherhood 153

Honoring Fathers 156

Chapter 11: Life's Journey and Meaning 160

A Personal Introduction to the Journey 160

Confronting Life's Impermanence 162

Finding Happiness in the Present.. 166

The Art of Being Present 167

Creating Your Life Map.. 169

What Truly Matters 171

Chapter 12: Ageing and Life Transitions 174

The Happier Decade 174

Loneliness and Ageing Care 178

Loneliness... 183

Talking About Dying.. 189

Time 195

Chapter 13: Loss and Grief 198

Losing Someone You Love... 198

Grief Comes in Waves 202

Losing Both Parents... 206

Reflections After Christmas.. 210

Chapter 14: Mental Health and Healing 215

Mental Health Support.. 215

Understanding Attachment Theory 220

Attachment, Fame, and the Price of Success............................... 225

A Moment of Human Connection 229

Domestic Violence: A Call to Awareness and Action 233

Chapter 15: Social Commentary and Justice 241

Fighting for Home and Community 241

The Economics of Inequality 246

Learning Respect and Understanding 250

The Cost of Conflict 257

Chapter 16: Cultural Observations and Celebrations 262

Superstitions Reflection 262

Easter 2025 265

April Fools' Day 266

Stonehenge 268

Trust Yourself This Christmas 269

Happy New Year 2025! 271

Reflection on the New Year 273

Chapter 17: Life Philosophy and Final Thoughts 275

Judging Others and Judging Yourself 275

When You Finally Wake Up 279

The Truth About Love and Appearance 282

Final Thoughts 285

Chapter 1: Understanding Yourself

The journey to understanding yourself is perhaps the most important work you will ever do. It forms the foundation for every relationship you will have, every decision you will make, and ultimately, the life you will create. In this chapter, we explore the essential building blocks of self-awareness, self-acceptance, and authentic living.

Who is Soledad Jewell?

Let me introduce myself and share why I've been exploring these different aspects of human experience.

I was born on the beautiful island of Gran Canarias, surrounded by incredible places that I didn't fully appreciate until much later in life. When you're young, it's easy to take things for granted, not realizing their true value until years down the line. I left Gran Canarias on July 19, 1989. I was very young then, but I still vividly remember those days. During my school years, my English teachers often encouraged me to learn the language. I would respond confidently, saying, "I'll never need English. I don't plan to leave this wonderful country."

However, life had other plans for me. I eventually decided to leave Spain and start anew after facing several personal challenges. It was an opportunity to rebuild my life. I packed four suitcases, took £200, and left everything I knew behind.

New Beginnings

Leaving Gran Canarias was bittersweet. My mother was heartbroken, and my father, feeling a mix of guilt and regret, boarded the plane to see me off. It was an emotional moment I'll never forget.

Adjusting to life in a new country wasn't easy, especially with the language barrier. I began learning English by listening to the radio, watching TV, and constantly asking questions. Determined to improve, I attended college to learn grammar, something I had been quite lazy about during school.

Life took an unexpected turn when I met and married an Englishman. We had three children together, but after 16 years, our marriage ended in divorce. That chapter of my life taught me resilience and the importance of finding purpose. As a single parent, I realized I needed to create a better future for myself and my children.

I worked part-time, raised my kids, and pursued further education. It was during this time that I first heard the question: "Would you like to be a counsellor or therapist?" At first, I misunderstood the role, thinking it was about telling people what to do. In reality, it's about listening, supporting, and guiding individuals through their own challenges. This realization sparked a passion in me.

A Journey of Growth

In 2007, I began studying counselling and therapy, completing my formal education in 2011. Since then, I've taken numerous courses—some lasting a year, others six to eight months—always striving to improve my skills and deepen my understanding. My hard work paid off, and I was able to support my children as they pursued higher education. My son studied Biology, one of my twin daughters studied Criminology, and the other pursued Sports Science. Encouraging them to prioritize education and understand its value was one of my proudest achievements.

Why I Started Writing

I began writing during one of the most difficult times of my life. On the 3rd of February 2022, my beloved mum passed away. It was heartbreaking not being able to say goodbye to her. The last time I saw her was in the mortuary, and the pain of not holding her hand one last time or telling her how much I loved her stayed with me deeply. Even though I never got to say it in person, I believe she knew.

Then, in September 2024—just a day after my birthday—my father passed away. This loss brought out a different kind of pain. I cried not only for his death, but also for the relationship we never truly had. After he passed, I felt like an orphan. I felt very low and lost.

It was around Christmas that something shifted. I started writing. At first, it was about love and how I felt about it. But soon, writing became my way of coping. It felt like I was a volcano, releasing years of emotions—grief, love, anger, sadness—all pouring out as words. The more I wrote, the lighter I felt. It became a beautiful and healing habit.

To my surprise, people began reading my words and sharing how much they related to them. Their kind comments showed me that my writing wasn't just helping me—it was helping others too. That's when I discovered I had a passion I never knew about: writing to connect, to heal, and to support others through shared feelings.

Now, I tell everyone: writing is a powerful way to heal. It lets you express emotions you might not be able to say out loud. It gives you a voice when you feel lost.

Through my work—especially with patients—I've seen how loneliness affects so many people. And I understand it, because I've lived it. I hope that through my writing, you find comfort, reflection, and maybe even a bit of laughter. If my words bring you even a small moment of peace, then I've done what I set out to do.

Self-Acceptance

Many people struggle with being themselves and constantly try to please others. Do you recognise this feeling? Have you ever felt that you are never good enough and that you must prioritise pleasing others over your own happiness?

Self-Acceptance and Having a Title

In a world that often values people based on their titles, it's easy to get caught up in defining ourselves by our roles—whether in our careers, education, or social status. But true self-worth comes from within, not from a title or recognition given by others.

Self-acceptance means embracing who you are, with or without a title. It's about understanding your value as a person, independent of external labels. Titles may bring respect in society, but real respect is earned through character, integrity, and how we treat others.

Ask yourself: Do you feel worthy only because of a title, or do you recognise your worth beyond it? True confidence comes from knowing that you are enough, just as you are.

Think about your relationship with yourself. How many times have you put others first just to be accepted by society, family, or friends? How often have you worried about stigma and what others might say if you didn't conform to their expectations? No matter what you do, people will always have something to say, and sometimes, you may feel left out of certain groups because of it.

Titles—how important are they when it comes to gaining respect and being valued? Without a title, how do people perceive you? Do titles make someone more or less valuable? What do you think?

One thing I have noticed is how much respect people give to those with titles, such as Doctor, Nurse, Teacher, or even Prime Minister. We often claim that everyone should be treated equally, yet those with prestigious titles seem to receive more benefits compared to people working in cleaning services or retail. This raises an interesting question: Do we truly treat everyone equally, or do we unconsciously place more value on those with certain job titles? I'd love to hear your thoughts on this.

Recently, someone I met online pointed out that, as a therapist, I share a lot about my personal life but not much about my relationships. They asked if I was hiding something. My first thought was that this person didn't know me at all. Yes, you can read about some of my experiences, but does that mean you truly know me? Do you know yourself fully?

This interaction made me reflect on how people perceive others based on limited information. Instead of focusing on the support and guidance I aim to provide, this person was more interested in analyzing me. But like everyone else, I have my own challenges. Despite my qualifications and title, my life is far from perfect.

I remember listening to a doctor talk about the dangers of smoking, only to later see the same doctor smoking at a bar. My initial reaction was to think he wasn't practising what he preached. But after reflecting, I realised that he, too, is human and has his own struggles. This made me understand that none of us have all the answers, and we certainly aren't perfect—we are simply doing our best.

Yes, I like to share parts of my life, but this isn't about self-esteem or insecurities. It's about being human. Despite my education and profession, I face family issues just like everyone else. I respect professionals who choose to keep their personal lives private, and that's their choice. However, I sometimes feel like I'm in a "damned if I do, damned if I don't" situation. Whether you keep your life private or not, people will always talk. Let them—because they are the ones wasting their energy and time with other people.

For me, writing is something I genuinely enjoy. More importantly, I do it to support others. If sharing my experiences can help even one person feel less alone, then it's worth it.

History has shown us examples of influential figures like Nelson Mandela, Eva Perón, and even members of royalty who have used their voices to speak on important issues. We often say we have freedom of speech, yet when someone expresses their feelings or discusses meaningful topics, it is not always well-received. This is a reminder to be mindful—both in how we share our thoughts and in how we respond to others who do.

While I share information through writing, my primary role in face-to-face work is to listen to my patients and support them to the best of my ability. My job is not to talk about myself or my life. When I need support, I seek my own therapy—because, at some point, we all do. We are not robots; we are human.

Value yourself—not based on a title, but for who you are. Respect should come from the person, not from what they present to the world.

I set clear boundaries with my patients, and they understand that if we cross paths in public, I will not stop for a casual chat out of respect for their confidentiality. The only time I would disclose confidential information is if there is an imminent risk to my patients.

The most important aspect of my work in mental health is ensuring that my patients feel truly heard. I listen attentively, summarise what they share, and reassure them that I fully understand them. I want to make this clear to everyone.

Finally, whether in relationships with family, friends, or colleagues, ask yourself: How often do you prioritise pleasing others over staying true to yourself?

Building on this foundation of self-acceptance, let's explore what it means to truly respect yourself in all areas of your life.

Building Self-Esteem: Finding Beauty Within

Let me share some thoughts about mental health and why so many people struggle with their well-being. My intention is not to disclose confidential information but to offer insights from the work I do with my patients every day.

As I've mentioned before, many mental health challenges stem from early attachment experiences, which can significantly impact adulthood, making it difficult to make the right choices in life. Think about the last time you wished you had chosen the right job, the right friends, or made better decisions that affected your well-being. Today, I want to discuss the importance of making the right choices for yourself and taking personal responsibility rather than shifting it onto others. Where in your life are you truly taking responsibility for your decisions instead of blaming others?

Many people carry emotional burdens that don't belong to them—thoughts, expectations, and judgments imposed by others. It can feel like carrying a heavy load on your shoulders, unable to put it down. Have you ever felt this way? What do you do when someone treats you with disrespect, lacks love and trust, and makes you feel like you are not good enough?

Do you express how you feel? Sometimes, no matter how much you try to change and show that you care, others keep holding you to your past, making it difficult to move forward. People often say, "You always talk about your past," but have they considered that some individuals are still grieving their experiences? Some behaviours, though not justified, stem from survival rather than malice. As a mental health professional, I see this struggle daily and work to help people navigate these challenges.

The truth is, no one is perfect. Yesterday, I watched a beautiful movie about an interracial couple in England who fell in love. Despite their deep connection, they faced countless obstacles due to societal prejudices. Many people projected their own negative thoughts onto them, trying to make them doubt their love. This happens all too often—we leave jobs, relationships, and opportunities because we listen to external negativity rather than believing in ourselves. If you truly want something, don't give up so easily. It takes effort, consistency, and self-validation.

Remember, anything worthwhile in life requires work. Don't allow others to define your worth or make you feel unworthy. No one can make you feel something unless you let them. You have the power to change your narrative. Surround yourself with positivity, even if it means setting boundaries with certain people, including family. Boundaries don't mean cutting people off completely; they mean protecting your well-being.

I hope this resonates with you, and I encourage you to reflect on where you can take responsibility for your choices and embrace the power to change.

How Do You Respect Yourself?

How do you communicate with others when you feel disrespected? Many people continue to give and give, avoiding confrontation because they want a peaceful life. But let's be honest—if you never speak up about how you feel, if you avoid difficult conversations like an adult and instead suppress your emotions like an angry child, then you allow others to dictate your feelings. You might even start believing it's your fault.

Even if someone else is right in a situation, we are all capable of change. Saying "sorry" should mean making a change, not just repeating the same behaviour. Otherwise, don't bother apologising.

When I work with my patients, I always remind them that therapy is not just about talking—it's about processing what's happening and taking action to make meaningful changes.

Yes, this can be hard to hear. Some people are simply not ready for change, and that's okay. Before change happens, we first need to understand our emotions and how they impact our lives. It's easy to criticise others, but have you ever stopped to consider why someone might be drinking too much, using drugs, or engaging in self-destructive behaviours? Blame won't help. If your family avoids talking about their struggles because they fear judgment, that is not your fault.

Start by respecting yourself. Listen to yourself. Validate your own feelings.

I know some people might be thinking, *It's not that easy.* I never said it was easy. What I'm saying is, if you want to change your life, you need to start with yourself. Once you do that, you'll know what steps to take.

Something I want to share—perhaps I've mentioned this before—is when I left my country, people told me I was crazy. I heard painful comments from the wrong people, but I never stopped believing in myself. I've faced many challenges, but I kept pushing forward. If one door closes, another will open.

Along my journey, I have met many people—some have taught me valuable lessons, while others have shown me what I do not want to carry with me. Both experiences have been learning opportunities.

Life is what you make of it—your choices, mindset, and actions shape your experiences. Even when things don't go as planned, you always have the power to learn, grow, and redefine your path.

Remember:
- RESPECT

- TRUST
- LOVE
- HONESTY
- CARING FOR YOURSELF

Even if others call you selfish for prioritising yourself, embrace it. Loving yourself is not selfish—it's necessary. Life is what you make. Congratulations on choosing you.

Self-respect forms the cornerstone of healthy self-esteem. Now let's explore how to build that foundation from within.

Building Self-Esteem: Finding Beauty Within

Self-esteem is an issue many people face, and it can be incredibly challenging. Often, those struggling with self-esteem feel unworthy or believe they must change themselves drastically to gain the approval or acceptance of others.

A thought that frequently crosses my mind is how this issue seems to affect women more than men. However, recently, societal norms have shifted, and more men are beginning to focus on their appearance and self-worth. In an effort to feel accepted, some people look to magazines, social media, and even undergo cosmetic procedures to match certain ideals.

Let me be clear: I deeply respect anyone's choice to make changes that help them feel good about themselves. However, I always remind my clients that true beauty comes from within. While outward appearances are visible, what truly matters is how we feel about ourselves inside. Many individuals—regardless of height, weight, or appearance—

exude confidence and happiness because they are content with who they are.

This inner contentment is rooted in self-esteem. Feeling good about yourself is not about looking perfect in the mirror, but about focusing on the positive things you tell yourself. It's about embracing who you are, regardless of societal expectations. What truly matters is how *you* see yourself, not how others perceive you.

Remember, physical appearances may change with time, but the essence of who you are—the kindness, strength, and uniqueness that define you—remains constant.

Signs of Healthy Self-Esteem

- Confidence in your abilities
- Acceptance of your flaws and mistakes
- Assertiveness in expressing your needs and opinions
- Feeling deserving of happiness and success

Signs of Low Self-Esteem

- Excessive self-criticism
- Difficulty accepting compliments
- Comparing yourself negatively to others
- Feeling unworthy or undeserving of good things

Ways to Improve Self-Esteem

Improving self-esteem is a gradual process that involves changing your mindset, habits, and behaviours. Here are some effective strategies:

Challenge Negative Self-Talk - Pay attention to the critical inner voice that says you're "not good enough" or "can't do anything right." Replace these thoughts with positive affirmations. For example, instead of saying, "I'll never succeed," say, "I'm learning and improving every day."

Focus on Your Strengths - List your achievements, talents, and qualities you admire about yourself. Celebrate small victories, and remind yourself of the value you bring to the table.

Practice Self-Compassion - Treat yourself with the same kindness and understanding you would offer to a friend. When you make a mistake, acknowledge it without judging yourself harshly.

Set Achievable Goals - Break your goals into smaller, manageable steps to build confidence as you progress. Accomplishing these goals, no matter how small, helps reinforce your belief in your abilities.

Surround Yourself with Positive People - Spend time with those who support and encourage you rather than those who bring you down. Avoid toxic relationships that make you doubt your worth.

Take Care of Your Physical Well-Being - Exercise regularly: Physical activity releases endorphins, which can improve mood and confidence. Eat a healthy diet and get enough sleep to maintain energy and focus.

Limit Comparisons - Social media can make it easy to compare yourself to others, often unfairly. Remind yourself that people often share only their highlight reels. Focus on your own journey and progress.

Learn New Skills - Engaging in activities that challenge you and help you grow can boost your confidence. Whether it's learning a new language, hobby, or skill, the sense of accomplishment strengthens your self-esteem.

Practice Gratitude - Reflect on things you're thankful for about yourself and your life. Keeping a gratitude journal can help shift your focus from what you lack to what you have.

Seek Professional Support if Needed - Therapy or counselling can help uncover underlying issues affecting your self-esteem. Cognitive Behavioural Therapy (CBT) is particularly effective in addressing negative thought patterns.

Many people struggle to value themselves and often feel like they have nothing to offer. They may experience feelings of inferiority, impostor syndrome, or a lack of self-love. Sometimes, they even internalise negative labels, saying things like, "I'm stupid," "I'm silly," or "I'm ugly," while also allowing others to reinforce these harmful beliefs.

It's important to look inward and practice kindness toward yourself. Start by replacing those negative labels with positive affirmations. Call yourself by kind and uplifting names, and you'll notice a profound change in your life.

Distance yourself from negativity and from those who try to bring you down. One simple yet powerful step is to tell yourself one positive thing every day. I encourage my patients to do this, and it can be a crucial step toward feeling better and improving your overall mindset.

Some young people have tragically ended their lives due to struggles with self-esteem and not feeling good about themselves. It's important to remind yourself: You are beautiful, not because of your appearance, but because of who you are as a person. Your value comes from your kindness, your unique qualities, and the way you make the world a better place. Never forget that.

Understanding the roots of shame is often essential to building genuine self-worth. Let's explore how shame affects our sense of self.

Shame

Have you ever wanted to do something meaningful in your life, but stopped yourself because you felt ashamed or because others made you feel that way?

Shame often begins in childhood. Think about how many times you may have heard, "Aren't you ashamed of yourself?"—perhaps for something that hurt someone else or went against what others believed was right. Over time, we start to carry this internal voice, a mix of guilt, embarrassment, and regret—like our conscience whispering, "That wasn't okay."

Ashamed is an emotion we feel when we believe we've done something wrong or when we fear being judged for being our true selves. Sometimes we end up hiding who we are or what we really want just to avoid upsetting others.

You might feel ashamed when:

- You hurt someone's feelings
- You fail at something and think you should have done better
- You get caught doing something you know is wrong

Can you relate to any of these?

For example, think about the moment when you had to tell someone you no longer loved them. It's painful—not because you want to hurt them, but because you know deep down it's the right thing to do. It takes courage to be honest in such moments, especially when the relationship no longer reflects the love and respect you know you deserve. Do you agree?

Other times, you may feel like a failure—at work, in your studies, or even in your relationships—because things didn't go as planned. Do you remember a time someone said to you, "Aren't you ashamed of yourself?" Maybe it was after a presentation, and instead of encouraging you, they criticised you. It can be deeply hurtful, especially when you've put in the effort and stepped out of your comfort zone to share something you're passionate about.

But when that happens, ask yourself: Is this really about me—or about them? Who is actually feeling ashamed—me or them?

I remember a time when I went out with friends, and the moment I heard a song I loved, I jumped up and started dancing. Some friends laughed and asked, "Aren't you embarrassed?" or "Have you been drinking?" I used to feel confused by those reactions. I'd respond, "No, I don't need alcohol to be myself or to enjoy the music."

Some might say people who express themselves openly are just showing off. I disagree. I believe those are the people who are confident and brave enough to be themselves, regardless of what others think.

And finally, I remember someone once saying:

"A real shame is stealing a chicken and then selling it back to the person you stole it from."

That made me laugh—it puts things into perspective, doesn't it?

Helping someone who feels ashamed takes empathy, patience, and care. Here are some gentle, meaningful ways to support them:

Listen Without Judgment - Let them speak. Don't interrupt. Don't rush to "fix" it. Just being there and listening with kindness can make a huge difference. Sometimes people just need space to express their shame without fear of being judged.

Say things like: "I'm here for you." "It's okay to feel like that." "Thank you for trusting me."

Remind Them They're Not Alone - Shame often makes people feel isolated, like they're the only one who messed up. Remind them that everyone makes mistakes, and feeling ashamed doesn't mean they're a bad person.

You can say: "Everyone struggles sometimes." "That doesn't define who you are."

Reinforce Their Worth - When someone feels ashamed, they often feel "less than" or unlovable. Gently help them reconnect with their value and remind them of their good qualities, strengths, or past growth.

Help Reframe the Story - Shame can trap people in a negative narrative about themselves. You can help them reframe the situation:

Instead of "I'm a failure," try "I made a mistake, but I'm learning." Instead of "I shouldn't have said that," try "I was being honest and brave."

Encourage Self-Compassion - Ask them how they would talk to a friend in the same situation. Most people are far kinder to others than to themselves. Help them turn that kindness inward.

Support Them in Taking a Step Forward - If they're ready, gently help them take a step toward healing—whether that's having a hard conversation, seeking forgiveness, writing their thoughts down, or just showing up the next day.

It's really hard, but it's important to accept that not every person is going to click with you—and that's okay! It doesn't mean you're a bad person. Some personalities just don't mesh, and that's a natural part of life.

You don't have to feel ashamed of being yourself or doing the things that make you happy. By accepting this, you can release some of the shame you may feel, because you'll realise that your feelings are completely normal. It's okay not to force connections or situations that don't feel right.

Have fun, and I encourage you to do the things that make you happy. Don't worry about what others think of you. Life is too short to focus on what others might expect. Just do what you believe makes you a better person—not what others want from you.

Sometimes the shame we carry stems from self-criticism that has become so ingrained we don't even notice it anymore.

Self-Criticism and the Impact of Others' Words

Others often make critical comments — and today, you might find yourself criticising your own worth. Have you ever wondered when was the first time you heard something negative about yourself? Can you remember how deeply it impacted you when others received praise, while your own efforts went unnoticed? How that moment quietly shaped your self-esteem?

Think back — maybe it was your best friend, or someone you trusted, who first made a hurtful comment. As children, we can't even see our own faces — we learn who we are through the eyes of others. When you started school, maybe you were the teacher's pet. Later in life, at work, you may have connected with someone while others made your professional journey difficult, projecting their own insecurities. They may have appeared confident, but deep down they were struggling, perhaps even more than you were.

Have you ever felt like that? Does this resonate with you?

I remember a colleague from my first school. She was overweight, and people often looked at her with judgment and disgust. The critical comments she received became unbearable. She started eating more — not because she didn't care, but because food became her voice, her comfort in silence. This was how she coped with a world that didn't listen or understand her pain.

It's painful but true: we're often quick to criticise others — so much so that we become experts at criticising ourselves. Can you hear your inner voice calling you names? "I'm stupid. Look at my belly. I need to change this or that about myself." These thoughts can become a constant echo.

Now, when we attend courses or meetings online, we don't even show our faces. The world has changed so much that we hide behind screens. We've stopped showing who we really are. Even when we meet someone for the first time, we share a photo taken 20 years ago, hoping to be loved for an image rather than our true selves.

All of this stems from a lack of self-belief — the fear that others won't love us as we are. We forget to fall in love with someone's kindness, heart, and mind. Instead, we fall for appearances, which will inevitably change with time. And then, later, we're left wondering: What did I really fall in love with? What did that person give me that made me believe in love?

Personal Reflections

I remember when I was a child, people used to say I had a big head, even though I was very slim. I remember asking my mum, "Do you think I am a good-looking girl?" With all her love, she would say, "You have beautiful skin." My family always laughed about this.

I also remember a teacher who really cared about me and loved me. Although what she did was wrong, I ended up paying the price for it — my mum and I had to deal with the consequences. I had to repeat a course even though I had earned the highest certificate in the entire year. Later, I found out that she had changed some of my answers after the exam.

I will never forget that I was only 10 or 11 years old at the time. I faced a lot of bullying from other kids because they said I was the teacher's favourite — the "teacher's pet." But the truth is, I was just being kind to people. Even though the teacher made a mistake, I'll always remember the moment when they called my name to receive the honor certificate. That was the best day of my life. I still remember it clearly.

Also, my family faced criticism from teachers who said things like, "Your daughters and son are not that intelligent." But today, I want to respond to that. I worked hard with my children and arranged private tutors to support their education because my English wasn't perfect, and I knew that with the right help, they would succeed. Even if they didn't use their certificates directly, they would have the skills to thrive in life. Today, all my children have gone to university and completed their courses.

My son, who was bullied by other children, is now working on discovering treatments for cancer and is currently pursuing his Master's in Artificial Intelligence.

As for me, I was told I would never earn any money from my studies. But here's what I want to say: don't listen to what others say. Be consistent and persistent in your life. Yes, challenges will come, and I can't even count how many times I had to rewrite some of my essays. But guess what? I did it. I kept working and stayed passionate about what I do.

Self-esteem comes from within — it's about believing in yourself. No one can take that away unless you give their opinions more power than your own belief.

Sometimes we learn to hide our true selves so well that we forget who we really are underneath all the masks we wear.

Wearing a Mask?

How many times in your life have you pretended that everything is okay? You wake up in the morning, go to work, and when someone asks how you're doing, you automatically say, "I'm fine." Can you relate to that?

You go home after a long day working with people you don't get along with, or after seeing friends you might not even like, but you keep pretending your life is fine. How often do you truly say what you feel? Many of us hold back because we're afraid that others won't like us if we show our real emotions. It's hard to be yourself when all you want is to be loved and accepted.

People often ask me, "How do I stop feeling anxious?" or "How can I stop people-pleasing?" These are big questions. To answer them, you need to reflect on when your anxiety started—and how you may have created or fed it. Ask yourself: how many masks do I wear to avoid showing my vulnerability, just to be liked or accepted?

The longer we pretend to be someone we're not, the more we lie to ourselves and others.

What would it feel like to actually say how you feel? I know—it might rock the boat. But isn't that part of being an adult? Being honest, instead of playing the role of a child who pretends everything is okay when it's not?

You might be suffering in silence because you don't feel safe expressing your emotions. But the beauty of adulthood is this: you can say how you feel. So, when someone asks if you're okay, it's perfectly valid to say, "No, I'm not okay."

Believe me, the more honest you are, the better you'll feel. Of course, we all want to be loved—but do you love everyone? Let's be real: even animals of the same species don't all get along. Neither do humans. And that's okay. We don't need to like everyone, as long as we respect one another.

A lot of issues arise because we only show what's on the outside. Many of us have become experts at wearing a mask. But at some point, it's important to take that mask off, be yourself, and allow yourself to be vulnerable. Sure, it's wise to choose carefully who you open up to—but that doesn't mean you have to convince the whole world that you're happy all the time. That's not real. Emotions are not permanent—they shift throughout the day, depending on how you handle what life throws at you.

Now, take a moment to remember the last time you were truly honest with someone about how you felt. What did it feel like? Liberating, right?

Expressing yourself and being authentic is freeing. Yes, it can be challenging—especially if it's with your boss or a close loved one. But think about what it's like to be in a relationship—professional or personal—where you can't speak your truth. That's exhausting. And it wastes so much energy.

Especially if you've lost a family member, you'll know that some days you're okay—and other days, you're not. But we often hide behind a mask, saying "I'm okay" when we're actually not. Why? Because we don't want to appear vulnerable, and we're unsure how others will react or what they might say.

So instead, we cover up our pain with a smile and pretend everything is fine. But what if, instead of pretending, you allowed yourself to say, "I'm not okay. I've had a really hard day."

Taking off the mask and being honest with yourself—and with others—can be the first step toward healing. It gives you permission to feel, to be human, and to stop carrying the pressure of always appearing strong.

Think about that. Maybe it's time to stop hiding and start allowing yourself to just be real.

So, take the mask off when you can. Be brave. Be real. Be you.

When we become comfortable with our authentic selves, we inevitably come to the question of who we are when all the pretenses fall away.

Be Yourself: The Key to Building Genuine Relationships

When we meet someone for the first time, why do we lie? Some might say it's to impress, to avoid rejection, or even to secure a short-term connection. Others may feel embarrassed about being themselves. Often, we overcompensate, saying or doing things that don't align with our true selves—all to gain someone else's approval.

But here's the catch: starting a relationship on a false foundation can lead to disillusionment and frustration. I've heard countless stories—and experienced it myself—of relationships changing dramatically once people start living together. Someone who claimed to love travelling or cooking suddenly reveals they have no interest in those things. Sound familiar?

It's easy to see how disappointment builds. Many believe their partner will change with time, but the truth is, people only change when they're ready—not because someone else wants them to. It's like fishing: the excitement of catching the fish fades once it's caught. Do you agree?

Why Do We Lie?

Lying often begins early in life. Think back to your childhood—did someone you loved ever tell you to keep a secret or to hide the truth to avoid hurting someone else? It's confusing, right? We learn to twist reality to fit social expectations, and this habit carries into adulthood.

I'll share a personal story: one of my daughters, when she was about five years old, had a habit of eating her twin's chocolate bar after school. One day, her brother asked, "Where's my chocolate bar?" She widened her eyes and said, "Maybe it ran away to the garden!" It was both funny and a teaching moment. I told her, "It's better to be honest. When you lie, people lose trust in you, and rebuilding that trust is hard." Eventually, she admitted the truth.

This childhood lesson reflects a broader truth: lying is often easier in the short term, but it erodes trust in the long run. Once trust is broken, it can take years—if ever—to restore.

The Importance of Reflection

When beginning a new relationship, I encourage my clients to reflect on these questions:

1. What do you want to change in this relationship?
2. What lessons have you learned from previous relationships, even if they were painful?
3. What responsibility can you take for the outcome of past relationships?

Blaming others might feel easier, but self-awareness is crucial for growth.

Why Authenticity Matters

Being yourself is liberating. If someone truly likes you, they'll accept you at your highs and lows. Pretending to be someone you're not will only attract the wrong people, and eventually, the facade will crumble.

My mom used to say, "A fish gets caught by its mouth," meaning that sooner or later, the truth will come out. Don't waste time pretending. Be genuine—it's refreshing, empowering, and the only way to build a strong, lasting connection.

The beginning of a relationship is a crucial time to be yourself. Sure, the other person might not contact you again if they don't like the real you—but isn't that better than wasting your time pretending?

For instance, they might say they love going out, but a few months after moving in together, they refuse to leave the house. Or perhaps they said they enjoy cooking, travelling, or other hobbies, only for those "passions" to disappear once the relationship gets serious.

Some people expect their partner to change over time, but the truth is, change only happens when someone is ready—not because their partner wants them to. Starting a relationship on lies is like fishing: the thrill of the catch fades quickly when the excitement wears off.

People often lie because it feels easier in the short term. But over time, lying can damage relationships beyond repair. Trust, once broken, is incredibly hard to rebuild. Most of us have experienced this to some extent—whether as the one lied to or the one telling the lie.

When supporting my clients in building new relationships, I always ask them:

- What would you like to change in your new relationship?
- What lessons have you learned from your past relationships, no matter how painful they were?
- What role did you play in your past challenges, and how can you take responsibility for them?

Blaming others is easy, but self-reflection and accountability are the keys to personal growth and stronger relationships.

The Power of Authenticity

Being yourself is refreshing and liberating. If someone truly likes you, they will accept you at your best and your worst. Wearing a mask and pretending to be someone you're not will only attract the wrong people, and sooner or later, the facade will fall apart.

As my mother used to say, "A fish is caught by its mouth." In other words, the truth always comes out eventually. So why waste your time—or someone else's—pretending?

Authenticity doesn't just help you find the right partner; it also strengthens your sense of self-worth. Being honest about who you are, what you want, and what you stand for will attract people who value you for exactly that.

Building a genuine relationship starts with being yourself. Let go of the fear of rejection and embrace the freedom of authenticity. In the long run, it's better to be alone and true to yourself than to be in a relationship built on false pretences.

So, take off the mask, be yourself, and watch how the right people naturally come into your life. It's not just refreshing—it's transformative.

Understanding ourselves—accepting who we are, respecting our boundaries, building genuine self-worth, releasing shame, silencing our inner critic, removing our masks, and embracing authenticity—these are not destinations but ongoing practices. Sometimes we might feel like frauds even when we're trying our hardest to be genuine.

Impostor Syndrome

Sometimes you might wonder why certain thoughts or feelings arise. When someone makes you cry, challenges your worth, or questions your abilities, you might find yourself thinking: Am I good enough? Do I deserve this success? What if they discover I don't know what I'm doing?

What is Impostor Syndrome? Impostor syndrome, also known as impostor phenomenon, is a psychological experience of feeling like a fraud despite evidence of one's abilities and accomplishments. You might feel that you have to work really hard to show that you deserve better things in life. Sometimes you might feel self-doubt and a fear of being exposed as unworthy or incompetent.

There are 5 different types of Impostor Syndrome:

1. The perfectionist
2. The natural genius
3. The rugged individualist
4. The expert
5. The superhero

What is the cause? Pressure from parents to do well in life. Low self-esteem and new responsibility can cause this issue.

How to fight this? Sometimes it's important to talk about this and to avoid comparison with others. You will need to know your own capacity and not pretend that you can do everything.

Sometimes we want to show that we are capable because we feel pushed to demonstrate to others that we can do it. When I work with my patients, I explore some of their feelings when they're feeling low about this, so I help them talk about it by helping them realise some of their feelings, so they don't need to blame themselves if they were unable to do it. By having some open conversations, we can help the patient understand that they have some talents, but it's okay not to do everything. They don't need to prove to the whole world that they are able to do everything.

Since I've had my children I have been trying to be perfect—well this is what I thought—but lately I realize that having to juggle a job, dealing with so many things in the house and more, dealing with our family to accomplish all the things that we need to do, to the point that sometimes I felt and questioned myself: have I been the best possible mother, worker and supported others properly during my work as a therapist?

During my work as a therapist, I have been told, "You have the answer for everything." Well, not really. I don't have the answer for everything, but my answer is I am good enough, so I don't want to pretend that I can do everything right. During my career, I have had to have my own therapy and today, sometimes I need to speak with other professionals to make sure that I am okay before I can support others. No, we are not perfect and no, we can't do everything to the best. I have been learning to take my mask off and sometimes I tell my patients that I don't have all the answers but I can support them to find their own answers. They can do it but they just need to take their time to process some of their feelings and understand how they feel when they are not able to do something, so they don't get stressed or have anxiety.

I always remember when I have to attend any training, how everyone is very quiet and don't ask many questions. I learned no questions are silly, so I will always put my hand up and ask questions even if they are not related to the learning.

The journey of understanding yourself is ongoing. There will be days when you feel confident and secure, and others when doubt creeps in. This is part of being human. The goal isn't to achieve perfect self-knowledge or unwavering confidence—it's to develop a compassionate, honest relationship with yourself that allows you to grow, connect with others authentically, and live according to your values rather than others' expectations.

Remember: You are not broken. You are not too much. You are not enough. You are a human being worthy of love, respect, and belonging—starting with the love and respect you give yourself.

With Gratitude, Love and Care.

Chapter 2: Setting Boundaries and Finding Your Voice

Learning to set boundaries and find your authentic voice is one of the most powerful gifts you can give yourself. It's about recognising your worth, protecting your energy, and refusing to accept treatment that diminishes your spirit. In this chapter, we explore how to establish healthy limits while maintaining your compassion and authenticity.

There It Is

Some people have asked why I write so much and what motivates me to do so. A friend of mine recently pointed this out, which inspired me to reflect on it. One common observation from friends is that I don't talk much about myself—I prefer to listen. This is true, and here's why: Although my sister thinks that I talk too much.

1. It's important to listen to others and, above all, to find people you can truly trust. However, even when we try to trust, some people let us down. That's just reality. I take these experiences as lessons, and I hope you do too.

2. I love supporting others because I know that many people go through life so busy that they don't even have time to reflect. I was once in that situation myself. Over time, I realised I had spent energy on people who were not really my friends—something I only recognized through their actions. As they say, actions speak louder than words.

3. Someone once wrote: "There it is—where they listen to you, where they dedicate time to you and show genuine interest, where excuses do not exist and the desire to be present is clear. Where they don't judge you but guide you with love and patience—that's where you belong."

4. I believe writing is therapeutic, and I always recommend it to my patients. It allows us to reflect, express ourselves, and connect with others who may be struggling without support. Someone once told me, behind every great reader, there is a great writer—and I truly believe this.

One of the biggest challenges in life is that we sometimes trust and confide in people we shouldn't. I focus a lot on setting boundaries, though I admit that even I sometimes slip. But as I always tell my patients, we are here to learn from our experiences. It's essential to be kind to ourselves because, at the end of the day, it's not about us—it's about them.

It is important to love yourself and part of that is being mindful of whom you share your secrets with. Sometimes, we confide in people we believe we can trust, only to realise that the best way to keep a secret is to keep it to yourself. As the saying goes, "A secret shared is no longer a secret." Once you involve another person, there is always a risk that it might spread.

One valuable lesson we all need to learn is to observe and listen carefully. Pay attention to what people say and, more importantly, to their actions—this can help you determine whether they are trustworthy.

Lastly, I just want to say thank you to everyone who reads these words. Remember, reading them is your choice, and I truly appreciate it. Wishing you all the best!

You Don't Have to Change Who You Are to Protect Yourself

Have you ever been told, "You need to change," or "Stop being so kind—this world will eat you alive"? Some people even say, "You're not Mother Teresa; you don't have to help everyone."

But here's a radical thought: maybe we need more people like Mother Teresa.

Imagine for a moment if we all chose to become hardened by our pain—if we let betrayal, disappointment, or cruelty turn us into bitter, selfish, cold versions of ourselves. What would the world look like if we all became bullies, cheaters, liars, or people who close their hearts out of fear? What if compassion, empathy, and care disappeared because someone hurt us once, or even many times?

Yes, life can be painful. People will let you down. They may lie, cheat, manipulate, abandon, or mistreat you—and yes, it's natural to want to shut down, to protect yourself by building walls instead of bridges. But here's the truth: you don't have to become what hurt you.

Feel the Pain, but Don't Let It Redefine You

We are human, and we feel deeply. When someone betrays your trust or disrespects your love, it wounds you. But we don't heal by mirroring that same pain back into the world. Healing comes from making space for your emotions—anger, sadness, confusion—and choosing not to let them destroy the beautiful parts of who you are.

Close your eyes for a moment and imagine doing to others what was once done to you. Now open your eyes. What kind of world would that create? Would you want to live in that world?

It takes strength to keep your heart soft in a world that can be harsh. But kindness doesn't mean weakness. Compassion doesn't mean you accept mistreatment. This is where boundaries come in.

Kindness Needs Boundaries

One of the most important lessons I teach my patients is that boundaries are not walls—they are bridges that protect your peace while still allowing connection. If you didn't grow up with healthy boundaries, they can feel unfamiliar, even wrong. You may feel guilty for saying "no" or feel selfish for protecting your time, space, or energy.

But the truth is, boundaries are a form of self-love. They are how you teach others how to treat you. They are not about being cold or distant; they are about being clear and respectful—of yourself and others.

Without boundaries, your kindness becomes something people take advantage of. But with boundaries, your kindness becomes something powerful and intentional. You decide when and how to help—not because you're being manipulated, but because it aligns with your values.

When the People Who Hurt You Are Still in Your Life

What if the person who hurt you is still part of your daily life? Maybe it's a family member, a partner, or a colleague. What if your partner had an affair, and people tell you to "get even," or "do the same"?

This is where self-awareness and emotional intelligence come in. Rather than reacting from pain, ask yourself: Do I want to reflect their behaviour or rise above it?

This isn't about excusing someone's actions. It's about recognising that repeating harmful behaviour doesn't bring healing—it brings more harm. Maybe the person who hurt you didn't have the courage to communicate honestly. Maybe they didn't love in a way that honoured the relationship. That's their work to do.

Your work is to decide what you will tolerate, how you will love, and how you will protect your peace.

Being Good Doesn't Mean Being Naive

You can still be a good person and say "no." You can still be compassionate and have high standards. You can still forgive and choose not to allow someone back into your life.

This is not weakness. This is wisdom.

Kindness without boundaries leads to burnout and resentment. But kindness with boundaries leads to strength, peace, and dignity.

Be the Light—But Protect Your Flame

You don't need to change who you are to protect yourself. You don't need to become cruel to survive. The world already has enough of that.

Instead, be the light—but protect your flame. Love, but don't let others drain you. Be generous, but know your limits. Offer support when you can—but never at the cost of your own well-being.

Don't let the world convince you to harden your heart. Instead, learn to care for yourself so deeply that your kindness flows from a place of strength, not sacrifice.

And remember: Being like Mother Teresa doesn't mean losing yourself—it means loving with boundaries, giving with intention, and living with courage.

You are a Priority, Not an Option

How many times have you heard someone say, "I was only with them to get over someone else"? Sadly, this seems to be happening more and more. People enter relationships not out of love or respect, but as a distraction from past pain. And in doing so, they hurt others—people who genuinely care—because they haven't healed from their own wounds.

Why do we allow ourselves to be treated this way? Where is our self-respect when we stay close to someone who doesn't see our value? Someone who doesn't love us the way we deserve to be loved?

It's heartbreaking to realise that some people will keep you around—not because they truly care, but because you are helping them feel better. You're their emotional crutch. They're angry, broken, or confused, and instead of healing properly, they latch onto someone else—often without any real consideration for that person's feelings. Is that right? What do you think?

Have you ever been in a relationship where the person says they're "not ready," yet they do just enough to keep you around? They take you out to dinner, buy you gifts, make you feel special—but only to a point. It's like you're a placeholder, a comfort object, something to display and use while they "figure themselves out."

And what about those mixed signals—texts filled with affection, attention, interest—but no real commitment? You're treated like a close friend, yet they don't want to lose you. They ask personal questions, show they care… but they still see their ex, or they're active on dating apps, chatting with other people.

What makes you stay in something where you are clearly not the priority? Are you hoping things will change? Do you believe they really care—or is it that they don't know what they want and you are the one left paying the emotional price?

You deserve better than this.

You deserve to be someone's priority—not an option they keep around just in case something better doesn't come along. You are worthy of love, respect, and someone who chooses you fully.

Why do you continue going out with people who don't truly value you or see your worth? Why aren't you putting yourself first? Don't you believe you deserve a relationship where someone accepts and loves you for who you are—giving you the attention, care, and respect you need?

You don't have to stay in situations like this. You have the power to walk away from anyone who treats you like an option or convenience.

Remember, time is valuable—but loving yourself is essential.

The message is simple: Stop letting others take you for granted. You are not a handkerchief to be used when someone feels like it, then tossed aside when they don't need you anymore. You are worthy of love, respect, and being someone's priority—not their backup plan.

What Truly Belongs to You

During my years as a therapist working with individuals struggling with depression—and reflecting on my own personal history—I have often observed how we fight over material things, sometimes to the detriment of our closest relationships. Families and friendships break down over disputes about possessions, especially during significant transitions like separations or divorces. For instance, I've seen countless cases where one partner insists on keeping the house or the car, with little thought given to how such decisions might affect their children. It's truly heartbreaking.

One lawyer once told me that when someone passes away, the reality of life's priorities becomes starkly apparent. People will often fight fiercely over the simplest things left behind. Have you ever thought about how everything you own is only yours temporarily? The things we acquire during our lives—the houses, cars, and other possessions—are fleeting. Yet, many of us act as though these things define us, even though we can't take them with us.

The Illusion of Ownership

People often claim that money isn't important. While it's true that money shouldn't define us, it can provide comfort and security if used fairly and responsibly. We can live well without obsessing over material possessions, especially if we start considering how our actions impact others. It's equally essential to care for ourselves, but this doesn't mean accumulating wealth or possessions at the expense of others.

From my own life, I remember watching my father build his business. He worked tirelessly, spending generously on friends and family to earn their love and respect. But in the end, despite all his efforts, he left this world with nothing. Everything he had worked so hard for was taken away. There are important lessons in this: the transient nature of material wealth and the futility of basing our worth on possessions.

The Cost of Competition

Why do we fight so hard for things that don't truly matter? We accumulate debt to buy the biggest house or the best car, often just to impress others. Yet, I've noticed more people now prioritising experiences over appearances. Many are beginning to ask themselves what's truly important in life. However, for those who feel compelled to always appear successful, this lifestyle can be exhausting.

Imagine if someone told you that you had only one day or one week to live. What would you do differently? Would the things you've fought so hard to obtain still seem important?

The Power of Saying No

A significant part of my work with patients involves helping them establish boundaries. When someone tells me they've learned to say "no" to others, I can see a light in their eyes. For the first time, they're prioritising their own needs and values. Of course, this can mean losing some friends or even family members who aren't used to these boundaries. But saying "no" isn't about upsetting others; it's about protecting what truly matters.

What Really Matters

When you're gone, the house, the car, and all the material possessions you've collected won't hold significance. What will endure are the relationships you've nurtured and the memories you've created with others.

What truly matters is how you treat others. This year, I've witnessed countless instances where people create illusions, offering promises they cannot fulfil—not because they are incapable, but because they aren't ready. Yet, in doing so, they build their own ego at the expense of others.

Take a moment to ask yourself: Is this okay? How would you feel if someone treated you this way? What's the purpose of making others suffer just to feel better about yourself?

Stop. Reflect. Change.

I was raised with the principle that you should never do to others what you wouldn't want done to yourself. I don't rely on karma, but I deeply believe that what you sow, you will eventually reap. So, be mindful of how you treat others. That's what truly matters.

As we approach another year, take time to reflect on what you want to carry forward in your life and what you're ready to let go of. What's truly important to you? How do you want to impact the lives of those around you?

Living Beyond Expectations

It has been a long day at work, but I wanted to take a moment to reflect on something that has been on my mind. How many of us have people in our lives who fail to meet our expectations? We often do so much for others, yet when we find ourselves in need of support, those same people are nowhere to be found.

Have you ever reflected on all the things you do for others, only to realise that when you are going through a difficult time, no one checks in on you or offers help? In my work with patients, I frequently notice how lonely they feel and how difficult it becomes for them to manage daily life when they believe no one is there for them. This isolation can be an incredibly hard and painful experience.

Often, I hear from patients who feel left out or unloved due to a lack of care and attention from those around them. For example, as people age or deal with serious health conditions, they may find themselves confined to their homes. In these moments, they notice that friends and family are too busy to reach out or offer support. Have you ever felt this way—stuck at home due to an illness or other circumstances, with hardly anyone reaching out to you? If so, you know how painful and disheartening it can be.

One of the strategies I suggest to my patients is to connect with others who are experiencing similar struggles. Finding a community of people who understand what you are going through can provide comfort and practical ideas on how to cope and move forward.

Think about the expectations you had for your first job, relationships, or even a first meeting with someone. How many times have you felt disappointed when things did not turn out as expected? Whether it's a job, a course, or a personal connection, unmet expectations can be frustrating. Someone once told me they never set expectations to avoid disappointment. While this might seem like a protective mechanism, in my opinion, it also means avoiding people, jobs, friendships, family, and new experiences altogether—just to escape potential pain. Is this truly living? Perhaps a better approach is to lower our expectations and adopt a more mature, balanced perspective to help us navigate life's challenges.

For instance, I once suggested to a patient that instead of waiting for someone to organise a party for her, she could plan it herself. While I was aware that she wasn't feeling well at the time, I encouraged her to consider this for the future when she felt better. Taking control of her celebration would allow her to create the experience she truly wanted rather than relying on others. Of course, in an ideal world, we all wish for surprise parties and grand gestures from loved ones, but reality doesn't always align with our desires.

There's something I always remember when flying: during safety instructions, we are told to put on our own oxygen masks before helping others. This advice extends beyond emergencies—it applies to life as well. Taking care of yourself first is not selfish; it is necessary. When you prioritise your well-being, you are better equipped to support those around you.

Something to Think About

Think about your first kiss, your first job—those moments filled with excitement and anticipation. But then, reality sets in, and you realise they weren't quite what you expected. The disappointment can be overwhelming, like a sudden awakening to a truth you didn't want to see. This is why some people retreat, locking themselves away, afraid of being hurt again and again.

If you let the fear of pain control you, you stop truly living. You hesitate to try new things or build new relationships, worried that someone else might hurt you. I see this often—so many people withdrawing from life because of past disappointments.

But here's the truth: do what you want to do, not because of expectations, but because it brings you joy. Set boundaries on who you support and why. You don't have to please everyone to feel loved. The most important relationship you'll ever have is with yourself. When you truly love yourself, you take charge of your happiness instead of waiting for others to provide it.

And remember, if someone truly cares about you, they will show it through their actions. Words are easy, but effort and time reveal the truth. Be kind to yourself, always.

Understanding and managing our boundaries and expectations requires us to look at ourselves honestly - often confronting uncomfortable truths about our patterns and choices. This brings us to the powerful influence of fear in our lives.

With Gratitude, Love and Care.

Chapter 3: Personal Growth and Life Lessons

True growth comes not from avoiding life's challenges, but from meeting them with courage, self-awareness, and a willingness to learn. This chapter explores the deeper questions of purpose, change, and personal evolution that shape our journey toward becoming who we're meant to be.

Overcoming Fear

Today, I worked with someone while exploring the concept of fear and its profound impact on our lives. Fear often influences our decisions, preventing us from overcoming challenges and moving forward. It is one of those emotions that can paralyse us, hindering us from pursuing the things we truly want to do.

Have you ever experienced this in your life? For instance, staying in a job you don't enjoy because you fear the uncertainty of finding another one. Remaining in a relationship because of your age, shared history, or fear of starting over. Not chasing your dreams because of the possibility of failure. Even in matters of health, fear can manifest as hesitation. For example, someone might avoid taking medication for fear of side effects, yet continue unhealthy habits that exacerbate their condition. I know of a family member with high cholesterol who relies on medication but refuses to change her diet. It's easier to depend on external fixes than to make meaningful changes within ourselves.

This led me to reflect on how often fear, whether ours or someone else's, holds us back. Fear is more pervasive than a virus because it fuels a host of emotions—dread, confusion, avoidance—that cloud our judgment. It agitates us, preventing rational thought and action. Our brains, as powerful as they are, can be influenced by the messages of others, keeping us from living a fulfilling life.

Happiness, like any other feeling, is not permanent. Fear, however, can weaken our ability to make decisions and embrace change. Isn't it sad to think about how fear affects our lives? Can you recall a childhood memory when fear—yours or someone else's—stopped you from doing what you truly wanted? It's heartbreaking to see people with extraordinary talent—in music, art, or other skills—who abandon their passions because someone, perhaps a teacher, parent, or peer, dismissed their potential. How often have we seen individuals pushed into careers or lives they didn't choose, all because of external expectations or family traditions? It's tragic, isn't it?

Imagine 100 babies born in a hospital. Now, picture 20 of them in separate rooms. Each of them is born with unique skills and potential. Yet many will never realize this potential because fear, instilled by themselves or others, will hold them back. Imagine carrying a metaphorical bag labelled "fear" throughout your life, a heavy weight preventing you from doing what you truly want. It's a sad thought, and I've seen it play out countless times in my work. So many people wake up each day regretting the life they're living, feeling trapped by the expectations of others—parents, teachers, friends, or society at large.

But here's the good news: we are all capable of change. One story that illustrates this beautifully is the tale of the elephant tied with a small chain. Despite its immense strength, the elephant doesn't break free because it believes it can't. That tiny chain represents fear—a powerful force in our minds that prevents us from seeing our true potential. Jorge Bucay wrote about this story, and it always reminds me to ask myself: what is my fear?

Fear has held me back in the past, too. Don't assume that because I work as a therapist, my life has always been smooth. I've faced my own fears. When I decided to move to England, my parents, especially my mother, were deeply upset. She cried and did everything she could to dissuade me. At one point, I almost gave in. But something within me pushed forward. I arrived in England with £200 and four suitcases, unable to speak the language. My journey started as an au pair, and from there, I moved through various jobs until I realised I needed to make a change. I wanted to help others, so I worked on myself to achieve that goal.

Today, I love what I do. The most rewarding part of my job is watching people confront their fears and make meaningful changes. It's incredible to see someone finally say "no" to others and start prioritising their own needs and dreams. They stop living under the shadow of fear—fear of judgment, rejection, or criticism.

Here's something I'd like you to remember: no matter what you do in life, people will always have opinions about you. So why let their opinions control your life? Stop letting fear dictate your decisions. Don't be like the elephant, held back by a tiny chain that exists only in your mind. Focus on your mental freedom and let go of the weight of fear. You can't change what others think, but you can change how you live.

I hope this resonates with you. Take a moment to reflect: what are your fears? Are they holding you back? You deserve a life free from the constraints of fear—a life where you can thrive, create, and truly be yourself.

Have You Achieved Your Dreams

Have you ever felt like you haven't achieved the things you truly wanted in life? Like somewhere along the way, you lost sight of your dreams? Do you ever feel like a part of you is missing—because, as a child, you followed the path others laid out for you? And now, you're stuck in a job you don't enjoy, repeating the same routine every single day?

Have you ever felt empty, as if the things you once loved no longer bring you joy? That passion and excitement you used to feel—gone, without you even realising when or why it faded?

How many dreams have you let slip away? How many things did you want to become, but never had the chance to pursue—because your life slowly became about fulfilling others' expectations rather than your own?

It's heartbreaking to see time pass by, feeling like you never had the freedom to choose your own path—whether because of family responsibilities or because your parents told you what you "should" do.

I've heard so many people share how unhappy they feel—how they're constantly searching for meaning, for a dream they can call their own. And the saddest part is feeling like they may never get to live the life they truly deserve.

Sometimes people say they are stuck in their job because of their finances and commitments and not able to leave just in case they are not able to find another job. We miss so many opportunities in life because of the unknown and not being able to bring food to their table, and they continue looking and dreaming but not taking any actions just in case. We tend to think it's better the devil that we know than to start something new. The fear of the unknown can be very challenging.

I heard so many times from people that had an operation or have been through difficult times, and they realise that life is short and they want to make some changes. But for some reason, they go back to the same routine and they don't take any action.

Do You Think People Can Change

What are your thoughts on this? Some of my friends tell me that people don't change, but on the other hand, during my studies with counselling, I was told that people have the capacity to change if they really want to. I was wondering what is your opinion on this?

So many people would like to see some changes within their family, partners and including people they work with all the time. Yes, this is correct, people get very frustrated to see that some of their colleagues make their life very difficult and they cannot wait for them to leave, or at some point of their life, they leave because they are not able to continue working under the same stress and they are feeling all the time worse about their job because of this.

Now imagine, at home when you are living and sharing part of your life (which is your precious time) with your partner and you are continually waiting for some changes but this never happens. I heard so many times things like, as soon as we move together, he or she will change, or when we have a baby there is hope they will change. Well, I am sorry to say about both of the examples that I have used, the first one, even if you move with your partner, unless he wants to change certain things, he will not change. Remember someone that was used to their parents doing everything for them, he or she will find it very difficult to be like their parents, so don't expect this to happen overnight. Additionally, having a child is not going to change the person. In fact, if your relationship is not strong enough, having a new family can be very challenging because of the nights that you will not be able to sleep and your partner might not be able to help you.

Now think before you think that you can change someone, and this is the majority of the issues - wanting to change someone instead of accepting the person that is living with you or working with you.

The reality is, the only person that can change is you. Yes, you. If you are in a relationship that you are not happy with, or if you are in a job that you are not happy with, none of these colleagues, family, or friends are going to do anything, but you can. Have you thought about this? We live with the hope that we can change the world. Yes, in a perfect world, I wish we could all do this, but sadly we are unable to change certain things because of the power of others and not letting you speak your mind.

One more time, you can make some changes by putting boundaries in your relationships with your friends, family, and partners. Trust me on this. So many people spend their whole life asking for changes from others, but they are not considering that unless someone realises how much damage they are doing in your life, this is going to be hard for you.

Life Teaches Us – And It's Never a Waste

Life always teaches us something. It's not a waste of time—far from it. Life helps us make better choices in our relationships, careers, and with our families. Why not embrace that?

All of my experiences have taught me to focus on the lessons, not the pain. Otherwise, holding on to anger and disappointment toward humanity becomes a waste of energy. Do you agree?

I used to think people didn't trust easily. But I've realised that people like me—who have trusted too many times—understand why others struggle with their own choices and the consequences they carry. It's heartbreaking to go through life trying to be a good person, helping others, and still ending up hurt.

It's devastating to think someone is your right partner—someone you've invested your time and emotions into—only to slowly discover their true self. You start to realise just how much of your life you've spent with people who haven't treated you well. And yes, it's deeply sad. Do you feel the same?

Sometimes I wonder: what makes people treat others like they have no heart? How do they justify such behaviour? It's disappointing, and the emotional pain they cause often leads others into depression, requiring support—or even medication—to cope.

Every time I see someone in my therapy room, I wonder: What's your story? What brought you to this place of pain?

As I listen, my heart sometimes breaks. And while I often hold back my tears, I feel every word. Because as a therapist, my life isn't perfect either. Far from it. I carry my own wounds while helping others heal.

And I do it with one hope: That someone, somewhere, will hear my words— "Take care of yourself. Love yourself. Choose the right people in your life."

Don't waste your time on people who don't deserve you. You are important. We all are. And no one has the right to tear you down because of their own unresolved pain.

You Matter - And That's Not Up for Debate

Often, I tell my patients: If you don't care for yourself, how can you truly care for others?

Life is a series of experiences. Some are incredibly painful—believe me—but I always say: Fall down. Get up. Get back on the horse.

Keep going until you find the job, friends, or partner that are right for you. And if you don't find them? That's okay. Because you still have YOU.

Remember that: YOU.

No one else can bring you happiness if you allow others to destroy it. And most of the time, they don't do it on purpose—it's their own pain, their own hardened hearts, that make them blind to the damage they cause. That's not on you. That's on them.

You will find your path. But first, you'll walk through many experiences. Every one of them prepares you for something better.

Unexpected Journeys

I never imagined that I would move to England and become a therapist. Never in a million years. I've always been a bubbly person, someone who loves to socialise. I thought I'd be working in tourism—travelling, making people laugh, singing songs on the bus with a microphone, helping them forget their problems.

And maybe I could've done well there—people often say I'm funny or that I have a warm presence that makes them open up. I don't know for sure. But what I do know is this: writing, and taking photos when I'm out in nature, brings me joy. That's something I now share with my patients.

Writing is healing. It's powerful. It gives voice to the pain and the lessons.

Sometimes I suggest writing a letter to yourself—one that someone else mails back to you a few months later. It's amazing to see what you were feeling in that moment and how far you've come since then.

Gratitude in the Pain

Yes, there is pain. There is disappointment. But if you can look back on your life with a bit of gratitude—even for the people who hurt you—you'll see they were teaching you something. Without them, you wouldn't know what to look for in the future. You wouldn't know what kind of love, friendship, and family you truly need and deserve.

Forgive them. But more importantly, forgive yourself.

Only then can you begin to truly move forward. And maybe one day you'll even be able to say, "Thank you" to those who hurt you—because they showed you what not to accept again.

Wish them well. They'll need it if they continue on the same path.

It's Okay to Feel Everything

You will cry. You will be disappointed. You will feel angry and broken. But if you work through those emotions instead of avoiding them, you will slowly heal. You will become a stronger, better version of yourself.

Even if that means staying in bed for a few days—do it. Talk to people who genuinely care about you. Surround yourself with those who uplift you.

Don't waste your time or your energy on people who don't see your value.

You have a choice now. You have the power to change things.

Trust me—I'm working on it too.

The Past – and How It Can Hold Us Back from Moving Forward

As we approach another season of reflection, I would like to take a moment to explore a powerful theme: "The Past – and How It Can Hold Us Back from Moving Forward."

Each of us carries experiences from the past. Some are beautiful and some are painful. Yet too often, we find ourselves stuck in those past experiences, unable to fully let go. It is not easy. Letting go requires courage. When we cling to what no longer serves us, we invite sadness, anger, resentment, and even hatred into our present lives.

Think about how often we hear phrases like, "During my previous marriage," or "In my last job," or "When I lived in my old house..." Instead of embracing the present moment, many of us unintentionally remain anchored in old memories.

I invite you to pause and ask yourself:

- How is revisiting the past helping me?
- What am I trying to achieve by bringing past experiences into current conversations or arguments?
- Is it contributing to healing, growth, or understanding — or is it holding me, and others, back?

Of course, our past is valuable. It contains lessons that shape us and helps prevent us from repeating old mistakes. But there is a fine line between learning from the past and living in it. If we continue repeating the same mistakes despite knowing better, how are we truly learning?

Often, I hear people say, "Remember what you did to me last week?" or "I promise it won't happen again," only for the cycle to repeat. And how often do we find ourselves reminding others of their past failures, rather than acknowledging the steps they are taking today to grow?

We are quick to recall the negatives, yet slow to recognise the positives. The truth is: as long as we keep dragging the past into every conversation, we are not allowing ourselves — or the people around us — to truly move forward. In doing so, we reveal that we have not fully forgiven. We hold others hostage to their former selves, and in turn, we stay stuck as well.

Ask yourself: Is this helping me in my current relationships — or hindering the new beginnings that could flourish if only I chose to let go?

Let us honour our past, learn from it, and then set it down — so that we can walk freely into the future we deserve.

Think about the last time something from your past resurfaced — for example, an old relationship. Now imagine you are in a new relationship, but during an argument, you bring up memories from the past and begin comparing your new partner to your previous one.

Often, this happens because we have not fully let go of the past. Maybe we are still grieving, and deep down, we weren't truly ready to start something new.

It's not easy — and I say this from my own experience. Sometimes, even small comments or situations in a new relationship can trigger old memories, making you wonder: "Am I in the right relationship?" "Is this going to end the same way as before?"

Even if we try not to think about the past, it can feel like we're carrying a heavy bag of memories everywhere we go. Imagine putting all your old experiences, pain, and memories into a backpack and carrying it on your back every single day. It's heavy. It's painful. And it prevents you from truly living in the present.

Ask yourself: What opportunity are you giving to the new person in your life if your heart and mind are still tied to your past?

Please know — this is not about judgment. I understand just how difficult it is to let go. But if we pause and reflect on how much our unresolved past can influence and even damage new relationships, we might realise something important: We need to take a leap of faith.

We need to give ourselves — and others — a real chance to start fresh, to live in the here and now.

There's a reason it's called the past. Of course, there are lessons we should take with us. But if we continue carrying all the hurt, anger, and negativity from what's behind us, it becomes almost impossible to build something beautiful and new.

Let's choose to leave the weight of yesterday behind — so we can walk freely into today.

Let It Go: Embracing Change and Moving Forward

What hurts or didn't work—let it go. This morning, as I reflected on conversations I've had with friends, patients, and even myself, I felt compelled to share these thoughts. It's both a personal reflection and a collection of insights that may resonate with you. Letting go is hard. We cling to good memories, the laughter, and the times we deeply loved someone. But have you ever considered that every challenge you face is an opportunity to learn and grow?

We often hold onto painful memories, as if punishing ourselves for what went wrong. Imagine holding something spiky in your hand—it hurts, doesn't it? Yet, you continue to clutch it tightly. This is what we do when we hold onto relationships or situations that no longer serve us. It's as if we're addicted to the pain because letting go feels even harder.

Have you ever thought that certain people come into our lives to teach us something about ourselves? Yet, we struggle to let them go. Take, for example, Richard Burton and Elizabeth Taylor. They married each other numerous times, yet even that wasn't enough to make it work. We're human, and we have habits that are hard to break. But is it healthy to keep repeating the same patterns?

Sometimes, we stay in relationships for the sake of our children. But what are we teaching them? That it's acceptable to live in pain and sacrifice our self-worth? By doing this, we model a narrative that says we are undeserving of happiness and love. If my parents had done this, I might have felt compelled to follow their example or vowed to do the opposite. If you're reading this, chances are you've encountered this dilemma yourself.

Love and Self-Worth

I've seen many couples who were unfaithful to each other. Infidelity is often a sign that something essential is missing. Yes, there may have been love, but not the kind of love you deserve. True love honours boundaries and respects intimacy. As I often tell my friends and children, "Your body is your temple." Intimacy is personal, and while I'm not here to judge, it's important to recognise its significance.

When you love someone deeply and purely, you don't seek fulfilment elsewhere. Instead, you work through the challenges together. If a relationship doesn't work out, celebrate the lessons it taught you. Whether it's a failed relationship, a job that didn't work out, or a broken friendship, these experiences shape who we are. Learn from them and move forward. Holding onto the past prevents you from embracing future happiness.

Embracing Emotions

It's natural to feel a mix of emotions when something ends—sadness, loneliness, frustration, disappointment, and more. Allow yourself to feel these emotions, but don't dwell in them. Letting go doesn't mean dismissing your feelings. It means recognising them, learning from them, and choosing to move forward.

During this process, take time to reflect. Ask yourself, "What did I do that contributed to this situation? What could I have done differently?" But remember, don't take on all the responsibility. Acknowledge the other person's role as well. Instead of labelling your actions as "mistakes," consider them valuable lessons. What did you learn from this experience?

Forgiveness and Growth

Don't chase something that continually hurts you. That person or situation was part of your life for a reason, and you likely had wonderful moments together. But now, it's time to prioritise yourself. Reflect on what changes you need to make, explore your choices, and work on forgiving yourself. Forgiveness is key—it's not about excusing what happened but about freeing yourself from the burden of blame.

Letting go is a journey. It requires courage, self-awareness, and a commitment to personal growth. But in doing so, you open the door to new opportunities, love, and happiness. Remember, you are worthy of all these things. Let go and embrace the future with hope and strength.

As we prepare to step into another year, let us celebrate the journey ahead. However, it's equally important to take a moment to pause, step off the train of life, and reflect on what we truly need for our everyday lives. Time is precious—never forget that.

Here are my final thoughts for all of you: Love is rooted in respect, kindness, care, attentive listening, and effective communication. These are qualities we all need to work on. Above all, remember that actions speak louder than words.

Your first love should always be for yourself. Embrace that love and let it guide you.

Living with Hope

How often have you found yourself in a relationship, holding on to the hope that the other person will change? You wake up every morning believing that today will be different — that they will finally see things from your perspective, behave differently, and become the person you've been waiting for them to be.

Many people even turn to prayer, asking for divine intervention, clinging to the belief that change will come. And so, they stay — day by day, year after year — filled with hope.

You try everything. You support them emotionally, financially, and spiritually, believing that if you give enough love, patience, and understanding, they will eventually change. But over time, you begin to notice that nothing changes. The person remains the same — perhaps still dishonest, still making promises they don't keep — and yet, you continue to hold on to hope.

It's exhausting. It's painful. And it's heartbreaking to realise how long you've been waiting for something that may never come. You've poured so much of yourself into someone who may not even see the damage their behaviour causes — someone who may not be ready or willing to change.

Then, one day, you wake up and realise: you can't wait any longer. You have to walk away, and this time, not look back. Because if you stay, you'll drown alongside someone who refuses to swim. The tears, the time, the love, the energy — it's overwhelming. But in the end, you must choose yourself.

You ask yourself: Why did I let this happen? Why didn't I trust my intuition? And the answer is often simple — because you loved them. Love has a way of blinding us to reality. But don't think the time was wasted. Think of it as an experience — a lesson that will guide you if you ever find yourself in a similar situation again.

The truth is, we are all capable of change — but only if we genuinely want to. No one can change for you. Change is a choice, an adult decision that only they can make.

So if you're in this situation now, take a step back. Reflect. Ask yourself if the person is truly making the effort to grow, or if you're simply holding on to potential that may never be realised.

Your time is valuable. Your heart is worth protecting. And your peace is worth choosing.

Ego Stages

As we approach a well-deserved break for reflection, I wanted to take a moment to share some thoughts about the behaviours we display and wonder: Why do we act the way we do? Often, we don't realise the deeper reasons behind our actions or reactions. Many of us grow up thinking we need to behave like our parents, yet at the same time, we say things like, "I'll never be like them." But the truth is, whether we like it or not, they were our role models.

That doesn't mean we can't change. Of course, we can—but it requires understanding where our behaviours come from and deciding what we'd like to change. There is nothing wrong with you, so please don't ever feel that way. Change begins with awareness and self-compassion.

Sometimes, children struggle to understand what's right or wrong because they've been told their way of thinking is "different" or not acceptable—especially when compared to their siblings. Have you ever heard someone say, "Why are you so different from your siblings?" or call you "the black sheep of the family" just because your perspective didn't match the rest of your family's?

Often, I hear people say things like, "I have to be good at what I do—otherwise, people will see me as a failure," or "I can't let anyone down." I wonder how much of this pressure comes from our upbringing—especially in cultures where the eldest child is expected to be a role model and take on adult responsibilities early. Many of us, as the oldest siblings, were taught to lead by example, to care for others, and to always "be strong." But in doing so, we may have missed out on parts of our childhood.

As adults, we might look back and realise we were never really given the space to just be children. This theme is explored in Transactional Analysis (TA), a theory developed by Eric Berne in the late 1950s.

Berne, a Canadian-born psychiatrist, was influenced by Freud's belief that our childhood experiences deeply shape who we become.

TA identifies three ego states that influence how we relate to others:

1. **The Parent Ego State** - Patterns of behaviour, thoughts, and feelings copied from our parents or authority figures.

2. **The Adult Ego State** - Behaviours, thoughts, and feelings based on the present moment and rational thinking.

3. **The Child Ego State** - Reactions and emotions replayed from our own childhood experiences.

It's fascinating how—even when we try to avoid becoming like our parents—we often find ourselves repeating their words or behaviours. When I used to work in a school, I noticed this during parent-teacher meetings. Children would mimic their parents' tone, language, and mannerisms. It reminded me how strong these unconscious patterns can be.

That's why understanding these ego states is so powerful. When we become aware of which state we're operating from, we can begin to make intentional, conscious choices—rather than simply repeating what we've learned.

Change is possible. It begins with reflection, understanding, and giving ourselves permission to grow.

Chapter 4: Health and Wellness

Our physical and mental health forms the foundation upon which we build our lives. Yet so often, we neglect these fundamental aspects of our well-being in favour of external pressures and demands. This chapter explores the vital connection between our bodies, minds, and spirits, and how caring for ourselves isn't selfish—it's essential.

You Are What You Eat

We are what we eat.

We wake up every morning, look in the mirror and often don't love ourselves—because we're trying to copy others, like celebrities, influencers and people we see in the media. We keep flipping through magazines, even though we know many of the photos have been digitally altered and retouched by professionals to make people look their absolute best.

So many people are suffering as they follow extreme diets, barely eating in an effort to shed extra pounds. Some even undergo operations to reduce the size of their stomach. While I understand that this is sometimes necessary for medical reasons, starving yourself or surviving only on liquids isn't healthy. Of course, you'll lose weight—but this is just a way of lying to yourself.

The real challenge begins when you start eating normally again. All the weight you lost so quickly tends to come back. That can be incredibly disappointing and frustrating, especially when your goal is to look like someone else instead of loving yourself.

Why do we eat foods we know aren't good for us?

Sometimes it's just because we enjoy sweet treats or junk food. Other times, it's because we've had a rough day and can't process what we're feeling. Food becomes an escape—we don't want to face our sadness, frustration, or anger, so we reach for comfort.

This behaviour can stem from many reasons, but in the end, it harms our health. Yes, it's true: we are what we eat. But please, don't be so hard on yourself. Even when we know what's best for us, change can be difficult.

Try being gentle with yourself. Speak to your inner child with kindness and compassion. Imagine walking into a shop and seeing a beautiful cake. Your inner child might say, "Go on, have it—you can start eating healthy tomorrow." But your adult self knows what you need and gently suggests something healthier.

Sometimes we need to have a loving conversation with that rebellious or hurt inner child, reminding them that everything will be okay. You don't need to eat that unhealthy food to soothe your pain—especially if you're already dealing with high blood pressure, diabetes, or high cholesterol. This is when your adult self steps in, reassures your inner child, and takes control with love and care.

This idea comes from Transactional Analysis (TA)—a psychological theory that explores how our inner child, parent, and adult selves interact. Working with these parts of ourselves can help us heal and grow.

So, remember: you are what you eat—but you are also worthy of kindness, care, and self-love.

The Major Illnesses of the 21st Century

Have you noticed how illness is on the rise across the world? More than ever, people are feeling overwhelmed, burnt out, and emotionally disconnected. While we often hear about diseases like cancer or autoimmune conditions, we must also speak about two powerful forces silently eroding our health: chronic stress and its impact on the immune system.

In fact, stress is now one of the leading causes of physical and mental illness in the modern world. We hear it every day: "I'm so stressed." "I can't cope anymore." "I feel exhausted all the time."

Sound familiar? Maybe you've even said it yourself.

The Ego and the Stress Trap

Stress is more than just a feeling—it's a physiological condition that affects nearly every part of the body. Often, our ego holds us in situations that increase our stress: needing to prove something, needing to stay in control, or fearing what others might think. But the more we allow stress to rule us, the more damage we do to our bodies and minds.

Stress raises cortisol levels. Over time, high cortisol interferes with sleep, digestion, blood pressure, heart health, memory, and emotional regulation. When stress becomes chronic, the immune system weakens, making us more vulnerable to infections, inflammation, and even long-term diseases like cancer.

Why Are We So Sick?

Even though people are visiting doctors more often, we are not making the deeper changes that truly support our health. We keep living in ways that wear us down—rushing, competing, staying in toxic relationships, and ignoring our emotional needs.

In my work as a therapist, I see this every day. People are living under constant pressure:

- Divorce
- Toxic work environments
- Domestic violence
- Sexual and financial abuse
- Ongoing criticism or lack of validation from family or partners

These experiences leave people feeling helpless, emotionally trapped, and physically drained. And our bodies were not designed to carry this kind of stress every day.

Think of an animal being chased by a predator. The stress response is intense—but short. Once the threat is gone, the animal relaxes, returns to safety, and the body resets. But humans often stay in that "chased" state for days, weeks, or even years, with no real chance to recover.

What do you think happens when you wake up every morning dreading the day? When you live in fear, criticism, or emotional neglect? This is not the way we are meant to live.

Medicine Can Help, But It's Not Enough

While medication from a GP may help reduce symptoms in the short term, it's often not enough on its own. Healing requires more than pills—it requires lifestyle changes, emotional regulation, and real self-awareness.

When patients come to me overwhelmed by stress, I often encourage them to:

- Take time off if possible

- Prioritise their emotional well-being
- Set clear boundaries
- Seek environments where they feel safe, seen, and supported

Yes, it's difficult. But in the long run, these changes can transform your life.

Think about it: how do you feel on holiday, when you're away from your routine and surrounded by people you love? Your stress levels drop. You sleep better. You laugh. You connect. But what happens when you return to the same stressful life? Your symptoms come back, often stronger.

Over time, this leads to:

- Poor concentration
- Hopelessness
- Depression
- Emotional disconnection
- Sleep problems
- Unhealthy coping mechanisms (e.g., overeating, under-eating, drinking)

What Can You Do?

So, ask yourself: When was the last time you truly felt calm and relaxed? What does stress feel like in your body?

Your body speaks to you. It tells you when you're overwhelmed. Don't ignore the signs. The more you suppress your emotions or "push through," the louder the consequences become—physically and emotionally.

Start by taking small steps:

- Breathe deeply and mindfully
- Rest when your body asks for it
- Surround yourself with people who uplift you
- Say no to what drains you
- Speak kindly to yourself

Stress is one of the most dangerous illnesses of the 21st century, yet it hides behind socially acceptable habits like overworking, pleasing others, or staying busy. But make no mistake—unchecked stress will eventually demand your attention through your health.

If we don't learn how to manage our stress, to let go of ego-driven pressure, and to live more mindfully, we risk not only our physical health but our emotional freedom and joy.

Remember: You are not meant to live in survival mode. Choose healing. Choose peace. Choose yourself.

Why Do We Drink or Use Substances That Harm Us

Yes, this is a serious global issue. Across the world, people are consuming increasing amounts of alcohol, drugs, food, and cigarettes—not because they want to, but because many of us are under immense pressure. We feel overwhelmed, unable to stop, and we turn to these substances in an attempt to manage our pain, emotions, and unspoken feelings.

We're not taking care of ourselves. Instead of confronting our problems head-on, we often try to numb them. Drinking becomes a way to forget, to escape—even if just for a moment—from the pain and worry that consume us.

There's also the pressure to please others—to be everything for everyone. In trying not to upset anyone or "rock the boat," we suppress our own needs and truths. It's like there's an elephant in the room that no one wants to acknowledge. We remain silent to avoid hurting others, yet in doing so, we continually hurt ourselves. Is that fair to you? Does that resonate?

How many times have you wanted to express how you feel, but instead, poured another glass of wine, took another pill, or ate more than your body needed—just to cope? We try to "swallow" the pain, the unhealthy relationships, the unresolved issues, the people we can't deal with. And at the root of it, often, is a simple truth: we struggle to say "No."

Saying no—and having a voice—is powerful. It's essential for your well-being. In my work, I often tell patients: it's not what you say, but how you say it. Yes, at first, it might feel uncomfortable to speak your truth, but over time, you'll experience a powerful shift. It's a feeling of freedom—something many of us long for, but rarely give ourselves permission to feel. We say we're free, but we aren't—not if we can't speak up or let go.

I'm not saying it's easy. It isn't. But many believe alcohol helps them forget. The truth is: alcohol is a depressant. It doesn't make your problems disappear—it only delays them, while silently affecting your brain and body.

The Science: What Alcohol Does to the Brain

Short-Term Effects (After 1-2 Drinks and Upwards):

When alcohol enters the bloodstream and reaches the brain, it acts as a central nervous system depressant, slowing down brain activity.

1. **Impaired Judgment & Inhibition** - Alcohol suppresses the prefrontal cortex, the part responsible for reasoning and self-control. This is why people often become more emotional, impulsive, or risk-taking.

2. **Slowed Reaction Time & Coordination** - It affects the cerebellum, responsible for balance and motor control, causing clumsiness and slurred speech.

3. **Dopamine Release (Temporary Pleasure)** - Alcohol triggers the reward system in the brain, releasing dopamine and creating a "buzz." But this effect is short-lived and decreases with tolerance.

4. **Memory Disruption** - Alcohol affects the hippocampus, which controls memory. Heavy drinking can cause blackouts, where you remain conscious but don't remember what happened.

Long-Term Effects (Heavy or Chronic Use):

1. **Cognitive Decline** - Prolonged use can reduce brain volume, impacting attention, learning, and memory.

2. **Addiction (Alcohol Use Disorder)** - Repeated exposure rewires the brain's reward system, leading to dependency and cravings.

3. **Mood Disorders** - Long-term use is strongly linked to anxiety and depression.

4. **Brain Damage (e.g., Wernicke-Korsakoff Syndrome)** - A severe condition caused by vitamin B1 deficiency, often due to

alcoholism, leading to memory loss, confusion, and in some cases, psychosis.

In Summary:

- **Low to moderate drinking:** May offer short-term relaxation or euphoria.
- **Heavy or binge drinking:** Affects memory, coordination, and judgment.
- **Chronic drinking:** Increases the risk of mental illness, brain damage, and addiction.

Reflection

Now take a moment and ask yourself: Do you really believe that drinking, using substances, or harming yourself is the answer? Deep down, you already know it isn't.

Sometimes we feel unheard, and that frustration can build up. But reacting with anger or silence doesn't help—true strength comes from calm, honest expression. If someone refuses to listen to your truth, perhaps they are not meant to hold space for it.

Don't destroy yourself for people who don't value you. Your body, mind, and life are yours alone. Use them well.

Think carefully:

- What would you like to change in your life?
- What would it look like to say no more often, and yes to yourself?

You can make different choices. You do have the strength. Wishing you peace, clarity, and the courage to move forward.

What Is Anxiety

Anxiety is a natural response to stress or perceived danger. It involves feelings of worry, fear, or unease, often about future events or uncertain outcomes. While it is normal to feel anxious before an exam, giving a presentation, or making a difficult decision, excessive or persistent anxiety may indicate an anxiety disorder.

If you've lived with significant stress or insecurity for a long time, it's no surprise that anxiety can develop. A lack of safety and stability, which are fundamental to a healthy life, can make anyone feel overwhelmed. When anxiety begins to interfere with daily life, it's crucial to seek professional help.

Causes and Triggers

For some, a family history of anxiety may predispose them to develop symptoms, but these may remain dormant until triggered by a major stressor. Others may experience anxiety due to prolonged exposure to toxic relationships, abusive environments, or chronic workplace stress.

For instance, imagine the challenges many faced during lockdowns: individuals trapped in abusive relationships, children subjected to domestic violence, or adults unable to escape hostile environments. The inability to leave home during these times exacerbated anxiety, creating a sense of constant fear and helplessness. Those who have experienced such situations understand what it's like to wake up each day wondering, "What kind of day will this be?"

The Generational Impact of Anxiety

Anxiety often spans generations, passed down without us fully realising the toll it takes. Watching others suffer from anxiety—whether a family member, friend, or colleague—can be deeply painful. Think about a time when you had a difficult meeting with your boss and received bad news about your job. The pressure of responsibilities at home and the uncertainty about the future could lead to anxiety or even panic. Without support from friends, family, or professionals, this kind of experience can leave someone feeling perpetually on edge, even in similar situations later on.

Effective Treatments

One treatment I often recommend to clients is Cognitive Behavioural Therapy (CBT). This therapeutic approach focuses on identifying and challenging negative thought patterns. Some people see the glass as half-empty, while others see it as half-full—CBT helps shift the perspective toward a more balanced, rational view of situations.

I encourage my patients to adopt a mindset that emphasises resilience and opportunity. For instance, when one door closes, another door opens. Often, we don't know what lies ahead until we try, and with the right tools and support, we can overcome the challenges anxiety presents.

How many of you remember the year 2000, when there was widespread fear about the "end of the world"? Many people felt anxious about whether they would wake up the next day. Anxiety can manifest in many forms and moments of life, and recognising it is the first step toward addressing it.

If this resonates with you or someone you know, remember that help is available, and recovery is possible. Don't wait another day and find the support that you deserve.

Understanding Cancer and Its Impact

This morning, I heard devastating news from a friend: her partner has been diagnosed with brain cancer. This prompted me to reflect on this challenging disease and its widespread impact on individuals and their loved ones worldwide. To my dear friend, I am here for you.

What is Cancer?

Cancer is caused by changes (mutations) in the DNA of cells, leading to uncontrolled cell growth and division. These mutations disrupt the normal regulatory processes that ensure cells grow, divide, and die in an orderly manner. Over time, this uncontrolled growth forms a mass of cells called a tumor, which can invade surrounding tissues and spread to other parts of the body (metastasis).

One in three people, 33% will develop cancer in their lifetime. This alarming statistic underscores the urgency of understanding this disease and its causes.

Causes of Cancer

The mutations that lead to cancer can arise from various factors, including:

1. **Genetic Factors:** Some individuals inherit mutations that increase their cancer risk.

2. **Family History:** A history of cancer in the family can indicate a higher likelihood of developing certain types of cancer.

3. **Environmental and Lifestyle Factors:** Exposure to tobacco smoke, harmful chemicals, and ultraviolet (UV) radiation significantly raises the risk.

4. **Biological Factors:** Chronic infections and hormonal imbalances can contribute to cancer development.

5. **Random Genetic Mutations:** Sometimes, cancer arises from random errors during cell division, independent of external or hereditary factors.

Understanding these causes and risk factors is crucial for prevention, early detection, and treatment. Simple steps like avoiding tobacco, limiting alcohol consumption, protecting against UV radiation, maintaining a healthy diet, and undergoing regular screenings can significantly reduce the risk of cancer.

Cancer's Mental and Emotional Impact

Cancer profoundly affects mental and emotional well-being, influencing patients and their families in diverse ways. Below are some key emotional responses often observed:

1. **Shock and Denial:** The initial diagnosis often triggers disbelief and denial.

2. **Anxiety and Fear:** Concerns about treatment, prognosis, and the future are common.

3. **Depression and Sadness:** The weight of the illness can lead to feelings of hopelessness and despair.

4. **Anger and Frustration:** Patients and their families may feel anger about the situation and its unfairness.

As a therapist, I have witnessed the emotional toll cancer takes on individuals and their loved ones. Hearing the diagnosis—often referred to as the "C-word"—is indescribably difficult. The impact reverberates not only through the patient but also through their family and social circle.

Communication Challenges

One of the most challenging aspects for families is knowing how to interact with someone diagnosed with cancer. Many feel paralysed, unsure of what to say or do. A dear friend who passed away once shared that people's comments were often inappropriate, even though they meant well. She considered writing a guide to help others avoid unhelpful or hurtful remarks.

Supporting a Loved One with Cancer

Supporting a loved one with cancer is an incredibly challenging and emotional experience. While the instinct to make decisions for them may be strong, it's essential to respect their choices regarding treatment and how they wish to live their remaining days. Here are some ways to offer meaningful support:

- **Listen Actively:** Allow them to express their feelings and decisions without judgment.
- **Respect Their Choices:** While it can feel powerless to step back, remember that it is their body and their journey.
- **Provide Emotional Support:** Be present, and let them know you are there for them.

Therapeutic and Holistic Support

In my work as a therapist, I've seen how addressing emotional needs can profoundly improve a patient's quality of life. One patient, after a long conversation, realised she had choices in her treatment and life, which brought her a sense of empowerment. Here are some effective ways to support emotional well-being:

- **Mind-Body Practices:** Techniques such as meditation, yoga, and mindfulness can reduce stress and build resilience.

- **Social Support:** Encouraging connections with loved ones or joining cancer survivor networks fosters emotional strength.

Recognising and addressing the mental health challenges associated with cancer is vital. Emotional well-being plays a significant role in improving the overall quality of life and can even influence recovery outcomes.

Cancer is not just a physical illness; it's a profound emotional journey for patients and their families. By listening, respecting choices, and offering holistic support, we can help ease the burden of this difficult journey. Together, with compassion and understanding, we can make a difference in the lives of those affected by this disease.

With Gratitude, Love and Care.

Chapter 5: Social Awareness and Kindness

In a world that often feels divided and harsh, our capacity for kindness and social awareness becomes not just important, but essential. This chapter explores our responsibility to each other—human and animal alike—and how small acts of compassion can create ripples of positive change in an increasingly complex world.

Why Are We So Cruel—to Others and to Ourselves

How many times have you heard heartbreaking stories of people suffering in silence? Children at school, for example, suffocating under the weight of cruel labels. "You're stupid, ugly, fat, weird, smelly." How many more could we list? Which one do you remember hearing the most as a child?

You went to school full of hope—to learn, to grow, to do well in life. But then someone, likely struggling with issues of their own, targeted you. They made you feel worthless. They made school feel like a battle, not a place of learning. Some of us left with poor results and shattered self-worth—not because we weren't capable, but because we were broken down by unkindness.

Why is the world so unkind? Why do we hurt each other so easily?

Jealousy. Insecurity. Pain passed from one to another. And yet we forget how powerful it is to simply be kind. Do you remember what it feels like to receive genuine care? To feel seen, loved, respected?

When you work in mental health, you see just how deep the pain goes. You hear story after story of people pushed so far by the cruelty of others that they consider ending their lives. And yes, I know—some are tired of hearing about this. But I ask you: how long does it take to be kind? A second?

This week, I was in a shop and a man walked in beaming with joy. He was so cheerful that the women behind the counter stopped and commented on it. "Did you see how happy he was?" they said, almost surprised. Joy like his seemed unusual to them.

Since COVID—and even before—we've been slipping further into disconnection, frustration, and emotional fatigue. People are more aggressive, more impatient. We are not getting better. And if we don't change, what kind of world are we leaving for our children and grandchildren?

I'm not here to judge. I'm here to reflect—with you.

When was the last time you said good morning, thank you, or how can I help you? Sometimes, we pass by people clearly suffering and do nothing. Why? Where has our compassion gone? When did we stop looking into the eyes of those in pain?

I used to work in a school, and I'll never forget what I heard from some teachers: "If you don't succeed, you'll fail at life." Or, "You're not smart," "You're lazy," "You're stupid." Labels, not lessons. Imagine a child already struggling with peer bullying—now also hearing this from adults meant to protect and guide them.

And what about the advice often given: "Just ignore the bullies." Is that really the solution?

Now imagine this: a child dealing with problems at home. School should be a safe space, a break from the stress. But instead, they face more hurt—rejected by peers, mocked, picked on because they seem "different" or "quiet." These are the most vulnerable students, and they're often targeted by others who are struggling too.

And what happens next? The child, already suffering, now has no one to talk to. They feel ashamed, embarrassed, alone. And sometimes, even their parents might say, "Just hit them back." But that only adds to the chaos. The child might be punished, suspended, and lose access to their education—not because they were wrong, but because no one gave them the support they needed.

It's hard. Really hard.

Can you put yourself in their shoes? Honestly—unless you've lived through something similar, it's difficult to truly understand.

But what you can do is choose to be kind. Choose to care. Choose to reflect.

The world doesn't change overnight. But it can start to change—with you.

If we can teach our children to be kind, loving, and caring—and to treat others with respect—then someone out there may grow up with a brighter future and a better education.

But here's the truth: children learn by example. If adults are not kind to each other, how can we expect the next generation to be any different? We are their role models. What they see at home becomes the foundation of who they become.

Think about this.

Being kind does not make you weak or naive. It means you have a heart. It means you choose compassion in a world that often chooses the opposite.

And if we all give up our kindness just to blend in with the rest of the world—what kind of world will we end up with?

So, ask yourself: What kind of example are you setting? What kind of world are you helping to shape?

It all begins with you.

Supporting Neurodivergent Students - Understanding Their Challenges

My primary job is as a therapist, but I also work as a mentor, supporting university students, particularly those with neurodivergent difficulties. This role can be both challenging and frustrating at times. Some students are unaware of the support available or struggle to ask for help, while others are aware but feel too embarrassed to seek assistance due to negative experiences throughout their education.

I felt compelled to share this because I know that many people live in fear—whether at work, with family, or among friends—simply because they are different. Social interactions can be incredibly stressful for them, as others may struggle to understand their conditions. As a result, they hide their challenges out of fear of rejection or being labelled as "weird," "freaky," or "strange." These hurtful labels contribute to their isolation and make it even harder for them to seek support.

I have heard many heartbreaking stories from my students about the difficulties they face in education. Sadly, some teachers and peers are unaware of the impact their words and actions can have. Comments—whether intentional or not—can be embarrassing and humiliating to the point where students no longer want to attend lessons. Some may even act out as a defence mechanism, leading to disciplinary action that further alienates them from learning.

Take a moment to reflect: How many of you have ever struggled to understand a lesson but remained silent out of fear that speaking up would invite ridicule? Imagine how it must feel for neurodivergent students who experience this on a daily basis. Some even start believing they are "stupid" or incapable of learning simply because they process information differently.

This is not meant to criticise but to raise awareness. While I understand that teachers have limited time and that it may not always be their responsibility to provide individual support, recognising when a student is struggling can make a huge difference. Taking just five minutes to speak with them outside of class or referring them to a professional could help improve their educational experience significantly.

By fostering awareness and understanding, we can create a more inclusive and supportive environment for all students.

Neurodivergent is a term used to describe people whose brain functions, cognitive processes, or behavioural traits differ from what is typically expected in society. It includes conditions such as:

- **Autism Spectrum Disorder (ASD)**
- **Attention Deficit Hyperactivity Disorder (ADHD)**
- **Dyslexia, Dyspraxia, Dyscalculia**
- **Obsessive-Compulsive Disorder (OCD)**
- **Tourette Syndrome**
- **Highly sensitive persons (HSP) or other cognitive variations**

Being neurodivergent isn't a disorder—it's a natural variation in how brains work. The concept promotes acceptance and understanding, rather than seeing these differences as something that needs to be "fixed."

Neurodivergence contrasts with **neurotypical**, which refers to people whose brains function in ways that align with societal norms.

If a parent is facing difficulties and struggling to find the right support, I always recommend going back to their GP and requesting an assessment. This can help identify the necessary emotional, physical, and additional support to ensure the individual has the opportunity to pursue their dreams or find a suitable alternative.

I remember working with a student who aspired to become a surgeon but was unable to do so due to dyspraxia, which affected his motor skills. Instead of giving up on his passion for medicine, we explored alternative career paths within the field at his university. This allowed him to stay connected to his interests while finding a role that suited his abilities.

Here are some specific ways you can help:

Communication & Clarity

- Offering concise, structured responses or breaking down complex topics into smaller, manageable steps.
- Using plain language when needed and avoiding unnecessary ambiguity.
- Adjusting the tone and style to match what feels most comfortable for you.

Reducing Overwhelm

- Summarising long information if needed.

- Providing visual aids, lists, or step-by-step guides when possible.
- Allowing pauses or slower-paced conversation if needed.

Flexibility & Customization

- Supporting alternative ways of learning or working (e.g., text-based over verbal, detailed over summarised).
- Helping with executive function challenges (reminders, planning, breaking down tasks).
- Encouraging self-advocacy and understanding of neurodivergent needs.

Emotional & Social Support

- Offering nonjudgmental advice and validation.
- Helping with scripts for social interactions if needed.
- Encouraging self-care and self-acceptance.

If you know someone who needs help, don't lose hope. Life can feel like a battle, but it shouldn't be that way. We all have the right to grow, develop, and pursue opportunities without feeling less than anyone else. Take your time, keep trying, and never stop believing in yourself or those around you.

Why Animals Hold a Special Place in Our Hearts

A friend recently asked me to write about animals, and I thought—why not? In my country, there's a saying: "The more I know people, the more I love my animals." And honestly, sometimes that feels true. Animals offer us things that even humans sometimes struggle to provide: loyalty, unconditional love, companionship, joy, and laughter. They bring a unique kind of warmth into our lives.

Although humans evolved from animals, I often think we've lost something along the way. Animals kill only to survive—humans often kill for other, darker reasons. Animals love without condition. They can sense when we're sad and often stay by our side quietly, offering comfort without asking for anything in return. If you feed them, care for them, and love them, they will love you back—deeply and without judgment.

I've heard many stories of dogs who grieve when their owners pass away. Some pine for days or even weeks. Others have been known to walk for miles in search of their beloved humans. This loyalty is incredibly moving when you think about it. One of my favourite moments is coming home after a long day—my dog is always the first at the door, tail wagging, thrilled to see me. Compare that with humans—sometimes we're home for hours before someone even notices.

That said, owning a pet is a serious commitment. If you don't have the time to care for one properly, it's better not to have one at all. Animals don't like to be alone for long periods. They're social creatures, just like us. If you work long hours, consider having two dogs so they can keep each other company. Imagine spending all day in silence, waiting to hear a single voice. It would drive anyone mad. Animals need walks, playtime, interaction—and most importantly, love.

I still remember my first dog, Coral. He was beautiful. One day, he showed up at our door, and my mum let him in. We never found his original owner, so we kept him. It was the first time we had an animal in our home. Unfortunately, my mum eventually realised she couldn't care for him properly—we didn't have the resources or time. I cried for weeks after Coral left. I even slept with his pillow. Now, as an adult, I understand why she made that decision. A pet deserves more than just scraps from the table. They need proper food, time, and attention.

Later in life, I faced the same painful decision. I had to rehome two of my dogs—one was very energetic and needed a life chasing rabbits and running outdoors, and the other came at a time when my parents needed care and attention. It broke my heart, but I had to think of the dogs' needs above my own. I didn't make a penny from giving them away, but I made sure they went to loving homes where they'd be well cared for.

If you're considering getting a pet, remember the old saying: "A dog is for life, not just for Christmas." Pets require love, patience, attention, and time. If you can't provide that, please don't abandon them on the streets or, worse, try to harm them. Take them to a rescue centre or find someone who can care for them. Dumping them in the woods or in bags is cruel and inhumane.

A vet friend of mine from Gran Canaria once said, "Why not go to a rescue centre instead of buying a dog? So many animals are waiting for someone to love them." And he's right. You don't need a fancy pedigree breed when there are countless beautiful, loving dogs in shelters just hoping for a second chance.

One thing I admire about living in the UK is how much people here care for their pets. It's inspiring to see how well animals are treated and cherished.

So, before you bring a pet into your home, take a moment to reflect. Ask yourself if you're truly ready. Animals give us so much—let's make sure we give them the love and life they deserve in return.

Having a pet is a long-term commitment. They need your time, care, patience, and love—every single day. In return, they give you loyalty, joy, and friendship like no other.

If you're not sure what kind of animal is right for you, visit a rescue centre and speak with professionals. They'll help match you with the perfect companion.

Understanding ourselves, setting boundaries, growing through challenges, caring for our health, and extending compassion to others—these are not separate endeavors but interconnected aspects of a life lived with intention and awareness. When we love ourselves deeply, we naturally extend that love outward. When we treat ourselves with kindness, we become capable of genuine kindness toward others. The journey of self-love isn't selfish—it's the foundation from which all other love flows.

Chapter 6: Understanding Love

Love is perhaps the most complex and beautiful aspect of human experience. It can lift us to incredible heights and challenge us in ways we never expected. In this chapter, we explore what love truly means, how to recognise it, and how to build relationships that honour both partners while fostering genuine connection and growth.

Love and Relationships

Do you love yourself? That's a question worth pondering. Shakespeare once said, "Journeys end in lovers meeting," and he also remarked that "Love is blind." He wasn't wrong. How often have you found yourself in relationships or situations where the love you offered wasn't reciprocated, or where you realised the relationship wasn't meant for you? Unrequited love can be one of the most painful experiences, leaving you feeling unseen and unloved.

As we near the end of another year, take a moment to reflect: How much love have you given to people who didn't deserve even a second of your time? How often have you waited for someone to love you the way you deserve, only to find that they couldn't or wouldn't? If you're in a relationship where your needs aren't being met, ask yourself—what do you do? Do you always initiate contact, hoping they'll eventually change and reciprocate your efforts? Do you keep giving your all, despite receiving little in return? These questions can be difficult but necessary to answer, especially during times that can be joyful for some yet deeply lonely for others.

Heartache and longing can feel sharper during certain seasons, particularly when love feels out of reach. For many, it's a painful reality to be apart from loved ones or to feel trapped in a one-sided relationship. I've had my own experiences with love that taught me valuable lessons. Let me share one with you.

I remember my first love—or at least, what I thought was my first love. I was very young. Can you imagine? At the time, I believed I'd found something truly special. They say everyone has a soulmate, but I've come to believe we may encounter more than one in our lifetime. Each relationship teaches us something and brings us closer to finding the person who truly complements us. That first love didn't last more than a few months before I fell in love again. Yes, that's possible. Sometimes we think we've found the one, only to realise later that they weren't right for us.

How many times have you believed you've found "the one," only to discover otherwise? It's both heartbreaking and humbling. Yet I love hearing stories from people who say, "I've met my soulmate, and I'm so happy." When you find someone who reciprocates your love, respects you, cares for you, and helps you grow as both an individual and a partner, you've truly found something precious. But let's be clear: love isn't a fairy tale. It's not about "living happily ever after" without effort. Maintaining a healthy, fulfilling relationship requires consistent work from both partners.

My sisters often tell me I'm a dreamer, probably because I adore films like Pride and Prejudice and You've Got Mail. During the COVID-19 pandemic, I must have watched those movies countless times. I even memorised some of the lines! My daughters would tease me, saying, "You're not watching that movie again, are you?" And I'd just laugh. Despite their teasing, those stories remind me of the beauty and possibility of love.

I sincerely believe love is out there for everyone. When you meet someone new, give them a chance. Trust your instincts, though—time is precious, and you deserve a love that uplifts you. But first, and most importantly, you must love yourself. When you prioritise self-love, you set the standard for how others should treat you. You'll no longer tolerate being treated poorly or settling for less than you deserve.

When you find the right person, love won't feel like a struggle. It will be mutual and natural. They will want to spend time with you, communicate with you, and be genuinely interested in your life. Love isn't complicated when it's right. You won't have to wait endlessly or chase after it. Trust me on this: the right person will make you feel seen, valued, and loved for who you are.

So as we approach a new year, take time to reflect on your relationships—past and present. Let go of those who don't deserve your love, and hold space for the ones who do. Most importantly, love yourself first. That's the foundation for finding and sustaining the love you truly deserve.

Understanding What is Love

This exploration is dedicated to a family member and to everyone who is going through similar situations every day. I have reflected on love in previous thoughts, but this focuses on understanding what love truly is.

When someone makes you cry, it is not love. When someone speaks to you in a derogatory or demeaning way, it is not love. Love does not insult you or belittle you. When someone hides you from others, that is not love. When someone constantly criticises you, that is not love. Love is not someone who speaks kindly to you one day and ignores you the next.

When someone tells you, "I am not ready," or "I can't see you because I'm stressed or have other things on my mind," that is not love. A person who truly loves you will make time for you. They will prioritise you because you matter to them. The person who loves you will make you feel like you are their priority—not their second choice.

Too often, we mistake lust, physical attraction, or dependency for love. Some people may use you because they have never truly been loved and don't know how to love. This is not about judging anyone, but understanding that love is something entirely different.

Love is not a fairy tale where everyone gets a perfect happy ending, but it is still profound and meaningful. Never beg for love. If you have to beg, it is not love. Someone is using you, and you need to recognise the signs.

Love is not jealousy, anger, manipulation, lying, disrespect, or shouting. None of these behaviours represent love. Please take the time to recognise the signs of unhealthy relationships and talk about them with someone you trust.

Types of Love:

1. **Romantic Love**: A deep emotional and physical attraction to another person, often involving intimacy, passion, and commitment.

2. **Platonic Love**: Affectionate love that is non-romantic, such as the bond shared with close friends.

3. **Familial Love**: The love and care shared within families, such as between parents and children.

4. **Self-Love**: Respecting and valuing yourself, which is essential for personal well-being and forming healthy relationships.

5. **Unconditional Love**: Love given without conditions or expectations, often associated with altruism or spirituality.

6. **Compassionate Love**: Empathy and kindness extended to others, including strangers or communities.

I have reflected on this before, but it is important to address it again because these issues continue to affect society.

Love is when someone truly wants to see you and be with you. You are their priority. They can't wait to spend time with you, to talk to you, and to share moments with you. They look at you with kindness, respect, admiration, and a genuine desire for your happiness. Love allows you to grow both as a couple and as individuals.

The person who loves you wants the best for you. They want to hear the good news in your life and support you through your challenges. Even if you are far away, they will wait for you because their love for you is sincere.

Can You Love Yourself This Way?

Please ask yourself: Can you love yourself in this way? If you are not able to love yourself, it's essential to work on building that love within before expecting it from someone else. Loving yourself first is the foundation for finding someone who will love you the way you deserve. Until then, you may find yourself in relationships that lack real love, mistaking unhealthy behaviours for affection.

Understand that love brings peace, tranquillity, and emotional stability. Mentally, it feels like a shower of endorphins when someone who truly loves you is around. They will want the best for you, no more and no less.

This year, dedicate time to loving and valuing yourself. When you do, you will come to understand what love truly is.

I'm sharing this to support you on this journey and to remind you that love starts within.

Quality in the Relationship versus Material Things in Life

This is one of those timeless questions: Why do I always end up with the wrong person?

But maybe the real question is—What are you actually looking for? Are you looking for the material things—the beauty, the house, the job? Or are you searching for kindness, compassion, genuine affection, and love?

Today, I had a conversation with one of my daughters about buying a car. She mentioned that she liked a certain car, even though it was about the same price as another one we had seen over the weekend. The difference? The one she liked was beautiful, but the quality was not as good. I asked her, "What do you really want from this car—beauty or quality?" Her answer made me stop and reflect.

As parents, we try to guide our children the best we can. But in the end, they have to make their own choices. We all know that. Still, it's hard to watch them make mistakes—mistakes we ourselves once made. That's how we all learn.

But there's a connection here, between how we choose a car and how we choose a partner. Too often, we go for the beauty—the dazzling car, the dream vacation, the perfect image—and forget to look deeper.

Beauty fades with time. But the quality of a person—their character, their values—those things remain. Maybe what we really need to do is look beyond what someone owns or how they appear on the outside.

Yes, we all want to enjoy nice things in life. That's natural. But let me tell you this: If you find someone who gives you love, patience, care, loyalty, and honesty—then you've already won the lottery. Everything else can be built together.

Look into their eyes. If you find someone who makes you laugh, who holds your hand, who goes to bed beside you each night with love and trust in their heart—then you've found your soulmate and best friend.

And that is worth more than anything money can buy.

Getting the Love You Deserve – Why Some Relationships Work and Others Don't

I hope everyone had a great time and enjoyed spending time with family, friends and yourselves. I thought to reflect on relationships and what happens when you are not getting the relationship that you deserve. Yes, this is right—we all deserve to be in an honest relationship and to feel secure and safe.

Sometimes we hold on to relationships that don't work and we find it very difficult to let go. To lose someone is difficult, but to learn to be with yourself is a necessity—it's a way of freedom.

Living by yourself is not a punishment. Sometimes we need to do this in order to find ourselves and to work on some of our behaviours. If someone says to you they love you but some days they don't love you, this is not love—this is a condition. I love you if you do what I say or what I want you to do. But how curious that we say to our children that we love them unconditionally and we accept certain behaviours because they are our kids. Other people have to work really hard to demonstrate their love. Are you not curious about our own behaviour and what we allow others to do, yet we excuse our own children?

I have experience of seeing couples fighting for their relationship with their own children, and not being able to have the same boundaries with their own children. It can sometimes be a bit chaotic when one of the parents sets one rule and the other sets a different rule, especially when the parents are divorced.

While each situation is different, there are a variety of reasons why some relationships don't work. Some of the main reasons why relationships fail:

1. Failure or loss of trust
2. Poor communication
3. Lack of respect
4. Differences in priorities
5. Little intimacy

And many more. The partner or friend is not listening and spending time with them and putting themselves in their shoes. I fully understand that sometimes we are not able to do this because we might be going through other issues, but if you are able to communicate with your partner or anyone else, this might help you with your communication and let them know that although you care for them, you are not able to support them because of your own circumstances.

We tend to open up to others and we don't talk to the person that we love, or at least we said that we do. In all my thoughts, I keep saying if you don't know how to love yourself, you are not able to love others. For example, if I don't drink water, how can I give water to another person? But even if you do, you are not taking care of yourself.

Some relationships work because from the beginning they are honest with each other, don't hide anything, and you are yourself. So when they choose you, they know what they are getting involved with. Relationship is a choice, but sometimes some of the choices are not the right ones because the other person is not telling you the truth about themselves. Yes, it is scary to be honest and say what you have done or who you are, but I can promise you any relationship started with a bad foundation will not go anywhere. It's like building a house—if you use the wrong materials, the house will fall down, so the relationship is the same.

We are going into a new year, or meeting new people. Think about how do you want the relationship to be? How would you like to build a new friendship? Are you scared to be yourself? If someone loves you, they will love you like they love their children—otherwise it's not love, it's a condition.

When the Romance Fades: Remembering Love and Choosing It Again

Can you remember the first time you went on a date with your partner? How they looked at you, smiled at you, treated you like you were the most important person in the world?

In my work with individuals and couples, I hear a recurring theme. People reflect on how things used to be—the little gestures, the attention, the love. And then they talk about what's changed. The silence. The distance. The absence of connection. They ask me, "Where did it all go?"

I remember a dear friend telling me how much she used to adore her husband in their early years. She laughed as she described how, on rainy days, he would get out of the car to wipe the water off the sunroof so she could see the sky. It was a small thing, but it meant the world to her.

Years later, she was heartbroken. The gestures stopped. The time together disappeared. The affection faded. She was left feeling unseen, uncared for, and alone—though still married.

This is a story I hear often.

Do you remember how your partner used to make you feel when you first met? Do you remember the excitement, the attention, the little surprises, the way they looked at you like you were the only one in the room?

And now, do you feel like something has changed? That all of that effort has stopped?

Sadly, many couples go through this transition. It doesn't happen all at once. Life gets busy. Stress builds up. Technology distracts us. And slowly, we stop looking at each other. We stop making the effort. We stop remembering why we fell in love in the first place.

As a therapist, I guide others through these struggles—but I'm also a human being. I, too, have faced heartbreak. I've had to walk away from relationships where I was giving and giving, only to realise the other person was only there for their own benefit.

Yes, it hurts. But these experiences taught me an important truth: It's better to be alone than to stay in a relationship where you're not respected, valued, or loved.

So, what do we do when love fades?

We talk.

We communicate our needs and feelings. We stop waiting for the other person to change and take ownership of what we can change. If your partner isn't willing to meet you halfway, then you have a decision to make—for your own peace and well-being.

Because waiting for someone to change who has no intention of changing? That's not love. That's suffering.

Love Doesn't Stop—But Effort Often Does

Some people joke, "Now that we're married, I've already won. I don't need to try anymore." But behind the joke is a painful truth.

Many couples stop dating after marriage. They stop showing affection. They stop complimenting each other, touching each other, making each other feel wanted. They stop looking into each other's eyes.

Instead, they sit in silence, in front of the television or behind their screens—while the person they once adored becomes like furniture in the room: present, but unnoticed.

To the Ones Who Feel Invisible

And what about those who feel stuck? Who don't leave because they've aged, gained weight, or have children?

Let me say this clearly: You are still worthy of love. You are still beautiful. You are still needed.

Don't ever let anyone—or yourself—convince you otherwise.

Love Is a Verb. Do the Work.

I often suggest to my patients: take your partner out once a week. Just the two of you. No distractions. Talk about your week. Ask what you need from each other. Laugh. Connect. Even once a month makes a difference.

Marriage is not the finish line. It's where the real journey begins.

Romance doesn't die; it's forgotten. And what's forgotten can be remembered.

Consistency, Not Perfection

So, what keeps love alive? It's not grand gestures once in a while. It's consistency.

It's showing up for your partner. Listening. Loving. Holding them when they need you. Seeing them for who they are, even as life and bodies change.

Yes, the hair may go grey. The bodies may soften. Life may bring stress. But that soul—the one you fell in love with—is still there. If you can see it, and nurture it, love can bloom again.

Don't wait until it's too late. Look at your partner. Touch their hand. Speak kind words. Laugh again. Love again. You can still choose each other.

And if you're no longer with someone who values you, let that pain guide you to a deeper truth: Loving yourself is the first step to being loved well by someone else.

With Gratitude, Love and Care.

Chapter 7: Finding and Building Healthy Relationships

The journey of love and connection is one of life's most profound experiences, yet it can also be one of the most challenging. In my years as a therapist, I've witnessed countless individuals struggle with questions about relationships—how to find the right person, how to recognise authentic character, and how to build something meaningful that lasts. This chapter explores these fundamental questions through both professional insights and personal reflections, offering you practical wisdom for creating the healthy, fulfilling relationships you deserve.

Finding the Right Person

As a therapist, I often reflect on how to support others without judgment—just listening and providing empathy. One of the recurring topics in my sessions is relationships, particularly the question: How do we find the right person? When discussing relationships with patients, family and friends, I often ask what has happened in their relationship. If a person claims they made no mistakes and places all the blame on their partner, my first question is: "What would the other person say about you?" This perspective can sometimes lead to confusion, as blame is frequently one-sided. However, a relationship involves two people, and its success or failure is rarely the fault of just one party.

Relationships are shaped by many factors, including communication, respect, honesty, and trust. Everyone seeks happiness, but emotions like joy, sadness, frustration, and anger are temporary. If you expect everlasting happiness, I regret to tell you that every relationship requires effort. A strong relationship is built on consistency, honesty, respect, and trust—these are essential elements for finding and maintaining a healthy connection.

One of the most challenging aspects of meeting someone new is discussing past relationships. If a person insists, they were perfect and did nothing wrong, the foundation of the new relationship may be built on a lie. Over time, as you begin to see things for yourself, disappointment may set in. This raises an important question: Have you been honest about your past? Have you truly reflected on your role in your previous relationships?

This principle applies to many aspects of life, including recovery programs like Alcoholics Anonymous, drug rehabilitation, and domestic violence counselling. Being upfront about both successes and failures is crucial. Many may resist this idea, fearing they will end up alone if they acknowledge their flaws. However, personal growth begins with self-awareness—recognising what needs to change in our approach to relationships. It takes courage, but honesty is the key to understanding who you are dating and ensuring a healthier connection.

Another important question to consider is: What changed from the beginning of your relationship? Many people start relationships with kind gestures and thoughtful words, but over time, these efforts fade. I recall a friend who told me that her boyfriend used to go out of his way to keep things romantic. However, as time passed, he stopped making the same effort, leaving her feeling disappointed. Relationships require ongoing effort to maintain the connection and appreciation that was present in the beginning.

Think about how often you used to compliment your partner compared to now. Relationships should be built on mutual support and encouragement. If your partner is controlling, manipulative, or disrespectful, it is important to set boundaries—or even walk away. Boundaries and open communication are essential in any relationship. Do not be afraid to be yourself and speak honestly. Yes, there is a risk that your partner may not like what they hear, but it is better to know if the relationship is built on honesty and a willingness to learn from mistakes.

I have made mistakes in my life, but these experiences have taught me valuable lessons. I have learned that in order to have a healthy relationship, I must be willing to grow and make positive changes. Self-awareness and honest communication are key to building strong, lasting relationships. Instead of blaming others, take a moment to look in the mirror and reflect on yourself. Be honest with others and give them the choice to be with you, knowing that sooner or later, the truth will come out, and they may walk away. Be gentle and kind.

Remember that love isn't just about one day of the year—it's about all 365 days. The daily choices we make, the consistent effort we put forth, and the ongoing commitment to growth and understanding create the foundation for meaningful relationships.

Recognising True Character

Understanding someone's true character takes time and careful observation. The early stages of attraction can cloud our judgment, making it essential to look beyond first impressions and examine the deeper qualities that will determine long-term compatibility. Getting to know someone deeply can be challenging, as a person's true character is often revealed over time, especially when you live with them. When we first meet someone and feel an initial attraction, we may think we love them, but this is just the beginning stage of a relationship. First impressions are important, but they can also be deceiving. People often present their best selves initially, which may not accurately reflect their true nature.

A psychologist once said that there are no truly toxic relationships—only incompatibility. Just as in the animal kingdom, not all species get along and even within the same species, conflicts arise. Similarly, in human relationships, compatibility is key. Therefore, before building any kind of relationship, whether romantic or platonic, observe how the person speaks, thinks, and reacts to different situations.

The way someone treats others says a lot about their character. Have you ever met someone who constantly speaks negatively about others and lacks empathy? Imagine how they might talk about you when you're not around. Everyone has moments of frustration or rudeness due to personal struggles, but ask yourself: if this person treats others poorly now, how might they treat you in the future? If they are consistently unkind, abusive, or lacking in empathy, it may indicate selfishness. Pay attention to how they interact with others—it can provide insight into how they will treat you.

Actions speak louder than words. Watch how a person takes responsibility for their choices and how they treat others over time. In the early stages of a relationship, everything may seem perfect, but as time passes, you may notice red flags that were initially overlooked. There is a saying: "The more I know people, the more I love my animals." While this may be extreme, it highlights the importance of thinking critically rather than idealising a person. Many people enter relationships hoping that love, a home, or even children will change their partner, but in reality, we cannot change others—we can only change ourselves.

Honesty is a fundamental trait in any relationship. If you notice inconsistencies in someone's words, pay attention. If a person frequently lies, even about small things, consider the potential consequences for your relationship. Dishonesty erodes trust, and if they lie to others, what stops them from lying to you?

Observing how someone handles challenges is crucial. Do they take responsibility for their mistakes, or do they always blame others? In my professional experience, particularly working with couples, I often see individuals blaming their partners instead of reflecting on their own actions. If someone constantly avoids accountability, they have not learned from their experiences. Instead of calling them mistakes, I prefer to view them as learning experiences. When evaluating someone's character, consider how they reflect on their own behaviour rather than how they judge others.

How someone treats their friends and family can reveal a lot about their character. Respecting boundaries and maintaining healthy relationships are key indicators of emotional intelligence and integrity. I recall an experience when I first arrived in England. I worked at a video rental store because I didn't speak English well and had to start somewhere. One day, a customer was browsing for a movie and talking to me when another person walked in. They greeted each other like old friends, laughing and chatting. I assumed they had a close bond. However, after the second person left, the first customer made a harsh, negative comment about them. That moment made me realise that if he could speak that way about his "friend," he could easily do the same to me.

By observing how someone speaks about and treats those close to them, you can gain valuable insight into their character. While no one is perfect, being mindful of these traits can help you make better decisions about the people you choose to have in your life. Remember to observe, listen, and think critically before deeply investing in any relationship. Life is a continuous learning experience, and we grow from our interactions with others.

Building Healthy Relationships

Understanding what makes a relationship truly healthy requires looking beyond surface attractions and examining the fundamental values that create lasting connections. In today's world, where many seek quick fixes and instant gratification, building something meaningful takes patience and intentionality. Since arriving in Gran Canaria, I've noticed how many people are searching for love and companionship. At the same time, I've also heard comments from people who prefer to stay single but enjoy weekend relationships or casual connections, often due to a fear of experiencing a negative relationship. Some opt for one-night stands or friendships with benefits. The world has changed so much—relationships don't seem to last, and it's sad that we often fail to communicate effectively when communication should be the foundation of any connection.

I've said this before, and I will keep repeating it: communication is essential. Don't pretend to be someone you're not. If you truly want to meet someone, be clear about what you want. Time is precious, and the energy you invest in relationships should be meaningful for both you and others.

Many people fear loving and not being loved in return, so they pretend not to care—but is that really true? Others seek status, wealth, or financial security in a partner. While I understand not wanting a partner who depends entirely on you, some people, conversely, look for someone they can depend on. I respect different perspectives, so please don't take this as judgment.

But ask yourself: What would it be like to choose a partner based solely on who they are rather than what they have? I've seen many couples form because of money, material possessions, or social status.

However, if you find the right partner, you can build these things together—and the satisfaction of growing as a team is immense. The belief that you must find someone to provide for you is outdated. I once spoke with a patient who told me her husband treated her poorly, but she stayed because he provided financial security. What do you think about that?

Now, imagine choosing a partner based on their values, morals, and ability to communicate and connect with you. Imagine being with someone who respects and admires you. That is worth more than anything money can buy. When you realise that you are capable of standing on your own, the fear of being alone disappears—because you know you will thrive, with or without a partner.

Yes, money rules the world, and I could write extensively on this topic. Lately, I've been deeply curious about human behaviour and what drives our actions. Where do these patterns come from? What shapes the way we approach love and relationships? I'd love to hear your thoughts. What is most important in your relationships? Do you value material things, or do you focus on the person? In my work with couples, I often see people staying together purely for financial stability and social status.

Take a moment to reflect—look at the clock and think: from the moment you are born, time is counting down, not up. I'm simply trying to be realistic about this. Lately, everything seems to revolve around money, and what stands out to me as particularly sad is how people use others when it benefits them. But in reality, when someone has nothing left to offer, many of those around them suddenly disappear.

We are not children—we are adults, so let's behave like it. Don't waste people's time because of your insecurities or uncertainty about what you want. Don't lie—you are not a child. But most importantly, don't fall in love too quickly. First, make sure you are in a good place emotionally, and second, be certain that the other person wants the same thing as you.

Too many people are talking to multiple others simply because they are lost and unsure of what they truly want. Some have been through so much that they no longer care if they hurt someone else. Remember, those who have been hurt or bullied often, without realising it, repeat the same behaviour.

Meet people, enjoy the process, but don't settle until you find the right one. One thing I've noticed—and something I find very interesting—is that as people get older, it often seems to get worse. They come up with endless excuses: I'm not ready, I need to find myself, I'm unsure, and so on. But the truth is, if someone truly likes you, they will never get bored of you. They will want more of you. If someone loves you, they will move mountains—you know this.

Value and respect yourself. Stop searching so desperately—the right person will find you in one way or another. I sincerely believe that we meet different people for different reasons, and each of them teaches us something. One important lesson I've learned in life is how to distinguish between those who genuinely want something meaningful with me and those who are just looking for a bit of fun. Now, it's up to you to decide what you want for your life. As I always tell my friends and family, the world is your oyster. It's your choice how you spend your time on this earth. Don't waste it on people who make you suffer, use you, or lie to you.

Move forward, and I truly believe—based on both my own experiences and the stories I've heard—that you will find the right person one day. But even if you don't, I'm sure you will have learned something valuable about yourself and others.

The Power of Communication

Effective communication forms the backbone of every healthy relationship, yet it's often the area where we struggle most. Understanding how to express ourselves authentically while creating space for others to do the same can transform not just our relationships, but our entire experience of connection. How do we truly connect with others? What do you say when you don't feel respected, loved, or cared for? Are you able to show vulnerability and express your feelings, or do you keep them to yourself for fear that others might take advantage of you?

I'm sure we've all experienced moments when we hesitated to express our emotions—perhaps because of fear, pride, or ego. Sometimes, we hold back even when something hurts, fearing that admitting it may make us seem weak. It's been said that words hold incredible power; they can either build someone up or tear them down. While physical wounds are visible, the damage caused by words often goes unseen—but it can be just as devastating. Many problems in the world arise from poor communication—misunderstandings, power struggles, manipulation, and control. Every day, I witness how painful it can be to see someone's life harmed by just a few careless words.

Many of us struggle with effective communication because of our upbringing. As children, some of us were taught to suppress our voices—to avoid speaking our minds for fear of judgment or punishment. We were told to be quiet, and over time, this silencing affected our ability to express ourselves. This suppression can lead to unhealthy communication patterns. Instead of calmly discussing our feelings, we may resort to shouting, just as children do. Adults should talk, but if we were raised in households where yelling was the norm, it can feel confusing to break that cycle.

Technology, too, has played a role in diminishing our communication skills. These days, gadgets often take precedence over face-to-face conversations. Many relationships falter because people are more focused on their screens than on each other. Another obstacle is self-esteem. We may fear saying the wrong thing and being laughed at or judged. I often tell my clients that it's better to express their thoughts and feelings than to keep them bottled up, as unspoken emotions can lead to anxiety and depression.

Additionally, fear of rejection or abandonment can make us hesitant to share our true selves with loved ones. We worry that being honest about our feelings may cause others to leave us. Even authority figures can unintentionally suppress communication. Many people assume that "the expert knows best" and don't question diagnoses or decisions. But I encourage my clients to trust their instincts and ask questions. You know your body and your experiences better than anyone else.

When you feel sad, worried, or unheard, try to express your feelings in a safe environment where the other person is fully present and attentive. Practice active listening by encouraging the other person to listen carefully by repeating back what they've heard. For example, one person speaks for a minute or two, and the other repeats what they understood. This ensures both parties feel heard and acknowledged.

Share how you feel and why certain words or actions have affected you. It's okay to be open and honest. For couples or close relationships, consider setting aside time to discuss what's going well and what needs improvement. Leave phones or distractions behind to focus entirely on each other. If you don't understand something, ask, "What do you mean by that?" Clear communication prevents misunderstandings and strengthens connections.

Speak your truth, but do so with kindness and consideration. Ask how the other person feels and what impact your conversations may have on them. My mother often said, "It's better to be red for a moment than yellow for a lifetime." What she meant was that it's better to speak the truth, even if it's uncomfortable, than to stay silent and suffer in silence.

If someone truly cares about you, they will listen and try to understand. Patience is key. Listening is one of the greatest gifts you can give someone. As a professional, I know how challenging it can be to tune into others' emotions, especially when dealing with my own thoughts and feelings. However, I've learned to leave my personal concerns outside the room to fully support my clients. When I make mistakes, I remind myself to apologise, because we're all human, and we're all learning.

Effective communication is the foundation of strong relationships. Remember to be kind and patient with yourself and others. Take the time to listen and express yourself honestly. If you need space, allow yourself to take it—but don't keep your feelings locked inside. Let's work together to create a world where everyone feels heard, valued, and loved.

Healing and Self-Awareness

The intersection of personal healing and relationship building is perhaps one of the most important aspects of creating lasting love. Before we can truly connect with another person, we must first understand ourselves—our patterns, our wounds, and our capacity for growth. The journey of therapy can be meaningful when someone chooses to open up and share their life with another person. For many, the idea of sitting with a therapist and speaking honestly about your struggles can feel daunting. It takes courage. And it's completely understandable to feel nervous or unsure in that space.

So often, we hear people say how hard it is to talk about their pain—their inner challenges, or as I sometimes call them, their "demons." But along with those struggles, we also carry goodness, strength, and resilience. Therapy is a space where both can be seen and held.

As a therapist, when I sit with someone, my intention is always to listen deeply. To offer presence, not just advice. Over time, I've learned that supporting others also invites me to reflect on my own patterns, my own history, and the importance of understanding how we all relate to one another—especially in relationships.

One question I often explore gently with clients is: "If your partner were sitting here, what might they say about you?" It's not a trick question, and it's never about blame. Instead, it's a doorway into self-awareness. We often think about what we want or need in a relationship, but we may not always reflect on how we show up, or how we're experienced by those we care about.

When I work with couples, I often say, "Let's begin with the idea that both people bring something to the dynamic. Let's call it 50/50—not to measure fault, but to explore together what's happening between you." This helps create a shared space for discovery, not judgment.

Behind most relationship struggles are deeper stories—about early attachment, unmet emotional needs, fear of abandonment, or the lingering effects of feeling unloved or unseen. For example, if someone learned early in life that love was conditional or inconsistent, it's understandable that they might struggle with trust or closeness now. And if someone carries unresolved anger, that too may affect how they connect with a partner.

Therapy can offer a place to begin making sense of these patterns. But meaningful growth often depends on whether we feel ready—not just to talk, but to truly reflect. Are we open to gently looking inward? Are we curious about how our past might be shaping our present?

These aren't easy questions. They require honesty, patience, and often a good deal of self-compassion. It's natural to want to talk about how others have hurt us. That can be a valid and important part of healing. But at the same time, we can also ask ourselves: What part might I have played in this relationship dynamic? Are there patterns that seem to repeat across different relationships? Have I had the space to work through my own pain before stepping into something new?

You don't have to have it all figured out. But taking time to pause and reflect—before starting or restarting a relationship—can be one of the kindest things you can do, both for yourself and for the other person. When we haven't yet healed, it's easy to carry old wounds into new connections, even when we have the best intentions.

This is something I've seen many times. People often come to therapy feeling stuck or frustrated, and sometimes hoping that I'll affirm their perspective. And while it's important to feel heard, I also try to gently invite them to explore the full picture. Not because they're wrong—but because deeper insight lives there.

It can be helpful to ask: Was I open and honest in my communication? Was I present when my partner needed support? Were there moments where I could have responded differently, with more care or awareness?

Taking responsibility doesn't mean blaming ourselves. It means recognising our power. When we acknowledge our part—without shame—we begin to reclaim the ability to make different choices moving forward. Just like in recovery programs where someone might say, "I'm learning to take responsibility for my actions," this kind of self-awareness is a powerful beginning. It doesn't mean we've failed; it means we're growing.

Relationships aren't about perfection. None of us have perfect attachment styles or perfect communication. But we can learn. We can get better at listening, at being present, at showing love in the way the other person needs—not just the way we've always known.

And if you're not quite there yet, that's okay, too. Healing is a process, and sometimes, we need time. But when we do begin to look inward—with honesty and gentleness—that's where change starts. That's when real connection becomes possible, not only with others, but with ourselves.

So, wherever you are on your journey, I hope you give yourself permission to grow, to be kind to yourself, and to take steps—however small—toward the life and relationships you truly want.

Love at Every Stage of Life

Love and connection remain vital throughout our entire lives, regardless of age or past experiences. The desire for meaningful relationships doesn't diminish as we grow older—if anything, the wisdom that comes with experience can make these connections even more precious and authentic. I started to reflect on how many people come to my country for the weather, which made me more aware of age. People in their 50s, 60s, 70s, and 80s are seeking happiness, sunshine, rest, and enjoyment. While observing and reflecting, I thought about Facebook and all the love groups for older adults. It made me wonder why so many people struggle to find love, even after multiple marriages and relationships.

Someone once told me that after a certain age, people in multiple relationships are just "the ones others didn't want." At first, I laughed at this comment, but then I thought, does this mean that after a certain point in life, we just wait for the end? Are we not deserving of love and connection anymore? I hope you don't agree with that statement.

Many believe that being married all your life means you've found the right person or that you are happy. But that's not always true. Some people stay in marriages despite unhappiness, while others divorce and continue searching for the right connection. I don't believe in the idea of a single soulmate; I think we have many soulmates throughout our lives. Everyone has flaws—we are all imperfect. But the desire to find love and companionship never fades, no matter our age.

Time moves forward, and we all reach our final destination eventually. Don't waste your time and life. Some people genuinely seek a deep connection, while others just want fleeting moments of passion or casual relationships. This frustrates many who are looking for something real, leaving them feeling disheartened and disappointed. Social platforms were created for meaningful connections, yet many use them irresponsibly, playing with emotions instead of being honest about their intentions.

If you're only looking for something casual, say it openly. Some people won't mind, but others will be respectful of their feelings. Consider this: if you had children, would you want them to be treated with dishonesty and disrespect? If the answer is no, then don't do it to others.

Many people come to me feeling heartbroken, struggling with self-worth, and trying to set boundaries. If you resonate with what I'm saying, please think about how your actions affect others. Last night, I was looking at pictures of myself taken in Gran Canaria and noticed how much younger I looked in some. It made me reflect on the way people present themselves online.

Whatever picture you post online, remember that you will eventually meet people in real life. If someone doesn't connect with you afterwards, ask yourself why. Love yourself as you are—whether small, large, young, old, beautiful, or imperfect. True beauty comes from within. As we age, our hair turns gray, our stomachs grow, and our skin wrinkles. Unless you spend a fortune on maintaining your looks—which I respect—it's ultimately about connection, communication, and emotional depth, not just appearance.

Physical attraction matters, but it fades with time. What remains is how well you connect, communicate, and share experiences with your partner. Don't fall for someone just because of initial attraction—get to know them first.

Of course, I see many people looking great in their 20s, 30s, 40s, and 50s. But whatever you do, do it for yourself, not for validation from others. Social media and comparisons have caused unnecessary pain, destroying many relationships and families.

When I see an older couple looking into each other's eyes with love and admiration, it's truly beautiful. Tell your partner they are beautiful or handsome, even with wrinkles. Make them smile every day. We are not young forever, and neither are the people in the perfect pictures we see online.

Find someone with similar interests. Differences are normal, but approach them with love and respect. Finally, relationships need nurturing. The beginning is always exciting, but like a plant, a relationship needs daily care to grow beautifully over time. Work on your relationship, cherish your partner, and remember that true love is built through kindness, communication, and mutual effort.

Chapter 8: Relationship Challenges

Even the healthiest relationships face difficulties, and understanding how to navigate these challenges can mean the difference between growth and destruction. The issues explored in this chapter—dominance, jealousy, infidelity, divorce, trust, and dishonesty—represent some of the most complex and painful experiences couples encounter. Rather than avoiding these difficult topics, we must examine them honestly, with compassion for all involved, and with the understanding that awareness is the first step toward healing and positive change.

Power Dynamics and Control

Have you ever been in a relationship where your partner always had to be right, no matter what you did or said? A relationship where you felt diminished, unable to be yourself because of the other person's constant need for control? How many times have you been at a party or event, only to find your partner taking over conversations and making you feel small in front of others?

This behaviour can be extremely damaging to the relationship. It can create deep feelings of inadequacy, slowly eroding your self-esteem and your sense of identity—especially as a woman or a man. For the partner who is more passive or sensitive, living with someone overly dominant can feel like having a strict father or mother figure at home, rather than an equal partner. It becomes very hard to feel confident and valued.

And how can intimacy flourish when one person feels like a child in the relationship, instead of an equal adult? Think about it: when your partner dominates your conversations with friends, leaving you feeling invisible, isn't that often the beginning of low self-esteem? You aren't treated as an adult; instead, you're pushed back emotionally into feeling like a powerless child. It's disappointing—and painful.

Sometimes, this dominance stems from past wounds—from childhood attachment issues, or from times when that dominant person once had no voice themselves. Ironically, they may have become the very person they once resented. They may shout, insult, or abuse you in subtle or obvious ways—and without realising it, you might begin to lose your own voice, too.

Respect is the foundation of any healthy relationship. Even if one person has a strong personality and the other is more fragile or timid, it's crucial to listen and honour each other's feelings. When one partner is always afraid of the other's reactions, it becomes a relationship ruled by fear, not love.

Remember this: You are just as important as the other person. You don't have to stay in a relationship where you are emotionally abused or treated as less. Maybe your partner was bullied once, but that does not give them the right to bully you now.

On the other hand, when both people in a relationship are dominant, it can also be exhausting. There can be a constant battle for control, with both partners fighting to have the last word. Can you relate to this in your own relationship?

As a couples counsellor, I often see this sad dynamic. Instead of treating each other with love and respect, they act like competitors, unwilling to listen or compromise. Sometimes, it feels like trying to mediate between two young children, each demanding their way without truly hearing the other's needs.

I find it very hard to witness situations where couples feel forced to take pictures or constantly update their partner to "prove" they are being faithful—like taking photos at the doctor's office or when they are out with friends. This often happens when one partner is overly dominant and struggles with losing control over the other person.

Living like this can be extremely humiliating. Being in a relationship without trust feels suffocating. I believe it's important to keep your partner informed about your plans out of respect, but it should never reach the point where you feel pressured or stressed to provide constant proof of your whereabouts. No one should have to explain every detail of their day just to avoid upsetting their partner. That is not love—and it's certainly not safe.

A healthy relationship is built on trust, respect, and freedom, not fear and control. Dominance isn't strength. Often it comes from fear, insecurity, or early life wounds, even if on the surface it looks like confidence.

Jealousy and Its Destructive Power

Jealousy and insecurity can be destructive, damaging both individuals and relationships. These feelings often stem from childhood experiences—such as a lack of parental affection or witnessing favouritism among siblings. When a child observes their parents treating one sibling differently from the others, it can leave a lasting impact, shaping their relationships later in life. This can even extend to their own parenting or how they behave when entering a relationship with someone who has children.

For example, if you are dating someone with children, unresolved jealousy can manifest in negative comments about their parenting.

Some individuals may feel envious of the bond their partner shares with their child, especially if they lacked such love growing up. However, it is essential to remember that love is not finite—there is enough love for everyone. If you struggle with feelings of jealousy or insecurity, open communication with your partner is crucial.

How beautiful it is to see a mother or father having a loving relationship with their child! The love they share with their children does not diminish the love they have for you. Never force your partner to choose between their child and you. Relationships are built between two people, but if children are involved, they should never feel like an obstacle. At the end of your life, your partner will be by your side, but if you have deep-seated insecurities or jealousy, seeking support is essential for your well-being and the health of your relationship.

Jealousy is a complex emotion that arises when a person feels threatened by the possibility of losing something valuable—such as a relationship, status, or possession—to someone else. It often involves feelings of insecurity, fear, resentment, or envy. Understanding its various forms can help us recognise when it appears in our lives.

Romantic jealousy involves fear of losing a partner's attention or love to someone else. Platonic jealousy creates feelings of being threatened in friendships due to the presence of a third person. Professional jealousy manifests as envy of a colleague's success, promotion, or recognition. Sibling jealousy creates competition for parental attention or favouritism. Material jealousy appears as envy of someone else's possessions, wealth, or lifestyle.

The causes run deep. Low self-esteem creates feelings of inadequacy compared to others. Past experiences of betrayal or abandonment leave lasting wounds. Insecurity leads to doubting one's worth in a relationship or situation. Comparison becomes a habit of measuring oneself against others' achievements or qualities.

The effects can be devastating. Jealousy can lead to conflicts, resentment, or toxic behaviour. It may cause anxiety, stress, or depression. Most importantly, it can damage relationships if not managed properly.

Learning to handle jealousy requires self-awareness—recognising and acknowledging your feelings. Improving self-confidence means focusing on your strengths and accomplishments. Open communication involves talking honestly with those involved. Practicing gratitude helps you appreciate what you have instead of comparing yourself to others. Trust-building strengthens trust in relationships to reduce insecurities.

Jealousy can be devastating and can harm both personal and familial relationships. I have seen many couples struggle with jealousy, especially in blended families where step-parents feel threatened by the love between their partner and their child. Some individuals, due to their own unresolved childhood wounds, expect their new partner to fill a void left by their parents. This can lead to tension within the family and, in extreme cases, cause children to feel unwelcome in their own homes.

Both partners need to communicate openly and honestly. Parents should never feel guilty for loving their children in front of their partners and no one should be forced to choose between their partner and their child. If someone asks me to choose, my children will always come first. Love should not be a competition.

If you feel the need for more love and reassurance, talk to your partner, but do not pressure them. Everyone has their own parenting style—rather than criticising, offer support. A strong relationship is built on mutual understanding, trust, and encouragement. Jealousy can destroy relationships, but with effort and communication, it does not have to.

Seek support if needed, and do not let jealousy take control of your life and happiness.

Jealousy and insecurities can be incredibly destructive. In extreme cases, they have led parents to harm their own children or even their spouses, often without realising the depth of their emotions until it's too late. These feelings can also create insecurity in others, sometimes forcing them to hide things from their own partners out of fear. Jealousy is an illness, and this can be treated if you find the right support and to talk about this. Part of my work involves helping people navigate some of the situations I have described here.

Take care of yourself and those around you. If anything in this resonates with you, please seek support if needed and talk to someone about it.

The Reality of Infidelity

Infidelity is a topic that many individuals and couples face at some point in their lives, creating difficulties that can deeply affect relationships. Why do men and women cheat? Have you ever pondered this, or do you know someone struggling with unfaithfulness in their relationship? It's easy to judge someone when we hear about infidelity, but it's crucial to approach this subject with understanding rather than condemnation.

It's often said that men cheat for reasons like pleasure, convenience, and novelty. For many, an affair may feel purely physical or superficial, leading them to claim, "You're the only woman I love," despite their actions. Women, on the other hand, tend to seek emotional connection and understanding in an affair. Their reasons are often more complex and tied to unmet emotional needs. Despite feeling guilty or remorseful during the affair, unresolved issues and a lack of effective communication in the primary relationship may still lead to its breakdown.

The reasons behind infidelity are deeply personal and influenced by various emotional, psychological, and social factors. While motivations differ for everyone, understanding common patterns can help us address underlying issues.

Emotional dissatisfaction often drives infidelity. Feeling unappreciated or emotionally neglected can drive someone to seek intimacy outside their relationship. A lack of connection or being undervalued can lead to seeking validation elsewhere. Physical dissatisfaction also plays a role—unmet physical or sexual needs may push a person toward infidelity, and a lack of compatibility in this area can contribute to the problem.

Poor communication about desires, concerns, or feelings creates emotional distance, making the relationship vulnerable. When couples cannot express their needs or resolve conflicts effectively, one or both partners may look elsewhere for understanding and connection.

Some people seek novelty or excitement. Boredom or the desire for something new and thrilling can lead to infidelity. Some individuals crave the exhilaration of a fresh romantic or sexual connection, especially when their current relationship feels routine or predictable.

Revenge or retaliation sometimes motivates unfaithful behaviour. Infidelity can stem from a desire to retaliate for perceived neglect, betrayal, or a partner's unfaithfulness. This reactive cheating often causes more harm than healing.

Low self-esteem commonly drives unfaithful behaviour through seeking external validation to feel valued or desired. When people don't feel good about themselves, they may look for affirmation outside their primary relationship.

Situational factors like opportunity, temptation, or proximity, coupled with the belief that they won't get caught, can lead to infidelity. Sometimes people find themselves in compromising situations and make choices they wouldn't normally make.

Some individuals struggle with commitment or feel constrained in a monogamous relationship. For these people, the structure of traditional relationships may feel limiting or uncomfortable.

Cultural or social norms can influence behaviour. In some cultures or social circles, infidelity might be normalised or less stigmatised, affecting individual choices. Personal traits or patterns also matter—traits like impulsiveness, narcissism, or a history of cheating can increase the likelihood of infidelity. Unresolved trauma or attachment issues might also play a role.

Alcohol or substance use impairs judgment and can lead to actions a person might not otherwise take. Finally, feeling stifled or controlled in a relationship may drive someone to seek freedom or autonomy through an affair.

While infidelity is complex and deeply personal, it is often a symptom of deeper issues in the relationship or within the individual. Understanding these root causes is crucial for healing and moving forward. Open communication creates a safe space for honest, non-judgmental dialogue about feelings and needs. Strengthening emotional bonds through quality time together nurtures emotional intimacy. Seeking professional help through therapy or counselling can address underlying issues and provide guidance. Setting clear boundaries involves discussing and establishing mutual expectations and boundaries in the relationship. Cultivating trust builds the relationship on mutual respect, trust, and accountability.

Infidelity is a significant challenge, but it's essential to reflect on the consequences of this behaviour. Is it worth risking your family and the person you love for fleeting pleasure? Relationships require effort, communication, and commitment to thrive. They need fun, passion, love, care, and understanding to grow.

Just like plants need water to survive, relationships need constant nurturing. If your relationship is struggling, invest the time and energy to address the issues together. If you can save your relationship, it's worth the effort.

When Relationships End: The Pain of Divorce

I write about divorce with deep empathy for those currently going through or contemplating this difficult experience. I know how emotionally draining this journey can be.

Think back to your first relationship, your first girlfriend or boyfriend, when you believed this was the person you would spend the rest of your life with. But life is unpredictable, and sometimes, the person you once saw a future with may no longer fit into your plans. Whether it's falling out of love, growing apart after many years together, or the strain of raising a family, relationships can change. Sometimes, relationships begin as arranged marriages, where love isn't the initial foundation; it's a choice made for you.

You may have had hopes that things would improve, but then realise that the love you once shared has faded instead of growing. And sometimes, a third party becomes involved in ways you never expected. Some people may even come to the painful realisation that their true feelings lie elsewhere—perhaps even with someone of the same gender. There are countless reasons for relationships to end.

It's often said that walking away from a relationship is easy, but I can assure you, it's far from true. It's not easy to wake up every day knowing that a relationship, once full of promise, is now broken, and that your feelings for that person have changed. But there are children involved, and the responsibility of not wanting to let them down can weigh heavily on your heart. We know that they're not at fault, but as parents, sometimes we feel the need to place blame somewhere as we make this difficult decision.

Leaving someone is painful, especially when you've shared a history with that person. The care may still be there, but the love has faded. It's heartbreaking to share a bed with someone, hoping that things might improve, only to realise that they won't. It's not easy knowing that people will judge your decision, often without understanding the full picture, and that judgment can be deeply hurtful. If you've never experienced this firsthand, it's hard to imagine the emotional toll it takes. But even when the love is gone, the care remains. You can still wish the best for someone, but it's not the same when you kiss them or share a life together.

In the movie Mrs. Doubtfire, there's a poignant moment when Robin Williams' character reads a letter to his children, explaining that sometimes it's better for parents to be apart if it leads to a happier life for everyone involved. Children should never have to witness constant fighting, emotional or domestic violence, or the toxic atmosphere that can result from two people who no longer love each other. Through my work, I've seen that when parents separate, it's often the best option for the children. They thrive in a stable environment where both parents are happier, even if that means living apart.

I know this may be hard to hear, but it's the truth. If you grew up in a home where your parents were unhappy together, you know how destructive that can be. It affects the whole family, especially the children. They grow up learning not to trust, and the trauma can impact their future relationships because of what they witnessed as children. Imagine going to school every day, wondering if your parents are fighting again. Or coming home, dreading the anger that might be directed at you. Children should never feel like they are caught in the crossfire of adult conflicts.

We need to stop pretending that staying together for the sake of the children is always the best choice. We need to think about the long-term impact of our actions. Children are incredibly perceptive. They can sense the tension and are affected by it. It's far more damaging to stay together out of obligation or fear of stigma, religion, culture, or financial reasons if it means subjecting children to an unhealthy environment.

The whole family deserves to live in a situation where they feel secure and loved, not one where they are trapped in the middle of adult conflicts. I know it's a hard truth to accept, but sometimes, divorce is the best option for everyone involved. Our children deserve to feel safe, loved, and happy, even if that means their parents are living separately.

This is a difficult truth to hear, but sometimes couples grow apart and fall in love with someone else. Whatever your struggles may be, remember that children should never have to witness pain, fighting, arguments, or a lack of respect between parents. They did not ask to be born, and while this situation may feel incredibly hard and painful—something no one should have to go through—it happens. More and more, we see this happening. But it's important to think about the consequences of staying together when it's no longer working.

Why stay with someone who no longer loves or cares for you the way you deserve? Yes, it will be hard at first—believe me, I understand. There will be many tears as things come to an end. But you and your partner can still choose how to end your relationship in a way that helps the entire family remain as strong as possible. Even if it doesn't feel amicable at the beginning, in time, you'll see the benefits of handling things in a respectful and thoughtful way.

One day, your children may meet someone and be able to trust again, knowing that relationships can be healthy and safe. Children need to understand that while their parents are no longer together, they are not being divorced from their love. On the contrary, parents can still offer safety, love, communication, and reassurance, letting them know that everything will be okay. Most importantly, show respect for each other, so your children can witness this. If one day, they find themselves in a similar situation, they'll know how to navigate it. Be kind to yourself and try to offer understanding, even though it may be painful.

Rebuilding Trust

Lately, I often hear people say, "I don't trust anyone." It's disheartening to hear this, as I believe much of this issue stems from early attachments. If you couldn't trust your parents—the first people in your life—then trusting others can become a challenge. As we grow up, disappointments from those around us can make us question who we can truly rely on.

A lack of trust can lead to constant caution, doubt, and even anxiety in relationships. It can mean questioning others' intentions, feeling guarded, or struggling to rely on people for support. This, in turn, can cause isolation, difficulties in forming close connections, and even loneliness. Often, distrust is rooted in past betrayals, disappointments, or personal insecurities. While a healthy level of scepticism can protect you, excessive distrust can make it difficult to build meaningful relationships.

I've often heard people say, "If someone talks about others behind their backs, be careful—they might do the same to you." While this can be true, I also believe that if a person struggles to connect well with others, they might unintentionally cause harm. My advice is to observe and listen carefully before making judgments about whom to trust.

One thing that always makes me smile is the way we teach our children not to talk to strangers—yet they see us doing exactly that. This can send mixed messages, so I always suggest being clear in our communication.

Now, let me ask you: Do you trust yourself? Who do you trust? And what do you do to make yourself trustworthy to others? These are important questions worth exploring and reflecting upon.

Learning to trust is a process that takes time and intentional effort. Trust doesn't have to be all or nothing. Begin by giving people small chances to prove their reliability. Observe how they respond and whether they keep their word.

Trust is a two-way street. Show honesty, reliability, and consistency in your own actions. When others see you as dependable, they are more likely to reciprocate. If past experiences have made you distrustful, ask yourself whether those fears still apply. Not everyone will repeat the mistakes of those who hurt you before.

Express your concerns and set clear boundaries. Honest communication helps prevent misunderstandings that can damage trust. No one is perfect, and mistakes happen. Instead of judging based on a single misstep, look for patterns of trustworthy behaviour.

Sometimes, distrust stems from not trusting our own judgment. Work on self-confidence and your ability to handle situations—even if someone does let you down. Would you say your struggle with trust stems more from past experiences, or is it a general difficulty in relying on others? Let's reflect on this together. These questions focus on personal experiences, what you have been through, and how you have dealt with them.

Lately, Facebook and online dating have been negative experiences for many people. You may start talking to someone, only to later discover that they have not been completely honest with you. Their intentions may not align with what you were expecting, which can be profoundly upsetting and damaging to your sense of trust.

On the other hand, such experiences can also be valuable lessons. They remind us not to open up too quickly to people we don't know well and to take our time in building trust. While these situations can be painful, they also provide opportunities for growth and self-protection.

Unfortunately, throughout your journey, you will encounter various experiences and difficult attachments. These moments can impact your expectations of others and cause pain when you discover that someone you trusted was not who you believed them to be. However, looking at the positive side, these experiences can make you stronger and teach you to take the time to process your emotions and learn from them.

Yes, it can be painful, but there are valuable lessons to take away. Start by trusting yourself and following your instincts—something we often forget to rely on. Work on building confidence in yourself first, and from there, develop trust in others. Observing and listening are crucial tools for navigating relationships.

The Complexity of Truth and Lies

Lying is an intriguing topic, one that deeply impacts our relationships and trust in others. Many people face emotional struggles in their relationships because of lies. It often becomes an issue of trust, creating barriers between people.

Imagine for a moment being a child, told by your parents never to lie. Yet, you observe them—or other adults—lying to others. How confusing must that behaviour be? We teach children that lying is wrong, but our actions can often contradict this lesson. To complicate matters further, we categorise lies as "white lies," "harmless lies," or even "colour-coded lies." Have you ever actually seen a lie in a specific colour? It's fascinating, isn't it?

Sometimes, it raises the question: is it better to remain silent than to lie? This question touches on the complex nature of truth-telling in human relationships.

Lying is a complex behaviour that serves various psychological, social, and situational purposes. While it is often viewed negatively, the motivations behind lies can range from self-preservation to altruism. People often lie for self-preservation—avoiding consequences by escaping punishment or negative repercussions, such as admitting to a mistake or breaking rules. They may also lie to protect their reputation, maintaining a positive self-image or avoiding embarrassment.

Lies can be used to gain advantage through manipulation, securing an upper hand in negotiations, competitions, or relationships. People may lie to achieve goals, securing opportunities or resources that would otherwise be inaccessible.

Sometimes lies serve altruism. People tell lies to protect others, sparing someone else's feelings or shielding them from harm. "White lies" are often used to maintain social harmony, avoiding conflict or smoothing over uncomfortable social situations.

Lies can help avoid complexity. In some cases, telling the truth can be cumbersome or time-consuming, so people opt for a quick lie to keep things simple. Lies can also deflect attention, redirecting a conversation or avoiding discussions about uncomfortable topics.

Social and psychological needs drive some lies. People might lie to fit in, appearing more interesting, competent, or aligned with a group. Lies can serve as a way to boost self-esteem, enhancing one's own sense of self-worth.

For some, lying can become compulsive or habitual. Pathological lying can become a habitual behaviour, even when there is no clear benefit. People with certain psychological conditions may struggle with impulse control issues that make it difficult to resist lying.

Fear or anxiety often motivates dishonesty. Fear of judgment, rejection, or harm can lead to lies aimed at avoiding perceived threats.

Humans are highly social creatures, and communication is central to our interactions. Lies can be a shortcut to managing social dynamics or navigating challenges. However, while lying can sometimes serve a purpose, it often erodes trust and has long-term consequences for relationships and self-perception.

Understanding the reasons behind lying can help us approach honesty more consciously and foster deeper, more authentic connections with others.

I remember a colleague from a previous job asking me for honest feedback. She wanted to know what she could improve physically to help her find a partner. Before responding, I asked her if she truly wanted my honest opinion. She assured me that she did. So, I gently suggested a few changes: switching from glasses to contact lenses to highlight her beautiful eyes, waxing her upper lip, and perhaps adding a touch of makeup.

She thanked me, and we returned to the office. Later, I overheard her telling others about the advice I had given. I was stunned but managed a smile when she shared the details. I reminded her, "You asked for my honesty. If you didn't want it, you shouldn't have asked." To my surprise, she took my advice, and the transformation was remarkable. Her confidence grew, and she looked amazing. Today, she is happily married with children. Seeing her self-esteem blossom was unforgettable.

Honesty takes courage, but it's often worth it. While the truth may sometimes sting, it's less painful than the betrayal of being caught in a lie later. When people discover dishonesty, it hurts far more than the initial truth might have.

That said, there are moments when lying is necessary. If someone's safety or well-being is at stake, lying might be the best option. But in most cases, honesty builds stronger, more meaningful relationships.

This subject challenges us to reflect on our values, choices, and the impact our words have on others. How do we balance honesty with kindness? And how do we teach future generations to navigate this complex aspect of human interaction?

Chapter 9: Dating and Modern Romance

After exploring the deeper challenges that relationships face, it's important to step back and examine the landscape of modern dating itself. The way we approach romance today—particularly in our later years—has evolved dramatically with technology, changing social norms, and shifting expectations. Yet beneath all these modern complexities lie timeless questions about authenticity, self-worth, and what we truly seek in a partner. This chapter takes a lighter but no less important look at the realities of dating in today's world, examining everything from the games people play to the double standards that persist, all while searching for genuine connection in an increasingly digital age.

The Reality of Mature Dating

I wanted to write something a bit lighter and humorous, and I hope this resonates with many of you—especially those navigating the world of relationships after 60. The other day, I had a wonderful conversation with a friend about dating and relationships. We discussed how many people in their 50s and 60s play games online, juggling multiple connections at once. And let's be clear—this isn't just about men; women do it too. This is not about judging anyone but rather reflecting on modern romance and the challenges of finding the right person.

It might sound a bit cynical or sarcastic, but wouldn't you agree that after experiencing several relationships and struggling to find the right one, you'd stop playing mind games? Wouldn't you reach a point where you no longer date multiple people just for fun or personal gain? I wonder—is that truly what you want for your life?

We've all had positive and negative relationships, but surely, we've learned something along the way. If you've dealt with infidelity, rudeness, dishonesty, or disrespect, wouldn't years of experience and failed relationships lead you to make some changes? Growth comes from learning, and part of that is adjusting behaviours that didn't work in the past.

Yet, many men and women continue playing games, not being honest about their intentions. One thing about Facebook, Instagram, and Messenger is that they reveal a lot. But when you directly ask someone if they are seeing or talking to others, many still choose to be dishonest. Is this really how you want to start a healthy relationship? Haven't we had enough life experience to act like adults—being upfront about our intentions, whether we're looking for something serious or just a casual encounter?

I understand that when you're young and inexperienced, you might engage in these games. But after going through a divorce or multiple relationships, shouldn't we break old patterns and embrace honesty? The hope is that with age comes wisdom—and a better way of building meaningful connections.

How many people today are going through divorce or separation simply because they keep repeating the same behaviours, yet wonder why their relationships fail? Some seek younger partners, while others prefer older ones—but what about focusing on finding a relationship that truly works for you? One where you can spend the rest of your years enjoying companionship, meaningful communication, and shared interests? Instead of prioritising physical beauty, perhaps it's time to see a person as a whole—beyond just their appearance.

I work tirelessly with men and women who struggle with these challenges, often feeling like failures because they couldn't be honest in their relationships. But remember, no one is perfect. The real question is: do you want to keep using others for the wrong reasons? Is that how you want to spend your final years—filled with regrets and no personal growth?

Take a moment to reflect on your last relationship. What worked for you? What didn't? Do you truly believe that constantly seeking new lovers will bring you happiness? As someone once told me, the truth about a person eventually comes to light.

I have done extensive work in relationships and have seen both men and women searching for the "perfect partner"—but the truth is, there is no such thing. Ask yourself: Are you perfect? If not, why expect perfection from someone else?

While no one is flawless, does that mean we should continue playing games and using online platforms to deceive others? Is that truly what you want? Many women post glamorous photos, and many men post pictures that don't reflect who they really are. But what's the point? Do you want to continue this cycle of dishonesty?

And remember—some women don't need private investigators; we are naturally good at finding the truth. So why not just be honest from the start? Being authentic and upfront about what you want is incredibly freeing. Honesty is a powerful thing. You don't need to copy other people's behaviours, nor should you continue playing the victim if things don't go your way.

I hope you don't find my words too blunt, but they are the truth. Would you agree? The day you stop playing games and truly embrace maturity is the day you'll find the right person to share the rest of your life with. Or, you can continue down the same path and see where it leads. The choice is yours.

Beyond Physical Appearance: Learning from Film

The entertainment industry often teaches us valuable lessons about love and relationships, sometimes more effectively than any textbook or advice column. I watched "The Mirror Has Two Faces" this evening, a beautiful film starring Barbra Streisand. If you haven't seen it, I highly recommend it—especially if you struggle with self-esteem or believe you need to be physically attractive for someone to fall in love with you.

This film reminded me that everyone has the capacity to fall in love, no matter what they've gone through—whether it's divorce, the end of a relationship, or simply not feeling happy with yourself. The story is a powerful reminder that love can begin with friendship, and that real connection isn't based on looks. As I've often said, physical appearance fades with age and time.

Many women forget how much they do to be liked and loved by others. No matter how much you spend on your body, your face, or cosmetic procedures, it often still feels like it's not enough. When you look in the mirror and still feel unloved or unattractive, it can be deeply upsetting.

It's painful to see how many people spend hours in the gym, constantly checking the mirror, seeking validation from others. It's also disheartening when someone is out with their partner but constantly distracted—checking out other people or chatting with others on their phone.

If you're in a relationship and find yourself doing this, please know it's deeply disrespectful to your partner. I don't believe people are inherently jealous—jealousy often comes from a lack of respect and consideration in the relationship. If you feel the need to look elsewhere, do it on your own time, not in front of someone you claim to care about. It is not okay.

To men and women: if you want your partner to look like a celebrity, be prepared to invest like one. But more importantly, ask yourself—are you valuing the person for who they are, or for how they look?

What I loved most about the film was that the male character wasn't looking for someone obsessed with beauty, hair, or nails. He just wanted someone he could talk to—someone with whom he could feel comfortable and connected. Women, I think many of you will agree: we want to be loved for who we are, not for how we look. Constantly trying to look perfect is exhausting and unsustainable.

The beautiful irony in the film is that when she changed everything about her appearance, it turned out that he had fallen in love with the woman she was before—when she was just being herself. Their emotional connection, their comfort with each other—that was the true beauty.

Sexual intimacy is important in a relationship for several reasons, but it's not the most important thing—it's one part of a much bigger picture. Sex can deepen intimacy and emotional bonding between partners. It's a form of physical affection that helps couples feel close and connected beyond words. A healthy sexual relationship often involves communication, trust, and vulnerability. Being able to express desires and respect boundaries strengthens mutual understanding.

Sex releases endorphins and other feel-good hormones like oxytocin, which reduce stress and increase feelings of happiness and relaxation. It's also physically healthy when consensual and safe. Feeling wanted by your partner is powerful. Sexual intimacy can be a way of saying, "I choose you," and it reinforces that attraction and connection are still alive.

Sometimes, a lack of sexual connection can be a signal that something else isn't working emotionally or relationally. It's not always about desire—it could be about unresolved tension, stress, or emotional distance.

That said, sex alone doesn't make a relationship strong or lasting. Trust, respect, communication, emotional support, and shared values are just as—if not more—important. Some couples have very little sex and still have deeply loving, fulfilling relationships, while others with an active sex life may feel emotionally disconnected.

What kind of relationship values are most important to you? The film beautifully illustrates how the man was looking for someone who wasn't focused on appearances—her hair, nails, or looks—but instead, someone he could genuinely talk to. He wanted a real connection, not a perfect image.

Yes, sex can be an important part of a relationship, as long as both people agree on what they want and need. But what's even more important is how well you get along, how deeply you connect, and whether you enjoy being around each other every day. That's what makes a relationship last.

Confronting Gender Double Standards

Society's treatment of men and women in matters of love and sexuality reveals deeply embedded prejudices that continue to shape how we view relationships and personal freedom. Yesterday, as I walked along the beach, I reflected on my week and some of the conversations I've been having. This morning, during a conversation with a friend, the topic shifted unexpectedly but powerfully toward the ways society treats women and men differently when it comes to personal choices, especially around relationships and sexuality.

That thought stuck with me, and it's the reason I want to address this important issue. Some people choose to live a more sexually open lifestyle and feel completely at peace with their decisions. They're not hurting anyone, and everything they do is between consenting adults. So why are we so quick to judge them? Is it because of outdated beliefs, cultural conditioning, or simply discomfort with someone else's freedom? Whatever the reason, judgment says more about the person casting it than the one living authentically.

Let's think about this: when a woman goes on a date, she often puts effort into how she looks—not always for others, but sometimes for herself, for confidence. A man might come prepared with charming words, but in most cases, it's the woman who decides what happens next. And that's not wrong.

Even in stories as old as time—take the biblical tale of Adam and Eve—it was Eve who made a choice. It wasn't Adam who seduced her. Women are often the decision-makers, whether society wants to acknowledge it or not. Yet, when a woman is open about her sexuality or desires, she's judged harshly. Why?

Let's be honest about the double standard that persists. If a man sleeps with many partners, he's often celebrated as successful or experienced. If a woman does the same, she faces harsh labels and social condemnation. Why is this acceptable?

Consider these realities: A woman often chooses the outcome of a date—not the man. History is full of examples of legendary lovers, but it's often the woman who holds the power of choice. Eve didn't get seduced—she made a decision. Women put effort into how they look not only for others but also for their own self-worth. Society teaches shame, while nature teaches freedom.

Consensual choices between adults should never be judged. Whether someone has many partners or none—that's their choice. If a woman chooses sex work, that is her profession and her decision. I'm not saying it belongs on a resume, or encouraging everyone to pursue it—but if that's her path, she deserves the same respect as any man making his own choices. Being a man doesn't mean you're allowed more freedom. Being a woman shouldn't mean less.

Respect is not gendered. It's earned by how we treat each other—not by who we choose to love or how many people we've loved. Have you ever felt judged for your choices? Let's stop judging and start understanding. Everyone deserves the freedom to choose—without shame, and without labels.

We are living in an era when it should be time to stop making anyone—woman or man—feel less because of their personal choices. Whether someone chooses to be intimate, whether it's a man or a woman, that decision deserves respect. No one should be made to feel ashamed for living their truth.

Both men and women are equal. As I've said before, I am the same as you, and you are the same as me. You are not better than anyone, and no one is better than you.

Understanding Love Beyond Commercial Traditions

The commercialisation of romance has created expectations and pressures that sometimes overshadow the genuine expression of love. With Valentine's Day approaching each year, I find it valuable to explore not just the traditions we follow, but the deeper meaning behind how we express and celebrate love.

Sometimes, we go through life following traditions without questioning their origins. Do you agree? I've heard many people express their expectations for this day, from romantic gestures to receiving flowers and chocolates—despite the rising costs! If you're as curious as I am, it's worth understanding where these traditions come from.

Valentine's Day is rooted in the story of Saint Valentine, a Christian martyr from ancient Rome. The exact origins blend history and legend. Saint Valentine was a priest or possibly a bishop in Rome during the 3rd century. The Roman Emperor Claudius II banned soldiers from marrying, believing single men made better warriors. Valentine defied this order and secretly performed marriages for young couples. He was arrested and executed on February 14, around 269 AD. While imprisoned, he allegedly healed his jailer's blind daughter and signed a farewell note, "From your Valentine."

Some believe Valentine's Day replaced Lupercalia, an ancient Roman fertility festival held from February 13-15. This festival involved rituals to promote fertility and matchmaking, which later evolved into a romantic celebration under Christian influence.

Valentine's Day traditions vary dramatically across cultures. In Latin America and Spain, Mexico and Colombia celebrate it as Día del Amor y la Amistad (Day of Love and Friendship), celebrating both romantic and platonic relationships, with gifts exchanged among friends and loved ones. Brazil celebrates Dia dos Namorados (Lovers' Day) on June 12, the eve of St. Anthony's Day, the patron saint of marriage. Spain has some regions that celebrate on April 23 (Día de San Jorge), where couples exchange books and roses.

In Europe, France hosts romantic festivals in Paris, the "City of Love," especially in the village of Saint-Valentin. Italy traditionally sees young couples get engaged on Valentine's Day and exchange Baci Perugini chocolates with love notes inside. Denmark gives pressed white flowers (snowdrops) instead of roses and sends humorous anonymous love notes called geekeries.

Asian celebrations are particularly interesting. In Japan, women give chocolates to men on February 14—either romantic (honmei-choco) or friendly (giri-choco). On March 14 (White Day), men return the favour with gifts, often of higher value. South Korea adds Black Day (April 14) where singles celebrate by eating jjajangmyeon (black bean noodles). China and Taiwan celebrate the Qixi Festival in August, China's version of Valentine's Day, based on the legend of two star-crossed lovers.

Other unique traditions include South Africa, where women pin the name of their crush on their sleeves, following an ancient Roman custom. The Philippines commonly holds mass weddings, with hundreds or even thousands of couples getting married simultaneously. Finland and Estonia celebrate Ystävänpäivä (Friend's Day), focusing on friendships rather than couples.

As you can see, while some countries celebrate Valentine's Day in similar ways, others have developed unique traditions that reflect their cultural values. Now, I'd like to share my personal view on this day. Some may say this is just my opinion, but I believe that love should be celebrated every day—not just once a year. If you love someone, show it 365 days a year. Why wait until February 14 to express your affection, go out for a meal, or give flowers?

Every year, I see people rushing to buy last-minute gifts out of obligation. Does this sound familiar? Learning about the origins of Valentine's Day has been eye-opening, and I encourage everyone to reflect on its true meaning. This is not about judging anyone, but rather encouraging reflection. In my work with patients, I often suggest making time for a romantic meal or a meaningful moment every week, rather than waiting for Valentine's Day. Regular communication and small gestures of love make a relationship stronger. Tell your loved ones how much they mean to you every day!

The pressure to perform romance on a specific date can actually detract from the spontaneous, genuine expressions of love that truly strengthen relationships. When we focus on authentic, daily demonstrations of care and affection, we build something much more valuable than any store-bought gesture could provide.

Chapter 10: Family Dynamics

The complexities of family relationships form the foundation of our emotional lives, yet they remain some of the most challenging dynamics to navigate. From the desire to become parents to the delicate balance between partnership and parenthood, from single parenting to understanding our own childhood attachments, family life presents us with profound questions about love, responsibility, and personal growth. This chapter examines these intricate relationships with honesty and compassion, exploring how we can create healthier family dynamics while honoring both our roles as caregivers and our needs as individuals.

Dreams of Parenthood and Life's Deepest Desires

As we welcome each new year, many of us reflect on what we wish to achieve. Some dream of a new car, a new house, a better job, or finding love. Others set goals to lose weight or even run a marathon. These aspirations, big or small, are vital because they give us purpose and drive. They shape the lives we want to lead.

But I want to write specifically for the women who dream of becoming mothers. For them, the wish for a child is as profound and deeply rooted as any other goal in life. Watching a film recently about the first baby born through IVF in 1978 brought back a flood of memories for me—memories of my own journey to motherhood.

I have three beautiful children now, but I was once told in Spain that I would never be able to become a mother. The news was devastating. When I moved to England, I tried to come to terms with this reality, and my partner was supportive. But deep down, I never gave up on my dream.

This isn't written to suggest that everyone who wishes to become a parent will succeed through medical treatments or otherwise. I was one of the fortunate ones. Despite the odds, I became a mother to three wonderful children. However, my journey was not without heartache: I endured two miscarriages and lost three babies along the way.

I share this because, while many people dream of material or career successes, some women yearn for what nature seems to deny them. For many, the desire to be a mother is a lifelong dream, instilled from childhood. My friends often tell me I'm overly protective of my children, jokingly calling me a "lioness." But few know the full extent of my struggles—the pain, the waiting, and the longing to hold my child in my arms. The day my first son was born remains etched in my memory as one of the happiest moments of my life. That feeling of overwhelming joy is something I wish for every woman who dreams of becoming a mother.

For some women, the journey to parenthood involves immense emotional and physical challenges. Many grapple with the heartache of infertility, questioning why they cannot conceive, while others, who may seem less deserving, can. These feelings can be incredibly isolating and painful. I deeply understand these emotions, and I encourage those in this situation to find someone they trust to share their feelings with. Talking can help ease the burden and provide comfort.

While I cannot promise that everyone's dream of becoming a parent will come true, I can say this: never give up on your dreams. Thanks to the opportunities I found in England, I was able to receive the help I needed to fulfil my dream of motherhood. I am forever grateful for this.

For those who are unable to conceive, adoption can be a beautiful alternative. Many children are in need of loving homes, and parenting is about so much more than biology. It's about love, care, and unwavering support. As I often tell my patients, being a parent isn't just about giving birth; it's about raising and nurturing a child.

Since the first test-tube baby was born, over 12 million IVF babies have entered the world. While IVF is a remarkable scientific achievement, it's important to acknowledge the heartbreak of those who cannot be helped. Patrick Steptoe, one of the pioneers of IVF, once said: "There are so many women that we won't be able to help, and for them, our existence is just another source of pain." His words resonate deeply, reminding us of the emotional complexities surrounding infertility treatments.

To anyone reading this who is facing challenges in life—whether related to parenthood or another dream—remember this: don't let anyone take your dreams away. Life's struggles may cause you to stumble, but each fall can make you stronger. Be kind to yourself, seek out the right support, and hold onto hope.

The Delicate Balance of Partnership and Parenthood

The relationship between parents and children reveals some of the most complex dynamics in human experience. Many parents express sadness when they realise that their children do not support them in the way they expected. This raises an important question: what is the difference between loving a child and loving other people in our lives? Who came first?

Before becoming parents, I hope that your first love was for yourself. Of course, you may have loved others and been loved in return. Eventually, you fell in love with your partner and built a relationship, forming a deep connection. From that love, you created your children. Many parents say that their children come first, which is understandable, but it is important to recognise that even in cases where someone becomes a parent without a partner, another person was still involved in creating that child.

What I observe frequently is that people tend to treat their children better than their partners. This often leads to feelings of neglect within relationships, and many wonder why their partner starts looking elsewhere for emotional fulfilment. I hope you don't mind my honesty in addressing this topic.

Children inevitably take up much of our time and energy, but later in life, many parents feel lonely and abandoned, wondering why their children visit only occasionally. This prompts an important reflection: did you have children with the expectation that they would provide you with the same level of care and support that you once gave them?

Consider this logically. Who did you start with? Many mothers say that because their child was in their womb, they share a special connection, which is true. However, it is also true that your partner was with you through the entire journey, supporting you during pregnancy cravings, mood swings, and many other moments.

We often forget to nurture our relationship with our partner, placing them last in our hierarchy of priorities. Yet, our relationship with our partner is the foundation upon which our family is built. I frequently hear couples say, "My partner treats our children better than me. They do everything for them but not for me." Is this a healthy dynamic?

Children are not inherently selfish; they are simply learning to look after themselves. As parents, our role is to help them become autonomous individuals, capable of surviving in this world independently. Over-supporting them can sometimes have the opposite effect, making them overly dependent rather than strong and self-sufficient. I know this from personal experience.

In my work with patients, I see this pattern repeatedly. It is particularly evident in cases where people have multiple marriages, searching for respect and love without fully processing the lessons from past relationships. Many people choose the wrong partners because they have not taken the time to understand what went wrong the first time. Therapists, including myself, also need to work on themselves—no one is perfect.

One of the most fascinating observations I have made is how often we put ourselves and our partners last. Parents frequently say, "Children come first." But have we ever stopped to ask what our children truly want? Many children grow up feeling obligated to fulfil their parents' expectations, sometimes leading to depression because they never discovered their own purpose in life.

The desire to have children is deeply rooted in human nature and shaped by biological, emotional, cultural, and personal factors. There's an innate evolutionary drive to reproduce and ensure the survival of our genes, influenced by hormonal changes that create a strong emotional pull toward parenthood. Many people dream of the deep bond and unconditional love that comes with raising a child, finding a sense of purpose and fulfillment that gives life new direction. The desire to pass on traditions, values, and wisdom can be a powerful motivator.

Cultural norms often encourage or expect people to have children as a part of adulthood, while family pressure and the desire for community belonging influence these decisions. Practical considerations include support in old age and building a family unit that provides security. The joy of watching growth and development, sharing life's milestones, and experiencing the unique challenge of parenthood drives many to become parents.

However, not everyone desires children, and that is entirely valid. The decision to have children is personal and influenced by individual circumstances, values, and goals.

Love yourself, and if you find love with someone, remember that a strong connection and a great relationship can last a lifetime. If you are single, focus on self-growth and engage in activities and communities that bring you joy. Do not wait for others to fulfil you—you have the power to create your own happiness.

From the moment a doctor cuts the umbilical cord, a child begins to breathe on their own. This is not selfishness; it is the natural course of life. It is heartbreaking to see parents in tears because their children are not present in their lives as much as they had hoped. If we look at nature, animals raise their young until they are ready, then let them go to live their own lives.

Focus on being happy and content with yourself. If you are in a relationship, invest in it—do not leave it for last. This does not mean you should not love your children, but rather that you should also prioritise your well-being and your relationship with your partner. Keep growing, and do not feel guilty for doing so.

The Strength of Single Parents

Being a single parent is one of the most challenging roles anyone can undertake. For those of you struggling without support, facing judgment from others who have no idea what it's like to shoulder this responsibility alone, this recognition is for you.

No one chooses this path lightly. When we marry, we dream of a lifetime together, building a family, and sharing the joys and challenges of parenthood as a team. Few of us imagine that one day, we might be doing it all alone. The reality of single parenting often comes as an unforeseen and painful chapter, filled with loss and heartbreak.

Without a partner to rely on, single parents often face societal judgment and unsolicited advice. Well-meaning or not, these opinions can sting deeply, especially when they come from those who have never walked in your shoes. Imagine the heartbreak of not waking up with your children on Christmas morning or missing their milestones because of custody arrangements. It's a pain only those who have lived it can truly understand.

To add to this, there are constant decisions to navigate—schools, activities, trips, and even basic daily routines. When two parents are no longer together, these decisions often become battlegrounds. The involvement of new partners can further complicate the situation, making compromise feel impossible at times. Does any of this resonate with you?

Living as a single parent can feel like a building collapsing around you, leaving you to gather the pieces to create a safe and stable environment for your children. It's no easy feat, and the emotional and physical toll can be immense. That's why setting boundaries and establishing clear communication with everyone involved—co-parents, family, friends, and even children—is crucial.

Boundaries ensure that relationships remain respectful and functional. It's important to decide who gets involved in your personal matters and how. Communicating effectively helps everyone—especially children—understand the new dynamics. Remember, children sense more than we realise, and changes in family structure can be confusing for them. Tailor your communication to their age and maturity level, and don't hesitate to seek professional support when needed.

As someone who has experienced single parenting and grown up in a single-parent household, I know these struggles firsthand. I still carry the memories of those tough days, even as my children have grown. One moment that stands out is when I was grocery shopping with my children, and someone asked, "Why don't you leave your kids at home?" Their comment stung. I thought, "If only you could walk in my shoes, you'd understand my situation." But instead of reacting, I smiled and continued shopping. Moments like these remind us of the strength it takes to keep going despite the judgments of others.

To every single parent reading this: I see you. I admire you. Your strength and perseverance are extraordinary. You are doing your best, often against overwhelming odds, and that deserves recognition. Remember some single parents don't have their family around and this is very hard.

If you're navigating this journey, remember to set boundaries with your family and friends. Communicate openly, especially when you're unhappy or overwhelmed. Involve your teenagers in discussions when appropriate—they're often more perceptive than we give them credit for. And if you know a single parent, don't judge—ask how you can help instead.

Most importantly, if you need help, seek it. Professionals, counselors, and support groups can provide invaluable guidance. Let your loved ones know you'll ask for help when needed, but be clear that taking sides or interfering isn't helpful.

To every single parent out there: You are not alone. Your efforts may go unnoticed by some, but they are deeply meaningful to your children and those who understand the challenges you face. Keep going, and know that you are seen, appreciated, and celebrated.

Children Come First... Or Do They?

What came first—the chicken or the egg? And in your relationship, what comes first: your partner or your children? This might be a controversial question, but after reflecting deeply on the nature of family, I believe it's time we ask ourselves: How do we really prioritise our lives—our children, our partner, and ourselves?

From generation to generation, we've heard the same saying: "Your children come first." But if they're always first, then where are you on the list? And where is your partner—the person who helped you create that family?

Without your partner—or at the very least, without their contribution—you wouldn't have had those children in the first place. Yet, once the children arrive, it often feels like the entire family must revolve around them, no matter the cost.

I've seen parents skip meals so their children can eat. But I often wonder—why not share the food equally? Why should one person go without? Why do we believe that children should always come first, even at the cost of our own health, well-being, or relationships?

What message are we sending when we do this? That their needs matter more than anyone else's? That their parents, as individuals or as a couple, are secondary?

Many husbands and wives feel emotionally abandoned when all the love, attention, and time that once existed in their relationship is redirected completely to the children. But think back: who was there first? The foundation of the family begins with the couple. If that connection breaks down, what remains?

As parents, we give so much. Our time. Our sleep. Our energy. We work hard to make sure our children never have to face the hardships we did. Some parents even take on debt to support their families, sacrificing long-term stability for short-term needs.

And yet, the most heartbreaking scene is one I've witnessed too many times: elderly parents, sitting alone in aged care facilities, waiting for their children to visit. And no one comes.

They are no longer able to do the things they once could. They spent decades giving everything for their children—and now they sit alone, sometimes without a partner, and often without the support they once gave so freely.

Let me be clear: this is not about choosing between love for your children and love for your partner. It's about balance. It's about remembering that your relationship matters too.

Without each other, your children would not exist. And while it's true that children grow up, start their own lives, and move on—that's the natural course of life—you don't have to lose yourself or your partnership along the way.

Take time to do things together as a couple. Reconnect. Nurture that bond. Don't just sit around waiting for your children to need you. You already gave them your best. Now you need to live, too.

Because I've heard it far too often: "My children don't come to see me anymore." And even worse: "You have to help me—we come first." Really? After all those years spent putting them first?

Love your children, absolutely. But love yourself. Love your partner. That bond is not secondary—it's central. It's what held everything together.

Yes, when children are young, they need more attention. That's only natural. But as they grow, they also need to learn respect, empathy, and appreciation for the people who raised them.

In the end, the answer is not simple. Life requires balance. But the truth is this: A strong family begins with a strong partnership. And self-neglect should never be the cost of parenthood.

So ask yourself honestly: What do you believe? Who truly comes first?

Understanding Our Earliest Bonds

I am writing this to support others who find themselves in similar situations and struggle to move forward because they feel they did something wrong or question why they grew up without a father or a mother. This is a deeply personal topic, but I hope that by sharing my thoughts, I can help others understand that it is not their fault.

When we are born, none of us have the ability to choose where we will live or who our parents will be. This is completely beyond our control. Unfortunately, many people feel rejected or abandoned by their own parents, leading to profound emotional pain. Can you relate to this?

Many people suffer because of early attachments—the relationships formed at the very beginning of their lives. Our parents, typically our first caregivers, are meant to love and nurture us. Mothers often help build a child's self-esteem, while fathers traditionally take on roles like teaching practical skills, reading bedtime stories, and providing protection. Sadly, not all parents are capable of giving their children the love and care they deserve, and this absence can have a significant impact on later relationships.

If your parents didn't provide the love you needed, how do you think this might affect your ability to connect with others? I know many stories of people who wake up each morning longing to see their father or mother, only to be reminded that their parent chose to leave or prioritise someone else over them. It's heartbreaking to hear people share how their mother didn't protect them or how their father walked away. The pain of feeling unloved and unprotected can run very deep.

The reason I am writing this is that I recently watched a touching film. In one scene, a daughter told her father, "You make me so mad because you drive so slowly." The father replied, "I only drive slowly when you're in the car." The way he looked at her brought tears to my eyes. It reminded me of how important attachments are and how the love we experience early in life shapes our sense of security and self-worth.

Without these foundational bonds, it can be hard to navigate life without feelings of rejection or abandonment. I also understand that not everyone has a natural maternal or paternal instinct. Some people have children because of societal expectations or pressure from their partners. They might think, "This is what we're supposed to do—grow up, get a job, get married, and have a family." Life feels mapped out, and they don't question it.

However, some people enter parenthood without truly wanting to. This can lead to strained relationships, divorce, domestic violence, and even heartbreaking situations of abuse. If you're in a relationship and considering having children, it's essential to have honest conversations about it. If necessary, take a parenting course to prepare yourself. Don't start a journey you're not ready for. And if you do separate from your partner, make it clear to your children that you are not leaving them. Children don't have the emotional capacity to understand the complexities of adult relationships unless it is explained to them. Sit down with them and provide clarity. If needed, seek professional family support to ensure your children don't grow up feeling that they are to blame. Children deserve to feel loved and to know they are worthy of love.

One of the challenges with attachments is the tendency to seek love from others in an attempt to fill the gaps left by our past, especially if we feel our parents didn't love us the way we needed. This can lead to a common mistake: expecting others to love us in a way that heals old wounds. When this happens, we often examine our relationships through a magnifying glass, constantly testing whether the love we receive is "enough," instead of focusing on understanding ourselves and the roots of our behaviours.

Rather than seeking constant validation—like needing someone to tell us they love us all the time, and interpreting silence as a sign of trouble in the relationship—it's important to turn inward. Reflecting on our past and understanding why we behave the way we do can be transformative.

We also tend to compare our relationships to others, which can lead to miscommunication and unmet expectations. Instead, the key is vulnerability: sharing your feelings openly and honestly with your partner. Talk about what hurts, express your needs, and allow space for understanding.

However, this kind of openness should happen within a safe and healthy relationship, where your partner is willing to understand and support you. With mutual effort and communication, you can begin to address these patterns and grow together.

One of the reasons I began studying human behaviour was to understand my own personal struggles. I wanted to know why people behave the way they do. My desire to understand myself led me to a path where I could also support others.

Through this journey, I realised it wasn't my fault. I've learned to be more compassionate with myself and to set boundaries so others don't take advantage of me. I'm now choosing how I want to live, rather than letting others make decisions for me.

If you are struggling with similar feelings, please know that you are not alone. You deserve love, and it's never too late to start healing. Find the support you need, whether through friends, family, or professionals, and remind yourself that your worth is not determined by the actions or inactions of your parents. You are capable of creating a life filled with love and fulfillment.

Writing this has helped me uncover many things, and I hope it helps you discover something about yourself as well. Perhaps it will guide you toward finding the answers you've been searching for.

Celebrating Motherhood

Being a mum is not an easy job. As women, we wear many hats—the Mum's hat, the Wife's hat, the Friend's hat, the Woman's hat, and many more. The journey begins when we find out we will be a mum. It brings a wave of emotions—happiness, excitement, fear, worries, and so much more. I have often heard that there is no book on how to be a perfect mum; instead, it is about being a "good enough" mum.

We wait for nine months to meet our beautiful baby, enduring countless medical appointments—scans, blood tests, and other procedures. Let's not forget the mums who undergo IVF and other treatments to fulfill their dream of motherhood. Unfortunately, some experience the heartbreak of miscarriage, a deeply traumatic event. Our bodies undergo immense changes, and we carry extra weight to bring our precious child into the world. The sleepless nights prepare us for the journey ahead, ensuring we can provide our baby with nourishment. It is truly a miracle how our bodies are designed for motherhood—something we often overlook.

Then comes the moment when we leave the hospital and take our baby home. Despite all the preparation, nothing fully prepares us for those first sleepless nights—crying due to colic, teething, or unknown reasons. I remember those nights vividly—the worry, the exhaustion, and the endless guessing of what my baby needed. Yet, I also cherish the beautiful moments—the evening cuddles, the bedtime kisses, and the pure love shared between mother and child. Time flies, and before we know it, our little ones grow up, leaving us with cherished memories of their early years.

We celebrate milestones such as the first words—"Mummy" or "Daddy"—the first crawl, the first steps, and even the first successful trip to the toilet. Some might wonder why a mother feels so much joy over something as simple as potty training. But only a mum knows the effort and patience it takes—countless accidents, outfit changes, and gentle encouragement.

Then comes the bittersweet milestone—the first day at nursery. Letting go of your child, even for a few hours, is heart-wrenching. I remember walking to the car with tears in my eyes, wondering if someone else could ever care for my child as I do. And so, begins a lifetime of letting go—bit by bit, step by step.

Motherhood is filled with moments of joy and moments of pain. Seeing your child hurt, especially at the hands of others, is one of the hardest parts. Bullying, unkindness, and exclusion leave scars, not just on children but on mothers who feel their pain just as deeply.

Then, one day, our children fall in love—not with us, but with someone else. It's a natural part of life, yet it tugs at a mother's heart. The child you've loved and nurtured since birth now shares their heart with another. It is both a moment of sadness and pride. But remember, motherhood is a choice we made, and our children owe us nothing. The love we give is unconditional.

Mother's Day is a wonderful occasion to celebrate and honour mothers, but appreciation should not be limited to just one day. Mothers sacrifice so much to provide their children with a safe home, food, clothing, and, most importantly, love. While it was their choice, and children are not obligated to repay that effort, a simple "I love you" or "I appreciate you" can mean the world to a mum. Grand gifts are nice, but heartfelt words hold far greater value. Don't wait for Mother's Day to express them—say them whenever you feel it.

It's important to remember that behind every mum is a woman who longs to feel love, appreciation, and recognition, both for her role as a mother and as an individual. Sadly, not everyone has had a positive experience with their mother. For those who have faced pain or neglect, healing often comes through understanding and forgiveness. In my opinion, if someone struggles to be a good mother, it is not entirely their fault—it reflects their own upbringing and a lack of awareness of how their actions impact their children.

Forgiveness does not mean forgetting or excusing harmful behaviour; it means freeing yourself from resentment. Forgiveness allows us to move forward, not for others, but for our peace.

Some people no longer have their mums with them. If this day is difficult for you, find something that brings you comfort. Always remember that your mum is still with you—not in person, perhaps, but always in your heart.

I no longer have my mum with me, but she remains in my thoughts and heart every single day. Life moves fast—family, work, and responsibilities often take over. That's why it is so important to cherish our time with our mums now, while we still can.

If you are fortunate enough to have your mum with you, tell her daily how much you love her. When you see her, hug her, listen to her, and support her—because you are her world. You only get one mum. Jobs, houses, and material things can be replaced, but a mother's love is irreplaceable.

I was incredibly lucky to have a wonderful mum—loving, funny, caring, and always there for us, even in her craziest moments. I'm grateful for every second I had with her, and I am happy to share this message with all of you.

To all the wonderful mothers out there—may you have a beautiful day today and every day.

Honoring Fathers

I would like to dedicate this recognition to celebrate fathers and their vital role in family life. This day is as important as Mother's Day because without their father, the children would not exist.

The role of a father goes beyond just providing for a family—it includes being a guide, protector and emotional anchor. A father plays many roles, including being a provider, ensuring the family's basic needs are met, including food, shelter and education. As a protector, he offers physical and emotional security, creating a safe environment for children. He serves as a role model, demonstrating values like integrity, responsibility and kindness.

As a supporter, a father encourages and nurtures children's dreams, interests and emotional well-being. He acts as a teacher, passing down wisdom, life skills, and discipline in a loving and constructive way. As a companion, he spends quality time, bonding through activities and building lasting relationships. Finally, he provides leadership, offering direction, making wise decisions and setting the tone for the family.

Ultimately, a father's role is to love, guide and prepare his children for the world while being present in their lives. The perspective on fatherhood varies based on culture, society and personal experiences, but at its core, it revolves around love, responsibility and leadership. Fathers are expected to be nurturing and emotionally supportive, not just disciplinarians.

A father plays a crucial role in shaping a child's self-esteem, confidence and emotional health. A loving and involved father fosters security and resilience in children. The absence or presence of a father figure significantly affects a child's mental well-being and life choices.

Some cultures view fathers as strict authority figures, while others encourage friendship and mentorship between fathers and children. The expectations of fatherhood differ across societies—some prioritize financial provision, while others stress emotional bonding.

Many religious traditions see fatherhood as a divine responsibility, emphasising guidance, love and moral teaching. Fathers are expected to lead by example in faith, ethics and family unity.

With evolving gender roles, many fathers are now stay-at-home dads or take on more domestic responsibilities. The role of a father is no longer defined just by work and authority but also by love, presence, and active engagement in a child's life.

Fatherhood is about balance—being strong yet compassionate, guiding yet allowing independence and teaching yet always learning. A great father is not just present but deeply involved in shaping his child's future.

Also, if you didn't have a good father, his actions don't define you. You have the power to break any negative cycles and build the kind of life and relationships you deserve.

If you were abandoned or unsupported by your father this can leave deep scars. If he was absent—physically or emotionally—it's completely understandable to feel hurt, angry, or even indifferent. A father's role isn't just about being there; it's about showing up in meaningful ways. When that's missing, it can leave a void.

But here's the thing: your past doesn't have to define your future. Recognizing where things went wrong is already a huge step toward healing and breaking the cycle. You deserve love, respect and stability, and even though your father failed you, that doesn't mean you have to carry his mistakes forward.

Healing from a painful past, especially one tied to a parent's absence or neglect, is never easy. It takes time, self-awareness and a lot of emotional work.

That's one of the hardest things to do—especially when the hurt runs deep. Forgiveness doesn't mean excusing what he did or pretending it didn't affect you. It's about releasing yourself from the weight of his actions so they no longer control your emotions and choices.

It might help to acknowledge your pain—your feelings are valid. What he did or didn't do hurt you and it's okay to admit that. Accept that he may never change—some people never become the parent we needed. That's not your fault. Forgive for yourself, not for him—forgiveness is about freeing you from resentment, not about making him feel better. Set boundaries—if he's still in your life, you can forgive while keeping your distance if needed.

The truth is, some people just aren't capable of being the parent their children need. Maybe he had his own unresolved pain, maybe he lacked emotional maturity, or maybe he was simply selfish. But none of those reasons excuse his absence and they definitely don't justify the hurt he caused you.

Not understanding why is one of the hardest parts. But maybe the real power comes in realising that you don't need to understand him to move forward. His failures as a father are on him, not on you. You deserved better.

If the first man in your life—your father—let you down, it's natural to struggle with trusting others. If he wasn't there for you, it can feel like no man will be. But that's his failure, not a reflection of all men.

It's not easy and I won't say it happens overnight. But you can rebuild trust and find someone who treats you the way you deserve. You're not alone in this. You're stronger than the pain you've been through, and you deserve love, respect, and happiness. If your father is no longer with you, remember to take care of yourself. If you had a great father, he will always be with you in your heart and in your thoughts.

Chapter 11: Life's Journey and Meaning

Life presents us with fundamental questions about purpose, meaning, and how to live authentically in an uncertain world. This chapter explores the deeper philosophical aspects of our human experience—from understanding our personal story and embracing the present moment to confronting life's impermanence and finding what truly matters. Through personal reflection and universal themes, we examine how to create meaning in our daily lives while accepting both the beauty and fragility of our existence.

A Personal Introduction to the Journey

My name is Soledad Jewell. I am Spanish and originally from the beautiful island of Gran Canaria. My journey into becoming a therapist began in 2007, but the story behind why I chose this path is deeply personal and rooted in my own struggles. At the age of 40, I found myself questioning everything about my life. Why was I repeatedly making mistakes? Why was I attracting the wrong people? Why was I facing difficulties that seemed never-ending? These questions haunted me, and I knew I needed answers—not just for my clients, but for myself.

When I first started my counselling course, I clearly remember a moment that made a lasting impression on me. My teacher asked why I had chosen to take this course. I wasn't ready to admit that it was for my own healing, so I joked, "I like to tell people what to do." Everyone laughed, including my teacher. Then he gently corrected me, saying that counselling wasn't about telling people what to do, but about truly listening. At that moment, I thought, "Oh dear, that's going to be difficult for me." But despite my doubts, I pushed forward. My marriage had recently broken down, and I was left to care for three young children. I was determined not to repeat the mistakes of my parents and to create a better life for myself and my family.

This book was born out of a period of profound change and loss. My father passed away on September 5th, and the grief brought with it a flood of emotions and thoughts. Over the years, I had supported many people through my work, but I realised I hadn't truly cared for myself. It was time to turn the attention inward and to find my own direction. Around that time, I reconnected with a friend back in Gran Canaria, a teacher who shared his own struggles and a passion for books. His encouragement inspired me to start writing—to channel my experiences, my pain, and the lessons I've learned into words.

Writing became my refuge. It was like water slowly breaking against rocks, each piece helping me to release some of the pain and fears I had carried for so long. I poured my heart into these writings, hoping that if someone else read them, they might find comfort and guidance, especially those who cannot afford therapy or don't know where to turn.

As the anniversary of my father's passing approaches, I find myself still shedding tears—not just for him, but for the father I never truly had. Through this process, I have found moments of laughter, healing, and hope. I want to share these with you. Life is incredibly difficult at times, and many of us want to give up. But I want you to know that it's possible to keep going, to find light in the darkness, and to create your own path to healing.

This book is for you—whether you are struggling right now or simply looking for a reminder that you are not alone. I hope you read it, laugh, reflect, and find a little hope along the way. And if you can, share it with others who might be going through their own battles.

Thank you for taking the time to read my story. I will continue writing because this has become a powerful way for me to release my pain and fears, and to transform them into something meaningful. Writing has given me a new voice and a new purpose, and I hope it can do the same for you.

Confronting Life's Impermanence

A few weeks ago, the world watched as we said goodbye to Pope Francis. There was a wave of sadness, a global mourning. People gathered, cried, and remembered all he stood for. But in what seemed like a moment, the grief gave way to cheers. A new Pope appeared on the balcony in Rome, and the crowd erupted with joy, chanting his name. It was a powerful moment—a reminder of how quickly life moves on.

This is life. Someone we thought irreplaceable is suddenly replaced. One chapter ends, and another begins, almost without pause. The people who once wept in sorrow are now celebrating a new beginning. This isn't heartlessness—it's human nature. Life doesn't stop for long. The world doesn't pause for any one of us.

And this truth should make us reflect. How often do we build our lives around others' expectations, around fear of rejection or judgment? We worry about being liked, being approved of, being remembered. But one day, just like those before us, we'll be gone. And the world will keep turning.

At work, someone else will fill your role. At home, the routines will resume. Friends will laugh again, find new friends, build new memories. Families will eventually smile after the tears. And the person who once felt central to everything becomes a story, a photograph, a memory that fades over time.

This may sound harsh, but it's not meant to be depressing. It's meant to set you free. You are not here to be everything to everyone. You are not meant to live your life constantly trying to please, impress, or fit into moulds made by others. Your time is limited. Your energy is sacred. Why waste it worrying about people who won't be there forever—or who may forget the sacrifices you made?

So many people say, "I could never replace you." Yet life often proves otherwise. I've heard it at funerals—"They were the love of my life"—only to see someone new arrive within months. This doesn't mean the love wasn't real. It means life is fluid. Time doesn't stop for mourning. We heal, and we move forward.

We are all temporary in someone else's world. But we are permanent in our own.

This isn't meant to be bitter—it's meant to wake you up. You are not here to live in fear of being forgotten. You are here to live. To truly, deeply, unapologetically live.

Stop spending your life chasing approval from people who will forget you. Stop sacrificing your dreams for people who would replace you in a moment. Don't give your peace to jobs that will post a vacancy within a week of your funeral. Don't give your time to people who drain your soul but never pour back into you.

Even fame doesn't guarantee lasting memory. Think of all the once-famous people whose names are now unfamiliar. Think of the teachers, mentors, and friends who meant the world to you once, and now you barely think of them. The same will happen to us.

And so, the point of this reflection isn't to create fear of being forgotten—it's to help you live more fully. The truth is: you are replaceable in the world, but you are irreplaceable in your own story.

You can't control what others remember. But you can control how you live. Live truthfully. Live boldly. Make choices that matter to you. Stop worrying about pleasing people who would forget you if you disappeared tomorrow. Don't give your best years, your best energy, to people or systems that wouldn't notice if you were gone.

Instead, be with those who value you—not just when they need something, but when you need them. Spend your time with people who love you as you are, not who want to change you. Create moments that matter, not for legacy, but for living.

And most importantly: let go of fear. Let go of guilt. Let go of the illusion that you must earn love or respect by sacrificing your truth. You don't owe anyone the version of you that silences your spirit.

Today, you are here. That's all that matters. Yes, someday you'll be a memory. But while you're alive—really alive—be present. Laugh loudly. Say what you mean. Follow that dream. Take that risk. Stop putting off joy. The clock is ticking, not to frighten you, but to remind you: this is your time.

So, when you see the Pope on the balcony, when you witness the world move from grief to joy, from past to present, remember this: life will move on without you—but you don't have to move through life without meaning.

Leave a mark not on history, but on hearts. And even if those hearts forget your name, the love you gave, the truth you lived, and the peace you found—those things echo, in ways you'll never see.

Your time is precious. Not just because it's limited, but because it is yours. Live for that. Live for you.

Choose you—now, not later. Don't wait for illness, heartbreak, or loss to shake you into living. You don't have to be cruel, selfish, or careless. But you do have to be honest. Choose people who choose you back. Choose a life that fills you, not one that drains you. Choose love over approval. Choose depth over popularity. Choose peace over performance.

Let go of those who only love the version of you that serves them. Walk away from situations that demand your silence in exchange for belonging. And don't be afraid to start over. The world forgets quickly, but you don't have to forget yourself.

And when you're gone, don't worry if your name isn't remembered by many. Worry only about whether you truly lived while you were here.

Every hour you spend doubting yourself is an hour you could have spent growing. Every day you spend trying to fit into someone else's version of "acceptable" is a day you could have used to build a life that actually fulfills you.

You have been told all your life that you need to be a certain way. That you need to achieve something, prove something, or be someone important to matter. But what if your value isn't in what you achieve—but in who you already are?

You don't need to be remembered by the world to have lived a meaningful life. You don't need statues, titles, or legacy. What you need is peace. What you need is truth. What you need is to lie in bed at the end of the day and say, "Today, I was myself. Fully."

Think about the people who once meant everything to you—do you still think of them every day? Do their names still pass through your lips, or have they faded like songs you used to love but no longer play? And yet, in their time, they were someone's whole world. That's how fleeting life is.

But fleeting doesn't mean meaningless. It just means urgent. This is life. We are all temporary in someone else's world. But we are permanent in our own.

Finding Happiness in the Present

During my recent trip to Barcelona, something deeply moving happened. I was standing in Tossa de Mar, surrounded by beauty—the sea, the sunshine, the charm of the town. As I stood there taking it all in, I heard a man singing on the street. His song wasn't just music—it was a message. He sang about the sadness in people's faces, about how many of us are walking through life looking down, disconnected, heavy.

I stopped and listened, and I felt something shift. There was truth in his words—a truth I've been noticing more and more.

I've spoken to many people lately. Some are doing well. Others are quietly struggling. Many live under constant pressure—from work, expectations, responsibilities—and they don't always know how to cope. Life feels repetitive, like we're waking up every day and running on autopilot. Even when we're doing things we once dreamed of, we're not always present. We're already thinking of what's next—tomorrow, next week, the future.

But the future doesn't always bring peace. Sometimes it only brings more pressure. The solution, maybe, is simpler than we think: to stop, to breathe, to notice what's happening now. Because even on the hard days, there's always something small to enjoy—a kind word, a warm coffee, a sunset.

Another thing I've realised is how often we compare ourselves to others. It's so easy to scroll through social media and assume everyone else is doing better—living more, smiling more, achieving more. But what we see online is a highlight reel. What we don't see are the arguments before the photos, the tears after the perfect moment, the struggles behind the smile.

The truth? Someone else's life doesn't define yours. It doesn't add value to your story. Only you can do that. We must remind ourselves: not every day will be good, but there is good in every day. And maybe that's enough.

What you see is not always the full story. You don't need to compare your life to others, because you never truly know what's happening behind closed doors. Focus on yourself, rather than getting caught up in the surface of what you see.

Appreciate every moment—because we never know when it might be the last time we get to laugh, to love, or to feel truly cared for.

The Art of Being Present

Looking forward to the weekend, I want to dedicate this reflection to each and every one of you. The theme is "Be in the Moment."

How many of us have been caught up in work, looking after others, supporting friends and family—and in doing so, completely forgotten ourselves? Forgotten to just be in the moment.

Have you ever felt like parts of your life passed by unnoticed? Then suddenly, you reach a stage in life where you stop and ask yourself:

"What have I done with my life?" "Who have I allowed into my life?" "Have I let others use me, manipulate me, and take from me—without even realizing—because I was too busy trying to give love to everyone else, forgetting to give it to myself?"

Someone shared with me recently that many people fall into the wrong relationships because they're searching for a love they never received in childhood. They end up choosing the wrong people, losing themselves, constantly worried about what others think, and unable to live in the moment.

When was the last time you truly appreciated your food? Every bite, every flavour—were you present? Or were you already thinking about your to-do list, forgetting the joy in the now, forgetting those who genuinely care about you?

How often do you find yourself working hard just to be liked? Can you recall the countless times you've pleased others, while putting your own needs on hold? That precious moment you gave away—could it have been a moment to rest, to connect with your children, or to be present with your parents?

Sometimes, we need to reclaim the energy we've given so freely. Not everyone will recognise your efforts, and in the process, you might miss the most meaningful moments in your life—all because you were worried about what others would say.

Does this resonate with you?

People often ask me if I want to save the world. My answer is no—I wish I could, but that's not my goal. What I want is to offer support, to encourage reflection. Even as I write this, I could be doing something else, but this—this moment—is important. Not just for others, but for me too.

This is not a waste of time. My time is precious, and I love what I do. Writing is therapeutic, and I recommend it to everyone. Put your thoughts on paper—your experiences, your feelings—it can help others, and it can heal you.

Even though I work as a therapist—both for a major organization in the UK and privately—this kind of writing brings me deep joy. It's incredible to witness the transformation in the lives of my patients. These moments are powerful. Because in truth, you cannot change anyone. You can only change yourself. You are responsible for you—and in doing so, you become a role model for others.

Living in the moment means walking slowly, kissing slowly, eating slowly. Savouring every second. These are the things that matter.

So, I invite you—right now—to sit down somewhere. Breathe. Don't rush. Walk and listen. Put on some beautiful music. Visit a place that brings you peace—like the beach or the countryside. Close your eyes, breathe through your nose, and really listen—to the wind, to the sounds around you. You'll understand what I mean.

Try to detach from all your worries in that moment. Stay in the present. Don't dwell on the past—it's already gone. Don't worry about the future—it hasn't arrived yet.

Just be here. Be now. Be in the moment.

Creating Your Life Map

I hope you're all having a wonderful weekend. As I was reflecting on what to share with you, I decided to explain the reason behind these messages. My intention is to offer support and encourage reflection on some of the issues we often overlook in the hustle and bustle of our daily lives—especially now, during busy seasons.

Imagine, for a moment, that you are sitting on a fast-moving train. Life often feels like this, rushing forward without pause. Now, picture yourself stepping off that train, finding a quiet spot, and taking the time to reflect on your life—your behaviours, decisions, and boundaries. If you could pause for just a moment and reconsider some of your choices, what would you do differently?

This week, I had a meaningful conversation with a friend who observed that my approach to my work is quite unique. My methods integrate various frameworks, including Gestalt therapy, Person-Centred therapy, Transactional Analysis, CBT (Cognitive Behavioural Therapy), and IPT (Interpersonal Therapy). I've also trained in working with couples, children, and adolescents, as well as coaching and mentoring university students with challenges such as Autism, Dyspraxia, ADHD, and other neurodivergent difficulties. My work is grounded in Humanism, and I am deeply passionate about what I do.

Since returning home, many of my friends have remarked that there is a real need for my skills and experience in Gran Canaria. I feel a strong calling to bring my expertise here, as I see so many people struggling without adequate support.

Take Christmas, for example. How many times have you celebrated this holiday under immense pressure to have the perfect food, gifts, and decorations? For many, January arrives with financial stress, and gifts are often exchanged or returned. The pressure can be overwhelming, leaving people feeling disappointed or exhausted.

I remember one year when I decided not to cook a traditional Christmas dinner. Instead, we ordered takeaway. It turned out to be one of the best Christmases we'd ever had—no stress, no frantic trips to the supermarket, and no pressure to recreate the idealized version of Christmas we see in the media. We spent the day playing games and watching funny movies. I'm not suggesting that everyone do this, nor am I judging anyone who loves a traditional holiday. I'm simply sharing how liberating it can be to step away from societal expectations.

When I reflect on my childhood, Christmas was about a few thoughtful presents, plenty of cake, and shared joy. Why wait until January 1st to make resolutions or changes? Why not start now?

One practical tool I recommend to my clients is creating a pie chart of your life. Use it to visualise the areas that matter to you—what feels fulfilled and what might be missing. What would you like to work on or change? This simple exercise can help you map out your journey and shape your own destiny.

I hope this message inspires you to pause, reflect, and consider what truly brings you joy and fulfilment this holiday season—and beyond.

What Truly Matters

I hope everyone had a wonderful day and enjoyed the weather. Here in the UK, we had a lovely weekend filled with sunshine, which makes such a difference to all of us.

Recently, I was reflecting on some of the things I've written and a conversation I had with a family member. During our discussion, a powerful question came up: What are you fighting for?

Looking back at my writings, I realised that many people fight for the "perfect" things—the perfect job, the perfect partner, the perfect house, the perfect children, the perfect car, the perfect holiday, the perfect body, the perfect life.

But while many people strive for these ideals, they often overlook something even more important: good health. We all want to be healthy, but how many of us truly appreciate it? My friend recently sent me something that made me reflect on this:

Visit a hospital and listen to the cries of those suffering, struggling just to feel better. Look into their eyes, filled with pain and sadness, as they fight for just one more day. Visit a prison and see the frustration of those who made wrong decisions—some by mistake, others because of their circumstances or their attachments. Visit a cemetery and reflect on the lives that have come to an end. Read the names, the dates of birth and death, and the messages left by loved ones. It makes you think: What have I done with my life?

Life is unpredictable—today we are here, but tomorrow is uncertain. Too often, we fight for the wrong reasons, even to the point of breaking family ties over trivial matters. But in the grand scheme of things, is it really worth it?

So, ask yourself: What are you fighting for? Every morning when you wake up, consider whether the things you invest your time and energy into truly matter. Are you prioritising the right people—those who value you as much as you value them? Or are you chasing things that won't bring real happiness?

It saddens me to see so many people struggling with mental health issues because they spend so much time trying to be the best version of themselves—not for their own happiness, but to please others. Anxiety and depression are on the rise, and much of this stems from allowing others to control, manipulate, and even gaslight us into believing they are right.

If you take a moment to reflect on what you're really fighting for, you'll realise that everyone just wants to be happy. But in order to truly find contentment, you must set boundaries. Without them, life can become overwhelming, making it difficult to slow down and focus on what truly matters to you. That's why I repeat myself so often—I want to remind you that it's essential to pause, reflect, and prioritise your well-being over others' expectations.

Without boundaries, it's nearly impossible to take care of yourself or fight for the things that truly matter in your life. Is this true for you? Think about how many times you've set boundaries with your friends, colleagues, and even your partner. If you've never done it before, it may feel difficult at first—but I promise you, it will help you in the long run.

In my work with patients, setting boundaries is a key focus. Many people feel mentally and physically exhausted because they're constantly doing things for others—just to feel liked or loved. But here's the truth: your love for yourself must come first.

Take a step back. Set your boundaries. Prioritize your happiness. Because you deserve it.

Life is fleeting. Make sure you're fighting for what truly matters.

Chapter 12: Ageing and Life Transitions

The passage of time brings with it profound changes that we often prefer not to contemplate. Yet ageing, loneliness, and even mortality are universal human experiences that deserve our attention and understanding. This chapter addresses these sensitive topics with the honesty they require, exploring how we can age with dignity, cope with isolation, and face life's inevitable transitions. Through personal encounters and professional observations, we examine the realities of growing older while offering practical wisdom for navigating these challenging but natural phases of life.

The Happier Decade

I want to dedicate this reflection to a dear friend of mine, who recently turned 60. Reaching this milestone often makes us reflect on how we feel as we transition into what many consider the third stage of life. It's a time when many of us start thinking about taking holidays, focusing on ourselves, and realising that our clock is indeed ticking.

I hope you don't see this as negative or morbid—it's simply an honest reflection on what this phase brings. I remember when I turned 40, my GP told me and everyone else, "Life begins at 40." That sounded wonderful at the time, but soon after, I began noticing the changes. My hair started turning gray, small wrinkles appeared, and I began experiencing back pain. For women, there are additional changes related to our physiology, and I'm sure men have their own unique experiences. It reminded me of being pregnant, forgetting appointments or losing track of time—only this time, the changes were different and permanent.

Everyone ages differently, and lifestyle plays a significant role in how we experience these transitions. However, both subtle and obvious changes will inevitably affect our physical and mental health. Some call this phase of life the "Happier Decade," though I often wonder what makes it happier when our bodies are clearly telling us a different story.

I wish doctors would elaborate more on what we need to do to embrace this stage of life positively. However, I'm not placing responsibility solely on them; we also need to educate ourselves and take accountability for our own well-being. The truth is, many of us reach this age unprepared for what it actually means to live in an aging body.

During my years working with older adults, I've observed that those who age most gracefully are often the ones who accepted these changes early and adapted their expectations accordingly. They didn't fight the gray hair or spend fortunes trying to look thirty again. Instead, they found new sources of joy and meaning that weren't dependent on physical appearance or the energy levels of youth.

Facing the physical changes that come with ageing can indeed be challenging. We may sweat more, lose some mobility, and notice weight gain, hair loss, or hearing loss. These changes can feel disheartening, especially in a society that celebrates youth and often treats ageing as something to be hidden or ashamed of. But they are part of life's natural progression. While we can't stop time, we can take proactive steps to maintain our health and manage these changes with dignity.

I've noticed in my practice that many people in their sixties experience a kind of identity crisis. The person they see in the mirror doesn't match the person they feel like inside. This disconnect can be profoundly unsettling. One patient told me, "I feel like I'm twenty-five inside a seventy-year-old body." This feeling is more common than people realise, and acknowledging it openly can be the first step toward acceptance.

Mentally, this stage of life can be even more impactful than the physical changes. It's not uncommon to feel that we're approaching the later chapters of our journey, and this awareness can lead to mood changes or even depression. The realisation that more time is behind us than ahead of us can be sobering. If you notice shifts in your mood or mental state during this transition, please don't hesitate to seek help. Speak with your GP—they can connect you with professionals or support groups to help you navigate these feelings.

What I've learned from working with people in this age group is that those who thrive don't ignore the reality of ageing—they reframe it. Instead of focusing on what they're losing, they become curious about what they might gain. Wisdom, perspective, the freedom that comes from caring less about others' opinions, the deep satisfaction of watching children and grandchildren grow. These aren't consolation prizes; they're genuine gifts that only come with time.

To support your mental health during this transition, it's crucial to exercise regularly, though this might mean adapting your activities to your current capabilities. A daily walk can be just as beneficial as the marathon running you did in your forties. Eating a healthy diet becomes even more important now, as your body may not process foods the same way it once did. Surrounding yourself with positive influences and socializing with the right people can make a tremendous difference in how you feel about yourself and your life.

I've observed that many people in this decade of life have spent so much time caring for others—children, aging parents, demanding careers—that they've lost touch with their own interests and desires. This can be an opportunity for rediscovery. What did you love doing before life got so complicated? What dreams did you set aside that might still be possible, perhaps in a modified form?

Many of us strive to look younger during this phase, but I encourage you to be mindful of the choices you make for your body and well-being. I've seen people spend thousands on procedures and treatments, only to end up looking like distorted versions of themselves. There's nothing wrong with wanting to look good, but when the pursuit of youth becomes an obsession, it often indicates a deeper struggle with accepting life's natural progression.

The physical aspects of intimacy during this decade also undergo natural changes that deserve honest discussion. Hormonal shifts affect both men and women, though in different ways. For women, menopause brings decreased estrogen, which may cause vaginal dryness or reduced libido. For men, declining testosterone levels can affect libido and erectile function. These changes are normal, not failures or inadequacies.

Sexual response patterns change, too. Arousal might take longer, and orgasms may be less intense or frequent. Men might experience erectile dysfunction or require more stimulation, while women may notice changes in vaginal tissues that can cause discomfort. Health conditions common in this age group—diabetes, heart disease, arthritis—can affect sexual function, as can the medications used to treat them.

But here's what I've learned from counselling couples in this age group: many find their intimate lives become more satisfying, not less. When the pressure of fertility and child-rearing is gone, when careers have stabilised, when there's more time and privacy, intimacy can deepen in unexpected ways. The key is open communication with your partner about these changes, maintaining overall health through exercise and good nutrition, and seeking medical help when needed.

Some couples discover that focusing on emotional intimacy and non-penetrative forms of affection opens doors to new experiences. Others find that accepting change allows them to explore aspects of their relationship they never had time for before. Professional help from sex therapists or counselors can address both emotional and physical challenges, while medical specialists can provide treatments tailored to individual needs.

What strikes me most about people who navigate this decade successfully is their willingness to grieve what they're losing while remaining curious about what they might find. They mourn the energy and appearance of youth without getting stuck in that grief. They adapt their expectations while maintaining hope for meaningful experiences ahead.

It's never too late to prioritise your mental and physical health. The choices you make today—about diet, exercise, relationships, and mental wellbeing—will significantly impact how you experience the years ahead. By making simple, intentional changes, you can embrace this stage of life with grace and vitality. Let's celebrate ageing as a journey of growth, wisdom, and resilience, rather than a series of losses to be endured.

Loneliness and Ageing Care

During a routine grocery shopping trip, I encountered a situation that stayed with me for days and ultimately inspired me to write about the profound loneliness many older adults face. I was in the clothing section when a mature woman—though I prefer not to use the term "old lady"—approached me for help. She was holding a pair of trousers and couldn't read the size label clearly. When I looked, I realised she had selected the wrong size and gently helped her find the correct one.

What began as a simple interaction became something much deeper. As we spoke, she began sharing details about her life with the kind of openness that often comes from people who rarely have anyone to talk to. She revealed that she had never been in a relationship, never married, never experienced romantic love. Surprised by this revelation, I smiled warmly and asked, "Never? Not even when you were younger?"

Her story unfolded slowly, painted with both sadness and acceptance. There had been someone once—a man she truly wanted to be with, someone who had captured her heart completely. But fate intervened cruelly when he had to leave for South Africa due to his failing health. The distance and his illness made maintaining their connection impossible, and he passed away soon after his departure. After losing him, she told me, she never opened her heart to anyone else again.

She spoke with a gentle smile throughout our conversation, but I could sense the underlying sadness that decades of solitude had woven into her spirit. The only visitors she received were her niece and her niece's husband, who came occasionally but lived their own busy lives with their own families and responsibilities.

I found myself drawn to continue our conversation because I could tell she was genuinely lonely and needed someone to listen. Human connection is something we all crave, yet for so many older adults, meaningful conversation becomes increasingly rare. By the end of our chat, she mentioned that she lived in a residential care facility where I had previously worked as a manager, supporting both men and women who could no longer live independently.

When I told her about my past role there, her face lit up with recognition and pleasure. She even took my name, promising to mention our encounter to other residents. She spoke fondly of the facility and said she was content where she lived, though she also mentioned how many people had passed away over the years—a reminder of the transient nature of relationships in these settings.

This encounter made me reflect deeply on the countless men and women who have dedicated their entire lives to caring for others—whether their aging parents, disabled relatives, or their communities—at the expense of their own personal lives and relationships. These are often the most selfless individuals in our society, yet they frequently find themselves alone in their later years, with no family of their own to provide the care they once gave so freely to others.

During my years working in elderly care, I witnessed this pattern repeatedly. There was Margaret, who spent forty years caring for her mother with dementia and never married because she couldn't leave her mother's side. There was Thomas, who gave up his chance at love to care for his younger siblings after their parents died, only to find himself alone when his siblings grew up and started their own families. These stories of sacrifice are both beautiful and heartbreaking.

While some people genuinely choose to live alone and find happiness in their independence, others find themselves trapped in loneliness, especially when they require care themselves. Many long for companionship and deeply regret not having the health or mobility to live independently, to make new connections, or to maintain the relationships they once had.

I remember walking through the beautiful facilities where I worked, seeing elderly people sitting in comfortable chairs, surrounded by nice furnishings and professional care, yet feeling profoundly alone. They would talk endlessly about their past lives—their marriages, their children who rarely visited, their friends who had died, or like the woman I met shopping, their lifelong solitude. It was heartbreaking to listen to their stories and witness their frustration with the passage of time, which truly spares no one.

The residents often shared their regrets with me. Some wished they had been braver about pursuing love when they were younger. Others regretted spending so much time working or caring for others that they forgot to build relationships that would sustain them in old age. Many expressed surprise at how quickly time had passed, how suddenly they found themselves elderly and alone when it felt like just yesterday they were young and surrounded by possibilities.

What struck me most was how hungry they were for genuine conversation, for someone who would listen to their stories without rushing away. In our youth-obsessed culture, we often dismiss the elderly as having little to offer, but spending time with them revealed incredible wisdom, humour, and insight. Their stories were fascinating, their perspectives hard-earned through decades of experience.

I want to dedicate this reflection to all the women and men who have never experienced romantic love—some by choice and others because they never met the right person, or because circumstances prevented them from pursuing it. It is incredibly sad to see people struggling with mobility issues, yearning for companionship but lacking the energy or opportunity to form new connections.

The loneliness I witnessed in these facilities was often compounded by the institutional nature of care. Despite the best efforts of staff, residents often felt like their individual identities were being erased, replaced by medical conditions and care routines. The woman who had been a talented pianist became "the lady in room twelve who needs help with her medications." The man who had run a successful business became "the gentleman who wanders at night."

If you know someone in this situation, I encourage you to offer your support. Even a small conversation can make an enormous difference in their day, their week, their entire outlook. Don't wait for holidays or special occasions—loneliness doesn't take breaks. A phone call, a short visit, or even just acknowledging them with a warm smile can remind them that they still matter, that their stories and experiences have value.

To all the men and women who feel alone, especially those in care facilities or living in isolation, please don't give up on connection. Love and friendship have no age limits. While romantic love might seem out of reach, human connection comes in many forms. Sometimes the most meaningful relationships begin with simple conversations, shared interests, or mutual support.

During my time working with retired people, I witnessed not only their loneliness and sadness but also their remarkable resilience. Many found ways to create meaning and connection even within the constraints of their circumstances. Some became mentors to younger residents, others started small groups around shared interests, and some found purpose in helping those who were even more vulnerable than themselves.

The fear I often saw in their eyes wasn't just about death—it was about being forgotten, about their lives having no lasting impact, about returning to a childlike dependence, but this time with far fewer people around to provide emotional support. Yet those who seemed to cope best were the ones who had made peace with their circumstances while remaining open to whatever small joys and connections were still possible.

When I meet someone like the woman in the store, I don't mind spending some of my time in conversation with them. If you look at their faces while you're listening, you can see how much they appreciate having someone who genuinely cares about what they have to say. These encounters remind me that we all have the power to ease someone's loneliness, even if just for a few minutes.

If you ever have the opportunity, take time to talk with elderly people in your community. You'll learn so much—they are often wise, full of stories, and frequently quite funny once they feel comfortable sharing. They've lived through historical events, survived challenges we can barely imagine, and developed perspectives that only come with decades of experience.

Remember to enjoy your own life while you can—time passes quickly for all of us. But also remember that the kindness you show to lonely elderly people today might be the kindness you hope to receive when you're in their position tomorrow.

Loneliness

Today, I felt compelled to write about loneliness because I understand intimately what it's like to feel this way, and because in my work as a therapist, I encounter it daily in forms both subtle and overwhelming. Sometimes, we can be surrounded by people at a party, at work, even at home with our families, and still feel utterly alone. Other times, during life's most challenging moments, loneliness feels so overpowering and profoundly sad that it seems to swallow us whole.

The loneliness I see in my practice isn't always dramatic or obvious. It's the successful businessman who has everything he thought he wanted but realizes he has no one to share it with. It's the mother who spends all day caring for everyone else's needs but feels invisible and unheard. It's the teenager surrounded by classmates who feels like no one really knows or understands them. It's the elderly person in a care facility who gets excellent medical attention but whose emotional needs go largely unmet.

As part of my work, I encounter patients with serious health issues who lack any form of emotional support. Hearing their stories repeatedly fills me with sadness that goes beyond professional empathy—it touches something deep in my own experience of isolation. I often wish I had a magic wand to take this pain away, not just for them, but for myself and others who have experienced similar feelings of disconnection and abandonment.

What strikes me most about loneliness is how it doesn't discriminate. Even those with seemingly perfect lives—the car, the house, the ideal job, the active social calendar—can feel low and profoundly disconnected. External circumstances, I've learned, are poor predictors of internal emotional states. Some of my loneliest patients have been people whose Instagram feeds would make others envious.

In an attempt to bridge this gap of connection, many of us turn to online groups or social communities. If you look closely at these platforms, you'll see countless men and women searching for the same thing—a genuine human connection. Yet somehow, despite all these people seeking the same thing, true connection often remains elusive. Isn't that one of the great ironies of our time? We're more "connected" than ever before, yet loneliness rates continue to climb.

I remember reading something that deeply resonated with me: even when you're sleeping next to your partner, living together, sharing physical space and even intimacy, it doesn't always equate to a genuine emotional connection. These interactions can become habitual, part of a daily routine that lacks real meaning or depth. True connection, however, is different. It's looking at someone and genuinely feeling seen and understood by them. Love is also about someone waiting eagerly to have a meaningful conversation with you, not just sharing space or going through motions.

How many times have you been in a crowded room—at a family gathering, a work meeting, a social event—and felt as though no one was truly listening to you? I experience this sometimes even in professional settings, where people ask how I am but don't really wait for or want an honest answer. We've created a culture of surface-level interactions that masquerade as connections but leave us feeling empty.

During my time working with older adults as a manager in residential care, I often saw residents who felt abandoned by their families, even when those families visited regularly. The visits had become obligatory, routine, lacking the warmth and genuine interest that create a real connection. It was heartbreaking to witness this daily. The residents could sense the difference between someone spending time with them out of duty versus someone who genuinely wanted to be there.

All I could do to support them was sit with them, share real conversations, and look at old photos as they reminisced about their younger years and the times they missed most. These weren't therapeutic sessions in any formal sense—they were human moments of genuine connection. I used to go home in tears, not just from sadness but from being moved by their stories, their resilience, their humour, even in difficult circumstances.

I encourage you to reflect deeply on this topic. Think about your parents, your friends, and your partner when they express feelings of loneliness. Often, we dismiss these expressions or try to fix them quickly rather than simply acknowledging and sitting with the person in their pain. Loneliness, I've learned, sometimes needs to be witnessed and validated before it can be addressed.

Loneliness can actually be positive for some people, offering necessary time for self-reflection, creativity, and personal growth. Solitude and loneliness are different experiences entirely. However, for others, chronic loneliness can be deeply harmful, even contributing to serious health problems if they don't find the connection they need. Studies have shown that prolonged loneliness affects physical health similarly to smoking or obesity. Remember, we're all different and unique in our needs for social connection.

Loneliness manifests in several distinct forms. Emotional loneliness involves feeling the absence of a close, intimate connection—the kind you might have with a romantic partner or very close friend. This type of loneliness often feels like a deep ache, a sense that no one truly knows or understands you at your core.

Social loneliness is different—it's lacking a sense of belonging to a group or community. You might have close friends but feel disconnected from any larger social network. This often happens when people move to new cities, change jobs, or go through major life transitions that disrupt their social connections.

Then there's existential loneliness, which involves feeling isolated on a broader, philosophical level. This is the loneliness that comes from questioning your place in the world, your purpose, the meaning of your existence. It's the kind of loneliness that can strike even when you're surrounded by loving family and friends.

Consider how many people around the world are actively searching for someone to connect with—dating apps, social clubs, online communities, religious gatherings. The number is staggering. Why, then, do we continue to feel disconnected? What is missing in our relationships that we can't seem to resolve?

I've observed in my practice that loneliness is sometimes a factor in relationship infidelity. When people aren't getting what they need emotionally or physically from their primary relationship, they may seek connection elsewhere. This doesn't excuse the behavior, but it helps us understand that human connection is a fundamental need that people will seek to fulfill somehow.

During my thirty-five years living in England, I've experienced my fair share of profound loneliness. My social media presence might look cheerful and connected, but behind those carefully curated posts, there have been moments of deep isolation that nearly overwhelmed me. Moving to a new country is an enormous challenge that people who haven't experienced it often underestimate. It's a traumatic experience that reshapes your entire world, often leaving you feeling like a stranger even to yourself.

When I first arrived in England from Gran Canaria, I couldn't speak a word of English. The very first word I heard at the airport was extremely rude, though I didn't understand its meaning until someone explained it later. That moment set the tone for what would be a long, difficult period of adjustment. Learning to navigate a new system, a different language, unfamiliar weather patterns, foreign food, and an entirely different culture was overwhelming in ways I hadn't anticipated.

The weather alone affected me more than I expected. Coming from the sunny Canary Islands to England's grey, damp climate felt like losing part of my identity. Simple things like grocery shopping became monumental tasks when you can't read labels or ask for help effectively. Social cues that seemed natural to everyone else were mysterious to me. I felt invisible and incompetent, despite being an educated, capable adult.

The loneliness of those early years taught me that isolation isn't just about being alone—it's about feeling fundamentally misunderstood and disconnected from the world around you. Even when kind people tried to help me, the language barrier and cultural differences created a sense of separation that was difficult to bridge.

Yet that experience also taught me that being alone isn't always negative. Sometimes, solitude can be refreshing and necessary, providing space for personal growth, reflection, and healing. I learned to distinguish between chosen solitude and imposed isolation. The former can be nourishing; the latter can be devastating.

For those struggling with loneliness, I want to offer some practical suggestions based on both my personal experience and professional observations. First, recognise that loneliness is not a character flaw or personal failure—it's a common human experience that serves an evolutionary purpose by motivating us to seek the social connections we need for survival.

Consider reaching out to old friends, even if you haven't spoken in years. Often, people are delighted to reconnect, and both parties have been thinking of each other. Join groups based on genuine interests rather than just the goal of meeting people—authentic connections form more easily around shared activities or values.

Volunteer for causes you care about. This serves the dual purpose of contributing to something meaningful while connecting with like-minded people. The shared sense of purpose often creates bonds more quickly than purely social activities.

If you're dealing with chronic loneliness, consider seeking professional help. Therapy can help you understand patterns in your relationships and develop skills for forming deeper connections. Sometimes loneliness is a symptom of depression or anxiety, which are highly treatable conditions.

I highly recommend reading "I'm OK—You're OK" by Thomas A. Harris. It's an excellent resource that explores how humans manage their emotions and develop healthier relationships with themselves and others. Understanding transactional analysis helped me recognise some of my own patterns that were contributing to my sense of isolation.

For those supporting someone who is lonely, remember that sometimes the most helpful thing you can do is simply listen without trying to fix or minimise their feelings. Loneliness often needs to be acknowledged and validated before it can begin to heal. Small gestures of connection—a text message, a phone call, an invitation for coffee—can have tremendous impact.

Let's remember to offer kindness, empathy, and genuine connection to those around us. We never know when someone might be struggling with isolation behind their public face. The elderly person in line at the grocery store, the colleague who always eats lunch alone, the neighbour you haven't seen in a while—these small moments of human connection can make a profound difference in someone's day or even their life.

Talking About Dying

The weather is improving, and many of us are looking forward to summer and some well-deserved rest. Yet today, I felt compelled to write about something that many of us actively avoid discussing—death—and how we feel when someone we love passes away. This avoidance is understandable but ultimately unhelpful, both for ourselves and for those we care about.

It's often said that grief is deeply personal, and we all grieve in different ways. This couldn't be more true, yet our culture offers few guidelines for navigating this universal experience. From the moment we are born, the clock starts ticking toward the day we will eventually leave this world. Yet, paradoxically, we often spend our time wishing for the next birthday, the next summer, or the next holiday, forgetting to appreciate the present moment that is the only one we truly have.

While we dream of turning eighteen, twenty-one, or thirty, we may be wishing away some of the most beautiful and meaningful years of our lives. I always tell people on their birthdays to enjoy it, remember it, and cherish the time they have with the people around them—because we don't know how many more birthdays, Christmases, or quiet Sunday mornings we'll share together.

Death is something we don't like to think about, and I completely understand that resistance. Some people say death is when we finally rest, free from suffering and struggle. That may be true, but I believe that if we learn to set healthy boundaries, surround ourselves with those who genuinely love us, and make choices that align with our values, we can live without excessive suffering, too. We weren't born to suffer endlessly—if you've been told that, or have believed it, know that you have the power to choose a different path.

In my work, I've noticed that people who have made peace with mortality often live more fully. They waste less time on trivial concerns and focus more intensely on what truly matters to them. This isn't morbid thinking—it's realistic wisdom that can enhance the quality of life we have.

It's also important to reflect on how our modern lifestyle might be affecting our health and longevity. With so many people being diagnosed with cancer, heart disease, diabetes, and other serious illnesses at younger ages, we should honestly ask ourselves: Are we living too fast, too stressed, too disconnected from our bodies and natural rhythms? What are we doing to our minds and bodies that might be contributing to illness?

I've observed that many of my patients who develop serious health problems have been living in chronic stress for years, eating poorly, sleeping inadequately, and ignoring their body's signals. While we can't control all factors that contribute to illness, we have more influence over our health than many people realise.

Death is an inevitable part of life. We don't know when it will come for us or our loved ones, but we can think deeply about how we want to live before it's too late. This isn't about becoming morbid or obsessed with death—it's about letting awareness of life's finite nature guide us toward more meaningful choices.

Imagine being told you have one week to live. What would you do differently? Who would you want by your side? What would you say to those you love? What experiences would suddenly seem pointless, and which would become precious? These aren't just hypothetical questions—they're invitations to examine whether your current life aligns with your deepest values.

Why wait for a terminal diagnosis to start living more authentically? Why not begin now to surround yourself with people who love and uplift you? Why continue to invest time and energy in relationships or activities that drain you rather than nourish you? Life truly is too short to settle for less than authentic connections and meaningful experiences.

Something else I want to address is what happens at funerals. Have you noticed the pattern? I've never been to a funeral where someone said the deceased was a burden or wasn't worth loving. Instead, we hear beautiful words, see lovely flowers, and feel the deep sorrow of loss. But often—and this is one of the most tragic aspects of our culture—the person who has passed didn't get to hear those words of love and appreciation while they were alive.

This disconnect breaks my heart repeatedly. Why do we wait until it's too late to say "I love you" "You matter to me" or "I'm grateful for what you brought to my life"? Why do we save our most heartfelt expressions for eulogies when the person can no longer hear them?

I've cried at every funeral I've attended, and sometimes I find myself wondering: Am I crying for the person who passed, or for myself because I won't see them again? Sometimes we cry because we wish we had done more, said more, or loved more openly. If you could have one more moment with someone you've lost, what would you do differently?

This question drives me to be more honest, more affectionate, and more present with the people I care about while they're still here. I try to hug like it might be the last hug, to say how I feel without waiting for the "right" moment—because we simply don't know how much time we have.

The global pandemic taught us this lesson in the starkest possible terms. Many people lost loved ones without being able to say goodbye, to be present during their final moments, or to have the closure that comes from expressing final thoughts and feelings. That time was traumatic for so many because it highlighted how fragile our connections truly are and how quickly everything we take for granted can be disrupted.

The pandemic also showed us how important it is to talk about death before it becomes imminent. Let's discuss what we want—whether it's the kind of funeral we'd prefer, what music should be played, whether we want to be buried or cremated, and what we want our legacy to be. Why not share those wishes openly? Why not be part of that conversation with the people we love?

I encourage families to have these discussions during calm, healthy times rather than waiting for crisis moments when emotions are high and time is short. Talking about death when no one is dying removes some of the fear and allows for thoughtful, meaningful conversations about what matters most.

One last thought about grief—please don't try to avoid it by immediately distracting yourself with holidays, redecorating projects, or staying constantly busy. While these activities might provide temporary relief, they can prevent you from processing the loss in a healthy way. Allow yourself to feel the pain. Work through it gradually. The intensity will ease in time, but only if you allow yourself to experience and process the grief rather than suppressing it.

Suppressing grief can lead to long-term emotional and even physical problems, including depression, anxiety, and various health issues. Your body and mind need to process loss, and grief is the natural mechanism for doing so.

I've noticed that people sometimes make jokes about negative traits they had in common with their deceased loved one, like being stubborn, because they find it difficult to express the full complexity of their feelings during the relationship. Grief often brings up not just sadness but also unresolved conflicts, regrets, and complicated emotions that are normal but difficult to discuss openly.

Find safe spaces and loving people with whom you can be vulnerable about the full range of your feelings. Talk about the person you've lost—both their wonderful qualities and their human flaws. Cry when you need to. Laugh when memories bring joy. Our tears serve a purpose—our bodies were designed to help us heal through the expression of emotion. Don't deny yourself this natural process.

I've experienced the loss of people I deeply loved, and that's one of the reasons I'm writing this—not just for my own healing, but hoping it might help others navigate their own experiences with loss and mortality.

It's not only acceptable but necessary to talk about death openly. It's healthy to feel sad when we lose people we care about. It's normal to experience pain during grief. These are human experiences that connect us all, regardless of wealth, status, or achievements.

No one, regardless of their fame or fortune, escapes this part of life. Death is the great equaliser that reminds us of our shared humanity. So ask your loved ones what they want, how they'd like to be remembered. We plan weddings and birthday parties with great care—why not extend the same thoughtfulness to end-of-life wishes?

Celebrate each day you wake up healthy and surrounded by people you care about. Celebrate each birthday, even if you're not thrilled about getting older, because reaching another year is actually an achievement worth acknowledging.

Life isn't perfect—it's not a fairy tale or cartoon fantasy where everything works out easily. But we can make it meaningful through our choices, our connections, and our willingness to love openly despite the certainty of loss. If you love someone, tell them. Spend quality time with them. Hug them. Don't wait to express your feelings after they're gone—let them feel your love now, while they're still here to receive it.

My mother used to say to me, "Sole, life is like a dream—by the time you wake up, it's already gone." I carry her words with me daily, and they remind me to make the most of my life and the precious time I have here with the people I care about.

Be kind and loving to yourself, and allow yourself to be fully human in all the messy, beautiful, painful, and joyful ways that entails.

Time

During the holiday season, I want to share a message for those who have lost someone they love deeply, but also for anyone who needs to be reminded of time's precious and fleeting nature. Christmas and other holidays can be beautiful times to celebrate with family and friends, but based on my experience as a therapist, I know they can also be stressful and emotionally challenging periods for many people.

While others celebrate with wonderful presents, delicious food, and joyful music, please remember that not everyone finds this season easy. For some, holidays amplify feelings of loss, loneliness, or disappointment. If this resonates with you, know that your feelings are valid and you're not alone in struggling during times that others celebrate.

Many of us reconnect with family members we haven't seen all year during holiday seasons, and while that can be lovely, it sometimes brings its own complicated dynamics. Old family patterns resurface, unresolved conflicts bubble up, and the pressure to be joyful can feel overwhelming when you're dealing with grief or other challenges. Despite everything, we often try to be on our best behaviour and make the most of these precious but sometimes difficult moments.

The purpose of this reflection is to encourage everyone to think of those who may not be surrounded by love or family during holidays and throughout the year. Some people are in hospitals, facing serious illnesses alone. Others are going through divorces, job losses, or other major life transitions that make celebration feel impossible. Still others are simply feeling lonely, even if they're surrounded by people.

A simple text message, a phone call, or even just thinking compassionate thoughts about someone can mean more than you realise. Don't wait until Christmas Day or other special occasions to reach out—loneliness and pain don't take holiday breaks. Consider taking time to reflect on your relationships and make a more consistent effort to contact people you care about, not just during holidays but throughout the year.

Time moves with such speed that it's easy to let weeks and months pass without meaningful contact with people who matter to us. We tell ourselves we'll call next week, send that card soon, visit when things slow down. But life rarely slows down on its own, and before we know it, years have passed and opportunities for connection have been lost.

There are also people who don't have any family at all—by choice, circumstance, or loss. Let's try to remember them and include them when possible, not just during holiday seasons but throughout the year. Even small gestures of inclusion can transform someone's experience from isolation to belonging.

I've learned that people who have experienced significant losses often develop a different relationship with time. They understand its scarcity in a way that others don't. They're more likely to prioritise meaningful experiences over material purchases, genuine connections over superficial socialising, and present-moment awareness over constant future planning.

During holidays, it's also important to take care of your own mental and emotional health. The pressure to be constantly cheerful, to create perfect celebrations, to buy expensive gifts, to attend every social gathering can be exhausting. Give yourself permission to participate selectively, to set boundaries around your time and energy, and to honour your own needs even if others don't understand.

Most importantly, try to enjoy yourself authentically rather than feeling obligated to perform happiness. Holidays and special seasons come once a year, but they're meant to enhance our lives, not create additional stress and financial burden.

Time is indeed precious, and we often don't realise its true value until it's gone or until we're facing its scarcity directly. Every moment we have with the people we love, every ordinary day of good health, every peaceful evening at home—these are gifts that deserve our appreciation.

The ticking of time isn't meant to create anxiety but to inspire gratitude and intentional living. When we truly understand that our time here is limited, we can make choices that align with what matters most to us rather than what others expect of us.

As you move through this holiday season and beyond, I encourage you to be generous with your time and attention toward others, but also protective of your own well-being. Reach out to those who might be struggling, but don't forget to nurture yourself as well.

Remember that the greatest gift you can give anyone is your genuine presence and attention. These cost nothing but time, yet they're often the most meaningful presents we can offer or receive.

Wishing you all love, care, and the wisdom to use your precious time in ways that bring meaning and connection to your life and the lives of others.

Chapter 13: Loss and Grief

Grief is perhaps the most universal yet profoundly personal human experience. It touches every life, yet each person's journey through loss is utterly unique. This chapter explores the raw reality of losing those we love most—the pain that reshapes us, the waves of emotion that continue long after the funeral flowers have wilted, and the complex process of learning to carry loss while still embracing life. Through deeply personal reflections on losing my own parents and observations from years of therapeutic work, we examine how grief changes us, challenges us, and ultimately, if we allow it, can teach us about the preciousness of love and the importance of saying what matters while we still can.

Losing Someone You Love

I want to dedicate this reflection to my mum, my sisters, and all those who have lost someone they truly care about. Today marks the third year since I lost one of the most important people in my life—my mum. If you have ever lost someone you deeply love, you understand that grief is incredibly difficult and that people grieve in completely different ways.

I remember listening to the priest at my mum's funeral, and his words have stayed with me ever since. He said, "We are all here for the same reason, but remember that we all grieve in our own way." His words were beautiful and empathetic, offering comfort to everyone present while acknowledging the deeply personal nature of loss. In that moment, surrounded by family and friends who all loved my mother, I realised that each person in that room was experiencing their own unique version of grief, colored by their own memories and relationship with her.

When we lose someone, we often feel that our tears are for them, but in reality, we cry mostly for ourselves. We grieve because we know we will never see them again, never hear their voice—whether they were scolding us for something we'd done wrong or speaking words of love and encouragement. We cry for all the conversations that will never happen, all the advice we'll never receive, all the moments of ordinary togetherness that we took for granted. That loss is profound in ways that are difficult to articulate to those who haven't experienced it.

Grief is a deep emotional response to loss, most commonly associated with the death of a loved one, but it can also be triggered by other significant losses—the end of a marriage, the loss of a job, a major illness, or any life transition that involves letting go of something or someone important. It manifests in countless ways, including sadness, anger, guilt, numbness, confusion, and even physical symptoms like fatigue, loss of appetite, or difficulty sleeping.

Many people are familiar with Elisabeth Kübler-Ross's model of the five stages of grief, which identifies denial, anger, bargaining, depression, and acceptance as common phases people experience. While this model can be helpful for understanding grief, I want to emphasise that these stages don't follow a strict order, and people often cycle through them multiple times, sometimes experiencing several simultaneously.

In my years as a therapist, I've learned that grief is much messier and more unpredictable than any model can capture. Some people get stuck in anger for months. Others skip certain stages entirely. Some experience acceptance early, only to find themselves back in denial years later when a particular anniversary or memory surfaces. The key is understanding that there's no "right" way to grieve and no timeline that applies to everyone.

My personal experience with losing both of my parents was one of the hardest journeys of my life. My first real encounter with profound grief was losing my mum, and it was devastating because I never got the chance to say goodbye. If you have been through this experience of losing someone suddenly, without warning or preparation, you understand how the shock compounds the pain. My loss happened so quickly that I felt completely unprepared, emotionally and practically.

I remember arriving in Gran Canaria late at night, with my family picking me up from the airport. I felt my stomach in my throat, knowing that the days ahead would be unlike anything I'd experienced before. The familiar island that had always represented home and happiness suddenly felt foreign and threatening, colored by the knowledge that my mother would never greet me there again.

Seeing my mum in her coffin was nothing like the way I had left her the last time we were together. I had left her believing, as we always do, that I would see her again, that there would be more conversations, more opportunities to tell her I loved her. Standing there, looking at her still form, the finality hit me with crushing force. This is why I always tell my clients and anyone who will listen: Never leave someone you care about without saying "I love you," because you truly never know if you will see that person again.

This experience taught me that life is far too short for grudges, unnecessary conflicts, or withholding affection. However, I've also learned that grief can lead people to set important boundaries and make necessary changes in their relationships, even with family members. Sometimes loss clarifies what truly matters and what relationships are worth our energy.

Someone told me after the funeral, "You will see the reality of life, and that is when you will need to decide how to move forward." Those words, though difficult to hear at the time, helped me realise the importance of valuing the people who truly matter and not wasting precious time and emotional energy on those who don't add value to my life. Believe me, experiencing profound loss changes everything about how you view relationships and priorities.

For those who didn't have a great relationship with their parents, grief can be equally painful but in a different way. Sometimes, the tears we shed are not just for the parents we lost, but also for the parents we never truly had—grieving both the actual person and the relationship we wished we could have had. This is a deep and complex kind of pain that deserves acknowledgement and professional support.

I've worked with many clients who struggle with what psychologists call "complicated grief" or "disenfranchised grief"—mourning someone with whom they had a difficult relationship. They feel guilty for grieving someone who hurt them, or they feel angry that death has taken away any possibility of reconciliation or closure. These feelings are completely normal and valid, though they can be particularly challenging to navigate alone.

One of the ways I encourage people to honour their grief and their loved ones is through meaningful rituals. For me, I light a candle and say a prayer for my mum and for myself each year on the anniversary of her death. I know that for my family, this day will always carry sadness, but we also celebrate the fact that my mum was deeply loved by many people whose lives she touched.

These rituals don't have to be religious or formal. Some people plant gardens, others donate to causes their loved ones cared about, and some simply spend the day looking through photos and sharing memories. The important thing is creating a way to acknowledge the loss while also honouring the love and connection that death cannot erase.

Coping with grief requires patience with yourself and often support from others. Allow yourself to feel whatever emotions arise, even if they seem contradictory or overwhelming. Suppressing grief can prolong the healing process and sometimes lead to more serious emotional difficulties later on.

Seek support from friends, family, or a professional therapist who understands grief. Talking about your loved one and your feelings about losing them is crucial for processing the loss. Take care of your physical health by maintaining as much routine as possible around eating, sleeping, and exercise, even when you don't feel like it.

Express your grief in ways that feel meaningful to you, whether through journaling, creating art, listening to music, or simply talking to your loved one's photograph. Find ways to honour their memory that feel authentic to your relationship and their values.

Remember that healing doesn't mean forgetting or "getting over" the loss. It means learning to carry the love and memories in a way that allows you to continue living meaningfully. The goal isn't to return to who you were before the loss—that person no longer exists. The goal is to integrate the experience of loving and losing into who you're becoming.

Grief Comes in Waves

If there's one truth I've learned about grief through personal experience and professional observation, it's that grief doesn't follow a straight line. It doesn't care about how much time has passed, how strong others think you are, or how much you believe you've "moved on." Grief comes in waves, sometimes gentle ripples that barely disturb the surface of your day, and sometimes massive swells that knock you completely off your feet without warning.

Some days you wake up and feel surprisingly okay. You can smile at a photograph, laugh at a cherished memory, and even feel moments of genuine peace or joy. These are the days when people might say you're "doing well" or "healing nicely," and you might even believe them. You start to think maybe you're through the worst of it, that you've found your footing on solid ground again.

But then other days, something seemingly insignificant—a particular song playing in a café, the scent of perfume that reminds you of them, an empty chair positioned the way they used to sit—can completely break you open. Suddenly, you're crying like the loss happened yesterday, not months or years ago. And this isn't because you're weak or because you're not grieving "properly." It's because love this deep leaves a permanent imprint on your heart that time cannot erase.

After losing both of my parents, I naively thought that time would make the pain easier to bear. And yes, in some ways, it does become more manageable. You learn how to carry the weight more efficiently, like strengthening muscles that have been asked to bear a heavy load. But the pain never really disappears completely. It just changes shape, becomes quieter and less sharp, but it remains present, woven into the fabric of who you are now.

Sometimes I catch myself reaching for my phone to call them, forgetting for just a moment that they won't answer. Other times, I experience something beautiful—a sunset, a piece of music, a moment with my children—and think, "They would have loved this" or "I wonder what they would say about this situation." These moments remind me that grief isn't just about missing the person; it's about missing their presence in your ongoing life, missing their perspective on your experiences, missing the comfort of knowing they're there even when you don't need them.

One of the most difficult aspects of grief that I've observed, both personally and professionally, is that you never stop needing your parents, regardless of your age. Society sometimes suggests that adult grief over losing parents should be more contained or manageable because "it's the natural order of things." But emotional need doesn't follow logical timelines. The forty-year-old who loses a mother still wants to call her when facing a difficult decision. The sixty-year-old who loses a father still wishes he could share good news and receive that particular kind of parental pride and approval.

I've learned that grief doesn't mean you're broken or stuck in the past. Instead, it means you loved deeply and authentically. It means that relationship had profound meaning and impact on your life. It means part of your heart is still actively loving someone, even though they're no longer physically present to receive that love.

Even though my parents aren't here with me in the way I desperately wish they were, I see them constantly in unexpected places. I hear my mother's voice in how I comfort my children when they're upset. I recognize my father's stubbornness in my refusal to give up when facing challenges. Their influence lives on in countless small ways that shape how I move through the world, how I treat others, and what values I prioritise.

If you're currently grieving, I want you to know that you are absolutely not alone in this experience. You're not "too emotional" when the waves hit unexpectedly. There is no correct timeline for healing, despite what well-meaning people might suggest. Society often pressures grieving people to "move on" or "find closure" according to arbitrary schedules that don't reflect the reality of human emotional life.

Let the waves of grief come when they come. Don't fight them or judge yourself for experiencing them. Feel the sadness, the anger, the longing, the confusion—all of it is valid and necessary. Trust that on the other side of each wave, there is still love, still connection, still meaningful memory that time cannot touch or diminish.

During my recent travels, I had an unexpected encounter that reminded me how grief connects us all and how people carry their losses in ways both visible and hidden. I was at a coffee shop, initially thinking a young woman nearby was just another customer enjoying her coffee outside. When she stood up to clear tables, I realised she worked there and we began chatting.

She had a lovely Scottish accent, and our conversation quickly moved beyond small talk. When I noticed her vaping, I mentioned that I used to smoke years ago and asked if she'd ever considered quitting. Her response opened a window into her story: she told me the vape helps her manage stress related to losing both parents—her mother when she was only five years old, and her father when she was fourteen.

The weight of what she'd shared left me momentarily speechless. Here was someone who had experienced more loss by age fourteen than many people face in a lifetime. She told me she'd moved to southern England alone at twenty, relying on an older sister who had cared for her after their father's death. As we continued talking, she showed me a small heart pendant containing some of her father's ashes—a tangible way of keeping him close.

When I asked about her mother, she told me something that shocked me: someone at her school had taken her mother's ashes and thrown them away. The casual cruelty of this act was heartbreaking. With a smile that didn't hide her pain, she added, "I broke her hand." While I didn't encourage violence, I understood her need to defend her mother's memory and told her honestly, "Your parents would be proud of you."

This encounter brought back memories of my own arrival in England as a young woman with very little, trying to build a new life in an unfamiliar place. I could see how she carried her grief—in small habits like vaping, in her fierce independence, in the pendant she wore close to her heart. Her story reminded me how fortunate I was to have had my parents for as long as I did, and how some people must learn to navigate life's challenges without ever having that foundation of parental love and support.

Grief changes you, absolutely. But so does love. And somehow, mysteriously, both can live side by side within the same heart. The capacity to feel profound loss is inseparable from the capacity to love deeply. Rather than seeing grief as something to overcome or cure, we might instead view it as evidence of our ability to form meaningful connections that transcend physical presence.

The waves will keep coming, probably for the rest of your life, but they don't have to overwhelm you. With time and support, you learn to recognise them, to ride them out, and to appreciate the love they represent. You learn that carrying grief doesn't prevent you from also carrying joy, hope, and new connections. They can all coexist in the complex, resilient human heart.

Losing Both Parents

This is perhaps the most personal piece I've ever written—about losing both of my parents—and if you're reading this, you might have experienced something similar. The journey of becoming an orphan, regardless of your age, is one that transforms you in ways you never anticipated.

Before I begin sharing this deeply personal experience, I want to express my gratitude to everyone who has taken the time to read my writings over the past months. I started writing after my father passed away, when the grief felt too large to contain within myself. Around that time, I reconnected with a friend who encouraged me to consider writing a book—a project I started and will continue—but somehow these individual reflections came first, flowing out of me like water finding its own path.

Writing became my primary method of healing, a way to transform overwhelming pain into something that might serve a purpose beyond my own processing. I thought that perhaps, if I could articulate these experiences honestly, my words might bring comfort or recognition to others walking similar paths.

I set an ambitious goal to write one hundred pieces before the anniversary of my father's death. This particular reflection represents number ninety-seven—just three more to complete this part of my healing journey. This process has been incredibly therapeutic for me, more powerful than I could have imagined when I began. I hope that in some way, these honest accounts of loss and resilience have brought connection or comfort to others who needed to know they weren't alone.

I lost my mum three years ago, an experience that remains one of the most challenging periods of my life. If you've ever lost someone you love deeply, you understand the emotional volatility that follows—how you can feel relatively stable one moment, and then a song, a scent, or even seeing someone who reminds you of them can trigger an overwhelming wave of grief that feels as fresh as the day they died.

For me, seeing someone sitting in a chair that resembles my mum's, or watching someone tenderly pushing their elderly parent in a wheelchair, can instantly transport me back to that raw place of missing her. I especially think of her during these moments of witnessing other people still having what I've lost—the ordinary, precious gift of a living parent.

She was truly an extraordinary woman—kind, gentle, and selfless in ways that shaped not only my understanding of love but also my approach to caring for others. She never spoke negatively about other people, always choosing to see the best in everyone she encountered. Her instinct was always to help, to give, to make others feel valued and cared for. She possessed a natural warmth that lingered with everyone who met her, leaving them feeling a little more hopeful about human nature.

What makes loss even more devastating is when you don't get the opportunity to say goodbye properly. During the COVID pandemic, countless people experienced this tragedy—losing loved ones without being able to kiss them, hold their hands, or share final words. That absence of closure leaves a particularly deep wound, a sense of unfinished business that can complicate the grieving process for years.

I wasn't able to see my mum while she was still alive, but I did see her in her coffin during the funeral. That moment completely shattered something inside me that I'm not sure has ever fully healed. I never imagined in my wildest nightmares that I would go through something like that—seeing the person who gave me life lying still and silent, beyond the reach of all the love I still had to give her.

When my father passed away last year, the experience was different but equally heartbreaking. I was able to say goodbye to him, which felt like both a gift and a torment. It happened on my birthday, a timing that felt cruelly ironic—celebrating life and mourning death on the same day. I still remember him asking for ice cream that final day, such an ordinary request that somehow made everything feel both normal and utterly surreal.

All my sisters were present during his final hours, which created a sense of completion that I hadn't experienced with my mother's death. His passing felt more peaceful in some ways, yet it was still devastating. I never expected to lose him so soon after losing my mum, as if life was systematically dismantling the foundation of my world.

If you've lost both parents, you may understand the strange, disorienting emptiness that follows. There's a particular kind of existential displacement that occurs—you feel like you've become an orphan regardless of your age, as if some essential part of your identity has been erased. Something fundamental feels missing, not just in your daily life but in your very sense of place in the world.

The people who gave you life, who shaped your earliest understanding of love and security, who knew you before you knew yourself—they're suddenly gone, and you're left holding all the memories, all the lessons, all the love, completely alone. It's a kind of responsibility that feels overwhelming, as if you're now the sole keeper of their legacy and your shared history.

As children, we never think this day will come. Even as adults, we avoid imagining it because the thought is too painful to hold. We live as if our parents will always be there, available for advice, comfort, or simply the reassurance of their continued existence. Even when loss does happen, part of you refuses to accept it as real, waiting for them to call or walk through the door as they always have.

But eventually, reality settles in with unforgiving clarity. And somehow, despite feeling broken and unmoored, we continue living—hoping, perhaps, that someday we might see them again. Whether you believe in an afterlife or simply hope that love transcends physical death, we carry that hope because the alternative feels unbearable.

This journey through loss has been extraordinarily difficult, but it has also taught me things about resilience, love, and the human capacity for healing that I never could have learned any other way. Writing through this process has been a lifeline, more transformative than any other healing method I've tried.

I want to encourage anyone reading this who has experienced similar losses to find their own path through grief. Whether through writing, talking to trusted friends, seeking professional counselling, joining support groups, or finding solace in spiritual practices—whatever feels authentic to your experience and needs.

The most important thing I can tell you is that you don't have to navigate this alone. Grief can feel incredibly isolating, but connection with others who understand can provide comfort and perspective that makes the unbearable slightly more manageable.

Whatever path you choose for healing, know that there is no timeline, no "right" way to grieve, and no expectation that you should "get over" losing the people who made you who you are. You're not trying to return to who you were before—that person existed in a world where your parents were still alive. You're learning to become someone who can carry their love and lessons forward while also embracing whatever life still has to offer.

Reflections After Christmas

Now that Christmas has passed, I hope you all had meaningful time with loved ones and found moments of joy despite whatever challenges this season may have brought. While holidays can bring happiness, they also invite deep reflection about the year that's gone by and, for many of us, acute awareness of who is missing from our celebrations. Though my thoughts are drawn from deeply personal experiences, I know they may resonate with others who have navigated holidays while grieving.

In England, we open presents on December 25th, but in Spain, the festive season stretches longer, with celebrations continuing until January 6th or 8th when gifts are traditionally exchanged. This extended celebration means holiday shopping, cooking, and social obligations linger for weeks. As I've grown older, I've become more aware—and perhaps somewhat cynical—about the sheer amount of work that Christmas requires.

Don't misunderstand me; I genuinely love Christmas and the warmth it can bring to relationships. But organising a meaningful celebration often feels like planning a wedding—except it happens every single year. While weddings might be once-in-a-lifetime events (or perhaps a few times, and I offer no judgment about that), the holiday season demands similar emotional and logistical energy annually, year after year.

When Christmas arrives now, I'm flooded with bittersweet memories of my mother and the sacrifices she made to create magic for us despite very limited resources. My mother always tried to give us presents, but her circumstances often didn't allow for much. I have vivid memories of her walking to the small shop at the end of our road to buy items on monthly payment plans, spreading the cost over several months just to afford small gifts for her children.

What stands out most clearly, though, are the things she made with her own hands—knitting jumpers and sewing clothes for us with such care and attention to detail. I remember one Christmas receiving a doll that came without any clothes, and my mother spent hours creating an entire wardrobe for it. These handmade gifts represented hours of love and effort that no store-bought item could match.

I never had a bicycle growing up, something that felt significant to a child who watched friends riding around the neighbourhood. I didn't actually learn to ride a bike until I was twenty-seven years old, living in England. These memories carry a tinge of sadness, but they also remind me of how much my mother gave us despite her struggles, how she made something from almost nothing through sheer determination and love.

I often wondered as a child why I couldn't have the kind of elaborate presents my best friend received—the expensive toys, the multiple gifts, the abundance that seemed so effortless in other families. It's a feeling many children from modest backgrounds might recognize, and I share this to acknowledge all the parents out there doing their absolute best with limited resources, just as my mum did for us.

Her love and effort, even when money was scarce, are something I appreciate more deeply now as an adult who understands the weight of financial responsibility and the lengths parents go to provide for their children. She gave us what mattered most—the sense that we were cherished and that Christmas was about love, not material accumulation.

Today, many of us overcompensate for what we lacked in childhood by giving our children far too much. I'm completely guilty of this tendency myself. I recognise now that this overcompensation creates unrealistic expectations that become harder to meet year after year. It can lead to serious financial strain, leaving families struggling to meet basic needs in January while still paying for December's excess.

I've heard heartbreaking stories of people having to sell household items just to afford groceries after the holidays, of parents going into debt to avoid disappointing their children, of family members feeling obligated to give gifts they genuinely cannot afford. The pressure to create perfect holidays can become overwhelming and ultimately counterproductive.

If you've experienced similar feelings, you may have noticed how some parents genuinely dread Christmas—not because they don't love their families or want to celebrate, but because of the enormous expense and the relentless pressure to please everyone. Some people give gifts they absolutely cannot afford simply to avoid the disappointment or judgment of others, creating financial stress that extends well beyond the holiday season.

While gifts can be lovely gestures that show thoughtfulness and care, it's often the intention behind them that matters more than their monetary value. I recently had this conversation with my son when he was choosing a gift for a family member. I reminded him that while we all appreciate nice things—especially those of us who grew up with less—the most meaningful gifts truly do come from the heart and show that you know and care about the recipient.

It doesn't matter if a gift costs one pound or one hundred pounds, as long as it demonstrates genuine thought and consideration for the person receiving it. Some of the most treasured gifts I've received have been handwritten letters, photographs, or small items that showed someone was thinking specifically of me.

Every year, as living costs continue rising while wages struggle to keep pace, families find themselves in financial difficulty that leads to stress, arguments, and sometimes lasting conflicts. I've heard stories of families actually falling out over unwanted gifts, inappropriate gifts, or the pressure to reciprocate expensive presents they couldn't afford to give in the first place.

This holiday season and going forward, I encourage everyone to give only what you can truly afford without creating hardship for yourself or your family. If someone genuinely values your relationship, they will understand your financial limitations and appreciate whatever gesture you can manage. The people who truly matter in your life will support you and value your honesty about what's possible for you.

Sometimes it takes losing someone precious to realise how little their gifts mattered compared to their presence, their love, and their availability for conversation and support. The most expensive present becomes meaningless when the person who gave it is no longer there to share experiences with you.

To those who feel ashamed about their financial limitations or pressured to spend beyond their means, I urge you to communicate openly with your loved ones about your situation. True friends and family will support your honesty and help you find ways to celebrate that don't involve financial stress. Sometimes having these conversations reveals that others are feeling the same pressure and relief comes from acknowledging it together.

Let's remember that the most valuable gifts we can offer are the moments we share, the kindness we show throughout the year, the attention we give when someone needs support, and the love we express not just during holidays but in the ordinary days when it's most needed and least expected.

Chapter 14: Mental Health and Healing

Mental health challenges touch every aspect of human experience, from our earliest attachments to our adult relationships, from our capacity for compassion to our ability to recognise when we're in danger. This chapter explores the complex landscape of psychological wellness through both professional insights and deeply personal encounters. We examine how childhood experiences shape our adult patterns, how understanding attachment theory can illuminate our relationship struggles, and how mental health challenges manifest in everything from celebrity culture to homelessness to domestic violence. Most importantly, we explore pathways to healing and the crucial importance of seeking support when life becomes overwhelming.

Mental Health Support

This week, I want to dedicate these thoughts to a beautiful friend of mine who has shown immense strength in the face of adversity. Even when things haven't gone her way, she continues to fight and provide love to others despite her own struggles. I also want to extend this dedication to everyone battling mental health challenges, as well as those who watch their loved ones suffer.

It is incredibly painful to witness someone you care about fighting internal battles, crying from exhaustion, feeling mentally overwhelmed, especially when you don't know what to do or where to turn for help. The helplessness you feel as a supporter can be overwhelming. You find yourself in a very lonely place when all you want is for your loved one to find peace and happiness, but you feel powerless to provide it.

We bring our children into this world hoping to give them good lives filled with love, opportunity, and security. However, many of us struggle to provide that foundation due to our own past experiences, lack of support systems, or simply not knowing where to seek help when problems arise. Sometimes, we aren't even ready to confront our own unresolved issues, which makes it even harder to assist others effectively.

These situations can feel isolating and overwhelming for everyone involved. Have you ever found yourself in this position? What has your experience been like supporting someone with mental health struggles? The weight of responsibility can feel crushing, especially when traditional support systems seem inadequate or inaccessible.

In my professional work supporting people with mental health challenges, I've encountered incredible difficulties, largely due to insufficient funding and resources within the system. I'm not here to place blame on individuals or even criticise the system as a whole, though the gaps in care are undeniably frustrating. To truly understand the depth of this crisis, you must witness firsthand what's happening in communities everywhere—why some people manage to recover and thrive while others continue struggling despite their best efforts and the support around them.

Mental health issues continue rising due to multiple interconnected factors: financial insecurity that creates chronic stress, job instability that undermines our sense of security, housing concerns, relationship breakdowns, social isolation, and the everyday challenges that life throws at us relentlessly. The human brain, despite being remarkably resilient, has limits to what it can process and manage effectively.

If we don't prioritize taking care of ourselves first, it becomes increasingly difficult to support others meaningfully. This isn't selfish—it's practical and necessary. Just as flight attendants instruct you to put on your own oxygen mask before helping others, the same principle applies to mental health support. You cannot pour from an empty cup, and attempting to do so often leads to burnout, resentment, and deteriorating mental health for everyone involved.

The statistics surrounding mental health are sobering and likely understated. Approximately 9.5 million adults aged eighteen or older seriously considered suicide in the past year, representing about 4.0% of the adult population. Around 2.7 million adults made specific suicide plans, accounting for 1.1% of the population. These numbers, gathered from various research sources, have likely increased significantly due to global events including the COVID-19 pandemic, economic instability, political upheaval, and ongoing conflicts worldwide.

The media plays a significant role in shaping our perceptions of reality, and often, we're not presented with complete, balanced information. News cycles focus on crisis and conflict, social media creates unrealistic comparisons, and the constant barrage of information can feel overwhelming. Even when we become fully aware of these issues and their scope, we sometimes feel limited in what changes we can actually make as individuals.

This is precisely why I emphasize the critical importance of self-care and learning how to support your loved ones without sacrificing your own wellbeing. While I wish I possessed some magical solution to fix the world's problems, I don't. Instead, I use my training, experience, and words to raise awareness and provide support where I can, hoping that small actions can contribute to larger positive changes.

As a therapist working with individuals struggling with various mental health challenges, I genuinely wish more funding and resources were available for comprehensive treatment and support. The reality is that mental health services are often overwhelmed, understaffed, and underfunded, creating waiting lists and limited options precisely when people need help most urgently.

If you have a loved one dealing with suicidal thoughts or serious mental illness and they seem unable or unwilling to help themselves, please understand that this is not your fault or failure. Many people don't know what to do in these situations because they're also struggling with their own challenges, fears, and limitations.

The first step is seeking support for yourself. Only when you have adequate support and coping strategies can you effectively help your family member or friend. However, be cautious of falling into what psychologists call the "Drama Triangle," which consists of three shifting roles: the rescuer, the perpetrator, and the victim. These roles can shift depending on the situation and circumstances, and becoming too enmeshed in this dynamic can negatively impact your own mental health.

No matter how desperately you want to help someone, you must also establish and maintain clear boundaries for your own protection and effectiveness. Communicate openly with your loved ones about your own struggles and limitations. Let them know when you're feeling overwhelmed, when you need support, and when you need space to recharge.

One resource I consistently recommend is "I'm OK, You're OK" by Thomas A. Harris. This book, translated into multiple languages and a New York Times bestseller since 1972, explores how individuals perceive themselves and others through the lens of transactional analysis. It offers valuable insights into human behavior and interpersonal dynamics, which can be incredibly helpful when navigating complex mental health challenges within relationships.

When someone becomes determined to end their life, preventing that outcome can be extremely difficult, and this is a painful truth that families and friends must sometimes accept. The best we can do is offer consistent support, encourage open communication without judgment, and guide them toward professional help while respecting their autonomy as adults.

However, if your loved one isn't ready to talk or accept help, remember that you can only do your best with the resources and knowledge available to you. It's crucial not to carry guilt or blame yourself if you feel unable to change their mindset or circumstances. Mental illness is complex, and recovery often requires professional intervention combined with personal readiness for change.

A practical tool I suggest for family members is keeping a detailed journal documenting changes in behaviour, mood, sleep patterns, eating habits, and concerning statements or actions. This documentation can provide valuable evidence when seeking professional support and help healthcare providers understand patterns and severity of symptoms.

Most importantly, don't neglect your own well-being during these challenging times. Supporting someone with mental illness can be emotionally draining, confusing, and frightening. You need and deserve support too.

Life presents challenges for everyone, and even as a trained therapist, I continue working on my own mental health and personal growth so I can better support my family and patients. We all juggle multiple demands: relationships, work responsibilities, friendships, self-esteem issues, and the unrealistic standards often promoted through social media that make others' lives appear perfect while ours feel inadequate.

The truth is that everyone faces struggles, but many people choose to hide their difficulties behind carefully constructed public personas. Social media particularly contributes to this illusion of perfection, creating additional pressure and unrealistic comparisons that can worsen mental health challenges.

If you have a loved one who is struggling, please don't give up on them, but also remember to take care of yourself. Progress happens one step at a time, often slowly and with setbacks. If one approach doesn't work, try another. Keep moving forward with patience and compassion for both them and yourself, remembering that recovery is possible even when it feels impossible.

Understanding Attachment Theory

Each year, as we mark another trip around the sun, many people arrive at my office with fresh ideas about what they want to leave behind and the changes they hope to make in their lives. The calendar changes, but meaningful transformation requires much more than a new date—it demands honest self-reflection and the willingness to examine patterns that may have been shaping our relationships for decades.

While gaining another year of life experiences can provide wisdom, true change comes from within, not from external circumstances or the passage of time alone. If you had just five minutes right now to reflect honestly, what would you most like to change about your life or about yourself? Remember this fundamental truth: we cannot change other people, and others will only change when they're genuinely ready and motivated to do so.

One of the most significant areas I explore with patients involves attachment and how their earliest relationships continue to influence their adult connections. Many people find it incredibly challenging to let go of their past experiences. They carry emotional baggage like a heavy backpack, and this weight prevents them from moving forward to embrace new experiences, career opportunities, healthier relationships, or different environments.

For example, ending a relationship with a partner who doesn't make you happy or treat you well can feel nearly impossible, even when you intellectually know it's the healthiest decision. The familiar feels safer than the unknown, even when the familiar is harmful or unfulfilling. I can certainly relate to this struggle—letting go is never easy, regardless of how clearly we can see what needs to change.

I often remind patients that we cannot alter what has already happened in our past. What's done is done, much like this chapter once you've read it—I cannot go back and rewrite these words. The only path available is forward: to reflect on our experiences, learn from them, and use that understanding to make different choices moving forward.

Attachment theory, first developed by British psychologist John Bowlby in the 1960s, provides a powerful framework for understanding how our earliest relationships shape our capacity for connection throughout life. Attachment refers to the emotional bond we form with primary caregivers, typically parents or guardians, during our first years of life.

Bowlby believed that these earliest bonds have a profound impact that extends throughout our entire lifespan, influencing how we approach relationships, handle separation and loss, manage emotions, and view ourselves in relation to others. He suggested that attachment behaviours serve an evolutionary purpose—keeping infants close to caregivers who provide protection, nourishment, and safety, thereby improving the child's chances of survival.

While earlier behavioural theories suggested that attachment was simply a learned response, Bowlby proposed that children are born with an innate biological drive to form these crucial bonds. Throughout human history, children who maintained close relationships with protective attachment figures were more likely to survive to adulthood and reproduce, passing on these attachment-seeking tendencies through natural selection.

There are four primary patterns of attachment that develop based on how consistently and sensitively caregivers respond to a child's needs:

Secure attachment, the healthiest and most common pattern, develops when caregivers are reliably responsive, emotionally available, and attuned to their child's needs. Children with secure attachment can depend on their caregivers for comfort and support. They show distress when separated but express joy and relief upon reunion. Although they may feel upset during separations, they fundamentally trust that their caregiver will return. These children feel comfortable seeking reassurance when frightened or distressed and generally develop a positive sense of self-worth and trust in relationships.

Avoidant attachment typically develops when caregivers are emotionally unavailable, rejecting, or punitive when children seek comfort or assistance. Children with this attachment style learn to suppress their attachment needs and often appear independent or indifferent to their caregiver's presence or absence. They show little preference between their caregiver and strangers and tend to avoid seeking help even when distressed. This pattern may result from repeated experiences of having their emotional needs dismissed or punished.

Anxious or ambivalent attachment occurs when caregiving is inconsistent—sometimes responsive and nurturing, other times unavailable or insensitive. These children become highly distressed when separated from caregivers and may be difficult to comfort upon reunion. They often cling to caregivers while simultaneously showing anger or resistance. This inconsistency leaves them uncertain about whether their needs will be met, creating ongoing anxiety about relationship security.

Disorganised attachment represents the most troubled pattern, often arising from frightening or traumatic caregiving experiences. Children with this attachment style exhibit confusing mixtures of behaviors—they may simultaneously approach and avoid their caregiver, appear disoriented or conflicted, or show concerning behaviors like freezing or repetitive movements. This pattern typically develops when the caregiver serves as both a source of comfort and fear, creating an impossible psychological dilemma for the child.

Your childhood attachment style significantly influences your adult relationships in ways you might not even recognise. Those with secure attachment generally find it easier to form healthy, stable relationships characterised by trust, emotional intimacy, and effective communication. They're typically more comfortable with interdependence—neither overly clingy nor excessively independent.

Adults with avoidant attachment often struggle with emotional intimacy and vulnerability in close relationships. They may prefer independence over connection, find it difficult to rely on others or allow others to depend on them, and tend to suppress or dismiss emotional needs—both their own and their partner's. They might withdraw during conflicts rather than working through problems together.

Those with anxious attachment frequently worry about their relationships and may require frequent reassurance from partners. They might become preoccupied with their relationship status, fear abandonment even when no real threat exists, and sometimes engage in behaviours that actually push partners away while desperately trying to maintain closeness.

Adults with disorganized attachment often experience the most relationship difficulties. They may simultaneously crave intimacy while fearing it, struggle with trust issues, and find themselves repeating chaotic relationship patterns. They might experience intense emotional reactions that seem disproportionate to situations and may have difficulty regulating emotions effectively.

Understanding your attachment style and its origins can be a vital step toward personal growth and healthier relationships. During my studies in England, I learned extensively about attachment theory and have since used these concepts to help patients identify the root causes of their relationship struggles. Together, we work to uncover what holds them back from letting go of pain and making the positive changes they desire.

For some people, unresolved attachment issues contribute significantly to challenges in forming and maintaining successful relationships. Recognizing these patterns doesn't excuse harmful behavior, but it provides a framework for understanding why certain situations feel so triggering or why particular relationship dynamics keep repeating.

The encouraging news is that attachment styles aren't permanently fixed. Through awareness, intentional effort, therapy, and healthy relationship experiences, people can develop more secure attachment patterns. This process, often called "earned security," demonstrates the remarkable capacity for human growth and healing.

Letting go of old patterns is often a difficult journey requiring patience, self-compassion, and usually professional support. But it's also a necessary journey for anyone seeking growth and healthier connections. Take time to reflect on your own relationship patterns: What would you like to change? What keeps you stuck in familiar but unhealthy dynamics?

Remember, meaningful change starts with honest self-awareness and a willingness to let go of what no longer serves your wellbeing or growth. If you need support with this process, don't hesitate to seek professional help. As I often tell my patients: "If you're not happy where you are, move—you're not a tree." You have more power to change your circumstances than you might realize.

Attachment, Fame, and the Price of Success

Over the weekend, I attended a Michael Jackson tribute show in London that left me with deeply mixed emotions. The performance itself was fantastic—a brilliant celebration of his incredible musical legacy and unparalleled talent. However, witnessing the portrayal of his life story was profoundly sad, highlighting how his extraordinary gifts were overshadowed by the struggles he faced due to problematic early attachments, the pressures of fame, and what appeared to be exploitation by those who should have protected him.

The show made me reflect on how many people, particularly celebrities, experience similar challenges with their mental health and personal relationships. The entertainment industry can be particularly brutal—the media has the power to elevate someone to incredible heights or completely destroy their reputation and well-being. Unfortunately, many people make substantial profits from tearing others down, creating a toxic environment where human beings become commodities rather than people deserving of compassion and respect.

One aspect that stood out most clearly was the role of early attachments, especially the complex dynamics between parents and children in high-achieving families. Sometimes, parents project their own unfulfilled dreams onto their children, pushing them to achieve what the parents themselves could not accomplish. This pressure can cause significant mental, physical, and even financial harm to young people who are still developing their sense of self and learning to navigate the world.

During the show, I noticed a woman crying during the final scenes, and I wondered whether she had experienced something similar in her own life—perhaps growing up with parents who prioritised achievement over wellbeing, or watching someone she cared about struggle under impossible expectations.

When early attachment relationships are characterised by conditional love—where affection and approval depend on performance or achievement rather than simply existing as a valuable human being—it can profoundly impact someone's ability to form healthy adult relationships. Children learn that their worth depends on what they can do or produce rather than who they are as people.

Many talented individuals have tragically lost their lives due to substance abuse or prescription drug dependencies because they couldn't cope with the immense pressure placed upon them by families, managers, record labels, and society. When people are forced to constantly please others and maintain an image dictated by external forces, they gradually lose connection with their authentic selves and their own needs.

I once overheard a parent discussing how their child was training for hours every day, sacrificing normal childhood experiences and social development, all in pursuit of success that might never materialise. Stories like these are unfortunately common—situations where a child's natural development and emotional needs are sacrificed for adult ambitions, often with financial motives playing a significant role in these decisions.

These dynamics aren't limited to entertainment industry families. Similar patterns occur in competitive sports, academic achievement, or any area where parents become overly invested in their children's performance. The child's value becomes tied to their achievements rather than their inherent worth as a human being.

By the end of the show, I felt simultaneously happy because of Michael Jackson's incredible musical contributions and deeply sad after gaining insight into what appeared to be a troubled and exploitative family system. The contrast between his public persona and private struggles highlighted how little outsiders truly know about what happens behind closed doors, even for people whose lives seem to be lived in the spotlight.

If you've struggled with difficult early attachments or felt pressure to meet others' expectations at the expense of your own well-being, seeking professional help can be incredibly beneficial. Sometimes, we unconsciously carry patterns from our childhood into our adult relationships, believing that conditional love or achievement-based worth is normal because it's what we experienced growing up.

These patterns might manifest as perfectionism, people-pleasing behaviours, difficulty setting boundaries, fear of disappointing others, or feeling like your value depends on what you can produce rather than who you are. You might find yourself repeatedly choosing relationships or situations that recreate familiar dynamics, even when they're harmful.

Having insecure attachment can significantly impact relationships, emotional well-being, and overall mental health throughout life. These attachment styles, developed in childhood based on caregiver interactions, often continue influencing how we approach romantic relationships, friendships, and even professional dynamics well into adulthood.

People with anxious attachment often experience fear of abandonment and need constant reassurance from partners. They might find themselves overanalysing relationships, feeling insecure even when things are going well, struggling with clinginess or difficulty being alone, and having strong emotional reactions to perceived rejection or criticism.

Those with avoidant attachment typically struggle with emotional intimacy and vulnerability in close relationships. They often prefer independence over connection, avoid deep emotional bonds even in long-term partnerships, and may shut down or withdraw during conflicts rather than working through problems together.

Individuals with disorganised attachment, often resulting from traumatic early experiences, may display a mixture of anxious and avoidant behaviours. They simultaneously want closeness but fear it, have difficulty trusting others, sometimes push people away to protect themselves, and often carry fear of being hurt or betrayed based on past experiences.

These insecure attachment patterns can affect multiple areas of life. In romantic relationships, people might struggle with trust, emotional closeness, or finding the right balance between dependence and independence. Friendships might be characterised by either excessive dependence or emotional distance. In workplace and social situations, individuals might avoid teamwork, struggle with criticism, or have difficulties with authority figures.

The mental health impacts can be significant, including higher risk of anxiety, depression, and emotional dysregulation. People with insecure attachment might experience more intense emotional reactions to everyday situations or have difficulty managing stress effectively.

However, healing is absolutely possible. Therapy, particularly approaches that focus on attachment and relationship patterns, can help process childhood experiences and develop healthier relationship skills. Mindfulness and self-awareness practices can help people recognise attachment triggers and respond differently in challenging situations.

Building relationships with emotionally secure people can provide healing experiences that gradually reshape expectations about how relationships can function. These healthier connections can serve as models for trust, communication, and emotional safety.

Self-compassion and inner work focused on healing fears of abandonment or intimacy can gradually build confidence and security. This process takes time and patience, but positive changes are definitely achievable.

If this discussion resonates with your experiences, consider exploring these issues in therapy where you can safely examine your relationship patterns and understand the underlying reasons why maintaining healthy connections feels challenging. Whether in romantic partnerships, family relationships, friendships, or your relationship with yourself, professional support can help you develop the tools needed for healthier, more satisfying connections.

Remember, you cannot change your past experiences, but you can absolutely work on your present responses and future choices. With time, effort, and appropriate support, you can develop more secure patterns of relating that will serve you throughout your life.

A Moment of Human Connection

I just returned from a wonderful trip to Spain, where I spent time with a dear friend and had the opportunity to meet some new people. It was fantastic to connect with others without constantly thinking about work—to simply be myself and have fun without the weight of professional responsibilities.

During my journey home, I had an encounter at the airport that has stayed with me and continues to influence my thinking about homelessness, mental health, and human compassion. I was trying to charge my phone at the terminal when I noticed a young woman with what appeared to be a male friend or partner. They had two shopping trolleys filled with their belongings, and she was writing intently in a notebook.

As I always do in public spaces, I remained aware of my surroundings while respecting others' privacy. However, something about this young woman drew my attention—perhaps her focused concentration on writing or the careful way she guarded her few possessions. Eventually, I found myself starting a conversation with her, which I know might seem unusual to some people, but I was genuinely curious about her situation and what she was documenting in her notebook.

What unfolded was one of the most heartbreaking conversations I've had in a long time. She explained that she comes to the airport because it provides a safe place to stay, as she had been abandoned by her father and her mother was not available to help her. She was somehow managing to send money to support five children in Spain, though the logistics of this seemed impossibly difficult given her circumstances.

As I listened to more details of her experiences—many too painful and private to share here—I was astonished to see how this young person, despite her own overwhelming challenges, remained concerned about her friend and was actively trying to take care of him as well. Her capacity for compassion in the midst of such personal struggle was remarkable and humbling.

She had the most beautiful smile, though her eyes carried unmistakable sadness as she spoke. When I asked where she sleeps, she mentioned trying to find safe places to rest and receiving some limited support from human rights organisations or similar services. The precariousness of her situation was evident—no guaranteed shelter, no security, no family support system to fall back on.

The reason I'm sharing this story is that it made me acutely aware of how often we take our basic securities for granted. We don't fully appreciate our ability to pay for a simple coffee, to have a bed to sleep in each night, to receive love and support from family members, or to feel safe in our own homes until something happens that makes us realise how fortunate we are.

There are countless people we walk past every day, often avoiding eye contact or treating them as if they're invisible or somehow contagious, without knowing anything about their stories or circumstances. While some people might argue that individuals experiencing homelessness are responsible for their situations, what I learned from this young woman was that her struggles began with depression and trauma rooted in childhood experiences where no one listened to her or provided adequate support.

We often don't realise how difficult life becomes for people when they lack family support, financial resources, or access to mental health services. Many turn to alcohol or drugs to numb emotional pain or forget traumatic experiences they couldn't process or cope with in healthier ways. While substance use isn't an effective long-term solution, it's important to understand what drives people to make these choices rather than simply judging their current circumstances.

Whatever has happened to someone, regardless of how dishevelled they might appear or how low their circumstances might seem, it's crucial to remember that every person experiencing homelessness was once someone's baby. They were children with hopes and dreams who encountered circumstances, trauma, or mental health challenges they couldn't overcome without proper support systems.

Many people have survived sexual abuse, domestic violence, financial exploitation, and other forms of trauma. When they haven't had parents or family members available to provide support—sometimes because those family members needed help themselves—it becomes incredibly difficult to find stable ground and rebuild their lives.

Someone once told me not to give money directly to people experiencing homelessness, arguing that they might spend it on alcohol or drugs. However, another person pointed out that if someone does use substances, at least they stay warm through the night and might avoid some of the physical dangers of sleeping outdoors. I'm not advocating for substance use, but I am suggesting we try to understand the impossible choices people sometimes face when basic survival is uncertain.

As I was leaving this remarkable young woman, I could see how genuinely worried she was about her friend's well-being. Despite her own overwhelming challenges, I witnessed the deeply human side of her character—someone who would clearly like to do something positive with her life but felt lost in her depression while still managing to support someone else who needed help. This kind of compassion in the face of personal struggle is truly remarkable.

I gave her my name and contact information in case she ever needed support or wanted to explore resources that might be available. She smiled and said she would try to contact me, though she didn't have access to a phone or reliable internet. The barriers to accessing help, even when help is offered, are enormous for people in her situation.

This encounter reminded me how much we take for granted—simply waking up each day in our own bed, having food available when we're hungry, feeling safe in our homes, having people who care about our well-being. These basics that many of us consider normal are actually precious gifts that not everyone enjoys.

We spend so much time worrying about relatively minor inconveniences or comparing our lives to others on social media, while there are people struggling with fundamental survival needs right in our communities. This perspective doesn't minimise anyone else's problems, but it does help put challenges in context and remind us to appreciate what we have.

I want to dedicate this reflection to that young woman, in case she ever finds a way to read this. I did ask for her permission to write about our encounter, and she seemed pleased that someone cared enough about her story to want to share it. Her resilience, compassion for others despite her own struggles, and determination to keep going in the face of overwhelming circumstances deserve recognition and respect.

If you encounter someone experiencing homelessness, consider treating them as the human being they are rather than looking away or making assumptions about their character based on their current circumstances. A simple acknowledgment of their humanity, a kind word, or even just eye contact that says "I see you as a person" can have more impact than you might realize.

Domestic Violence: A Call to Awareness and Action

As we move through the year, I felt compelled to address one of the most serious and widespread issues affecting families and communities worldwide: domestic violence. If you are currently in an abusive situation, I urge you to seek professional help, find support systems, and make plans to leave safely. You deserve a life free from abuse, filled with respect, safety, and genuine love. While leaving can seem impossible and terrifying, there is support available, and there is hope for a different future.

Domestic violence often has its roots in early childhood experiences and attachment patterns. Growing up in a household lacking love, respect, and emotional safety can significantly influence how you view relationships in adulthood. Your early attachments—whether secure, avoidant, anxious, or disorganised—can profoundly shape your expectations about how people should treat each other and what constitutes normal behaviour in intimate relationships.

If your parents or caregivers did not treat you with kindness, respect, and consistent care, it might have established patterns where you unconsciously accept similar treatment from partners later in life. When children grow up with criticism, yelling, threats, physical violence, or emotional neglect, these experiences can normalise unhealthy relationship dynamics.

Think back to the first time someone shouted at you, called you names, or made you feel worthless. How did you react? If you were very young, you might have believed you deserved that treatment. Perhaps you thought, "My parents are supposed to love me, so if they're treating me this way, I must have done something wrong." Let me be absolutely clear: this is not love, and this kind of treatment is never normal or acceptable.

Over time, such experiences systematically erode your self-worth and make you more likely to believe others' negative opinions about you are valid and accurate. You might develop a voice inside your head that echoes those early messages, telling you that you're not good enough, that you're too sensitive, that you deserve poor treatment, or that no one else would want to be with you.

Now, try to contrast that with moments when someone has treated you with genuine respect, love, and care. Can you visualise what that feels like? For many people who grew up with dysfunction, receiving kindness feels uncomfortable because it's unfamiliar. Some of my patients have told me they actually feel uneasy when receiving compliments or genuine affection because it doesn't match their internal sense of what they deserve.

This response is heartbreaking but also a clear sign of how deeply early experiences shape our sense of self-worth. However, just like my patients, you can learn to accept kindness, recognise your inherent value, and understand that you deserve to be treated well simply because you exist as a human being.

Growing up in an environment lacking love and respect makes abusive behaviour seem normal and familiar. When you become an adult, you may unconsciously seek similar relationships because they feel comfortable in their familiarity, even though they're harmful. If you find yourself in such a situation, it becomes crucial to start paying close attention to how others talk to you, treat you, and behave around you.

Trust your instincts—we all have an internal alarm system that alerts us when something feels wrong or unsafe. This intuition is often your first line of defence, though people who grew up with dysfunction may have learned to ignore or doubt their instinctual responses.

Unfortunately, abusers often mask their control and manipulation as expressions of love and care. For example, they may isolate you from family and friends under the guise of wanting to spend more time together. They might monitor your activities, phone calls, or social media claiming they're being protective. They could dictate how you dress, whom you talk to, or where you go, framing these controls as caring about your safety or reputation.

You might find yourself thinking, "He or she must love me so much because they're so concerned about me and want to protect me." However, this is not love—it is control and manipulation designed to make you dependent and unable to seek help or leave. Genuine love involves trust, respect for your autonomy, and support for your individual growth and relationships.

If you recognise these patterns in your relationship, the safest approach is to begin planning your exit strategy carefully and seek professional guidance. Leaving an abusive relationship can be the most dangerous time for victims, so safety planning is crucial.

It's important to recognise that abuse takes many different forms, and physical violence is only one aspect of a broader pattern of control and intimidation. Physical abuse includes hitting, slapping, punching, choking, throwing objects, or any other form of physical harm or threat of physical harm

Emotional abuse involves insults, belittling, humiliation, intimidation, constant criticism, or threats designed to destroy your self-esteem and confidence. This type of abuse can be particularly insidious because it leaves no visible marks but can cause profound psychological damage.

Psychological abuse includes manipulation, gaslighting (making you question your own perceptions and reality), isolation from friends and family, threats to harm themselves or others if you leave, or creating an atmosphere of fear and walking on eggshells.

Sexual abuse involves forcing or coercing someone into sexual acts without consent, using sex as a weapon of control, or violating someone's sexual boundaries and autonomy.

Financial abuse means controlling access to money, preventing someone from working or pursuing education, stealing their money or benefits, or ruining their credit to create financial dependence.

Digital abuse has become increasingly common and involves using technology to stalk, harass, monitor, or control someone through their phone, computer, social media accounts, or other digital platforms.

There are numerous warning signs that indicate someone may be experiencing domestic violence. These include a partner who exhibits extreme jealousy or possessiveness, trying to control your activities, relationships, or appearance. You might find yourself feeling isolated from family, friends, or support systems because your partner has systematically undermined or eliminated these connections.

You may feel afraid of your partner or unsafe in their presence, walking on eggshells to avoid triggering their anger or violence. There might be frequent unexplained injuries or you find yourself making excuses for marks, bruises, or behavioural changes that others notice.

You might observe sudden changes in your own behaviour, confidence, or mood as you adapt to living in a climate of fear and control. Your personality may seem to have changed as you suppress parts of yourself to avoid conflict or violence.

If you recognise these patterns in your own life or someone else's, it's crucial to understand that help is available and leaving is possible with proper support and safety planning. However, it's also important to acknowledge that leaving can feel overwhelming and dangerous, which is why professional guidance and support are so important.

People experiencing domestic violence often face numerous barriers to leaving, including financial dependence, fear of retaliation, concern for children's safety, social isolation, cultural or religious pressures, immigration status concerns, or genuine fear that they won't be believed or supported.

These barriers are real and significant, but they're not insurmountable. There are organisations specifically designed to help people navigate these challenges safely. Remember, you are not responsible for fixing or changing your abuser. People only change if they genuinely want to and are willing to do extensive work on themselves, and many abusers never change despite promises or temporary improvements.

Your priority must be protecting yourself and reclaiming your life and safety. Statistics show that approximately 1 in 4 women and 1 in 9 men experience severe intimate partner physical violence, intimate partner contact sexual violence, or intimate partner stalking. Tragically, many lives are lost each year due to domestic violence, making it crucial to take threats and controlling behaviour seriously.

If you know someone who might be experiencing domestic violence, please offer support without judgment and help them connect with professional resources. However, exercise extreme caution to ensure the abuser doesn't become aware of your involvement, as this could escalate the danger for the victim.

Every year, countless young women and men lose their lives to domestic violence, leaving behind shattered families who often tried to help too late. Victims frequently believe their abuser's words, thinking they are loved despite the abuse, and that no one else cares for them or understands their situation.

This belief becomes deeply ingrained, particularly when it builds upon trauma experienced during childhood. The abuser systematically reinforces these messages through isolation, manipulation, and intermittent reinforcement—periods of kindness mixed with abuse that create powerful psychological bonds similar to trauma bonding or Stockholm syndrome.

Even those who had secure attachments in childhood may fall prey to abusive relationships, influenced by life stresses, vulnerability during major transitions, or simply encountering a skilled manipulator during a period of emotional openness. The abuser's lies become believable through repetition and the systematic dismantling of the victim's support network and self-confidence.

It's crucial to recognise the warning signs early and seek help immediately. Don't ignore red flags or delay taking action because you hope things will improve or because the person seems loving at other times. The cycle of abuse typically escalates over time, and what begins with emotional manipulation often progresses to physical violence and potentially life-threatening situations.

Domestic violence affects people of all genders, ages, socioeconomic backgrounds, and educational levels. No one deserves to endure abuse regardless of their circumstances, choices, or perceived contributions to relationship problems. If you or someone you know is experiencing abuse, taking action today could literally save a life.

The barriers to leaving are real and significant, but they can be overcome with proper support and safety planning. Professional organizations understand these challenges and have resources specifically designed to help people navigate them safely while protecting their children and rebuilding their lives.

You deserve to live in an environment filled with genuine love, respect, safety, and kindness. These aren't luxuries or unrealistic expectations—they're basic human rights that everyone deserves in their most intimate relationships.

For those currently in abusive situations, please know that the abuse is not your fault, leaving is possible with proper support, you deserve better treatment, and there are people trained specifically to help you navigate this process safely.

If you're supporting someone in an abusive relationship, remember that leaving is a process that often takes multiple attempts. Continue offering non-judgmental support, help them access professional resources, respect their autonomy and decision-making timeline, and prioritise safety over pressure to leave immediately.

Resources for immediate help include national domestic violence hotlines that provide 24-hour support, local shelters and safe houses, legal advocacy services, counselling and support groups, and safety planning assistance. Many of these services are available at no cost and can provide guidance even if someone isn't ready to leave immediately.

The most important message is this: domestic violence thrives in secrecy and isolation. Breaking the silence, seeking support, and creating safety plans can literally save lives and create pathways to freedom and healing.

Chapter 15: Social Commentary and Justice

Sometimes, the work of understanding ourselves and healing our relationships must extend beyond the personal to examine the broader social forces that shape our lives. This chapter addresses some of the systemic issues that affect our collective well-being—from economic inequality and housing injustice to discrimination and conflict. These are not abstract problems but lived realities that impact mental health, family stability, and our ability to create meaningful connections. Through personal observation and social analysis, we explore how individual healing intersects with the need for social justice and collective action.

Fighting for Home and Community

I hope you are all doing well and having a meaningful week. I am writing this to raise awareness and support for my family and many others in Gran Canaria who are facing an unjust and heartbreaking situation that goes far beyond individual circumstances to represent a broader pattern of displacement and inequality affecting communities worldwide.

If you have ever visited Gran Canaria, you know how breathtakingly beautiful this island is. The dramatic landscapes, pristine beaches, and year-round sunshine make it a paradise that draws millions of visitors annually. But beyond its stunning natural beauty, this island is home to countless families who have built their entire lives here—creating memories across generations, raising children who consider this place their only home, and working tirelessly to secure a future in the place they love.

Now, these very families are at risk of losing everything they have worked for, not due to natural disasters or economic hardship, but because of decisions made in boardrooms by people who will never experience the consequences of their choices.

Several years ago, the government of Gran Canaria announced that residents in certain areas of the south would have to leave their homes to make way for private development projects. These aren't vacant lots or abandoned properties—these are homes where families have spent years, even decades, working, investing their life savings, and building with their own hands, brick by brick, the places where their children took first steps and celebrated birthdays.

The families now face forced relocation under what can only be described as inhumane conditions. They are being offered inadequate compensation that wouldn't allow them to purchase comparable housing elsewhere on the island. No alternative housing is being provided that would keep families in their communities, near their schools, jobs, and support networks. Most devastating of all, there is no genuine support system to help them navigate this upheaval or rebuild their lives elsewhere.

This decision will have devastating ripple effects that extend far beyond the immediate housing crisis. Children will be uprooted from schools and friendships. Elderly community members will lose the neighbourhoods where they have lived their entire lives. Local businesses that depend on these residential communities will collapse. The social fabric that took generations to weave will be torn apart permanently.

Many families are fighting tirelessly to protect their homes, organising community meetings, seeking legal representation, and trying to navigate bureaucratic systems that seem designed to wear them down through sheer exhaustion. But the pressure from government and corporate interests is relentless and well-funded. Some families are even facing heavy financial penalties simply for refusing to abandon their homes, as if defending their right to shelter is somehow a criminal act.

It is deeply unjust that homes built with decades of hard work, sacrifice, and love are being taken away simply to increase corporate profits and facilitate luxury tourism development. These aren't investment properties owned by wealthy speculators—these are family homes where people have raised their children and planned to age in place.

The human cost of this displacement extends far beyond the financial losses. Forced relocation is recognized by mental health professionals as a significant trauma that can trigger depression, anxiety, and various stress-related health problems. Children who experience housing instability are more likely to struggle academically and socially. Elderly residents who lose their long-term community connections often experience rapid deterioration in both physical and mental health.

We cannot remain silent in the face of such injustice. This situation is not merely about property rights or zoning regulations—it is fundamentally about people, families, dignity, and the basic human right to secure housing within the communities where they have built their lives.

I urge anyone reading this, whether you live in Gran Canaria, elsewhere in Spain, or anywhere in the world where similar displacement occurs, to take this issue seriously and find ways to support these families. Housing displacement for private profit is a global phenomenon affecting communities from San Francisco to London to Cape Town, and the patterns are disturbingly similar everywhere.

Imagine if government officials arrived at your home tomorrow and ordered you to leave within months, offering compensation that wouldn't allow you to remain in your community, simply so a private company could develop your neighborhood for wealthy buyers. Imagine being fined and penalised for refusing to abandon the place where you have invested your life savings and raised your family.

Where is the justice in systems that prioritise corporate profits over human welfare? Who is truly listening to these families when they explain that their roots, their children's schools, their elderly parents' medical care, their employment, and their entire support networks are tied to these specific places?

This is not progress in any meaningful sense—it is a step backwards toward a feudal system where ordinary people have no security or rights when their presence conflicts with the profit motives of the wealthy and powerful. We cannot allow people's lives to be destroyed in the name of economic development that benefits only a small elite while devastating entire communities.

The fear and distress these families are experiencing daily is unimaginable for those who have never faced housing insecurity. They wake up each morning uncertain whether they will still have their homes next month, next year. They watch their children's anxiety increase as friends move away and familiar places disappear. They feel powerless against forces much larger and better funded than themselves.

This is happening in 2025, in a European Union nation with strong legal protections for human rights, yet these families are being forced to live in constant fear while facing severe financial penalties if they do not comply with orders that will destroy their communities.

If you are reading this and have ever visited Gran Canaria as a tourist, I ask you to look beyond the beautiful beaches and resort hotels to see the reality of what tourism development costs when it displaces existing communities. Ask yourself how this kind of systematic displacement can be legal under any constitution that claims to protect human dignity and property rights.

The constitution of Spain, like most democratic nations, guarantees the right to adequate housing and protection from arbitrary displacement. Yet here we see those protections being circumvented by legal and bureaucratic mechanisms that serve corporate interests rather than community welfare.

This injustice is being carried out with the cooperation of multiple levels of government and institutions that should be protecting residents rather than facilitating their displacement. It represents a fundamental failure of democratic governance and a betrayal of the social contract between government and citizens.

We need to come together across geographic and economic boundaries to stand against this pattern of displacement and demand better from our institutions. Enough is enough—we cannot continue to allow economic systems that treat housing as a commodity rather than a human right. It is time for coordinated action, legal challenges, international attention, and sustained pressure on the institutions enabling these injustices.

Please share this story widely and help spread awareness of the injustice these families are facing. No community should have to endure this kind of treatment simply because their homes occupy land that could generate more profit in different hands. We must stand together and demand systems that prioritise human welfare over corporate profits.

The Economics of Inequality

In previous discussions, I mentioned that I might explore the role money plays in shaping our world and how financial instability affects people's mental health, relationships, and overall quality of life. The economic pressures facing individuals and families today have reached a crisis point that demands honest examination.

The growing wealth inequality in our societies has created a situation where some people accumulate far more resources than they could ever use, while others struggle to meet basic needs like housing, healthcare, and nutrition. We are systematically destroying the middle class that once provided economic stability for the majority of people, creating a polarized system where you are either wealthy or struggling, with very little space between these extremes.

This economic polarisation affects every aspect of human wellbeing. People are losing their jobs daily due to automation, corporate restructuring, outsourcing, and economic instability that treats human workers as disposable resources. Many families now require multiple income sources just to maintain what previous generations could achieve with single incomes. The psychological stress of this constant economic insecurity contributes significantly to rising rates of anxiety, depression, and relationship breakdown.

The exploitation of workers to maximise profits has become so normalised that we barely notice it anymore. People work longer hours for wages that have not kept pace with the cost of living, while corporate profits and executive compensation reach unprecedented levels. This creates a cycle where people become increasingly desperate and willing to accept worse working conditions, fewer benefits, and less job security.

The history of money reveals how we have moved from systems based on tangible value to purely abstract financial instruments that can be manipulated by those with power and access. Understanding this evolution helps explain how wealth concentration has accelerated in recent decades.

Before money existed, people used barter systems, directly exchanging goods and services. A farmer might trade wheat for a blacksmith's tools, but this system had significant limitations since both parties needed to want what the other offered, making trade inefficient and limiting economic development.

To overcome these problems, societies developed commodity money using objects with intrinsic value like shells, salt, gold, silver, and livestock. These commodities were widely accepted and had practical uses beyond exchange, but they remained inconvenient to transport and divide for smaller transactions.

The development of metal coins around 600 BCE in Lydia marked a major advancement. Made of precious metals like gold, silver, and bronze, coins had standardised values that made trade much more efficient. Ancient civilisations, including the Greeks, Romans, and Chinese, adopted coin-based monetary systems that facilitated expanded trade and economic development.

China pioneered paper money during the Tang Dynasty in the 7th century CE, with widespread adoption during the Song Dynasty in the 11th century. This innovation spread to the Middle East and Europe through trade networks. European banks, particularly Italian families like the Medicis, began issuing banknotes in the 1600s that could be exchanged for gold and silver, creating the foundation for modern banking.

During the Renaissance, banking systems became more sophisticated, allowing people to deposit money and receive promissory notes that functioned like early checks. The establishment of central banks, such as the Bank of England in 1694, created institutions designed to regulate money supply and facilitate economic stability.

The 19th-century gold standard linked paper money to fixed amounts of gold, which helped stabilise economies but became difficult to maintain during economic crises like the Great Depression. This system ultimately proved too rigid for modern economic needs.

After World War II, countries gradually abandoned the gold standard entirely. In 1971, the United States fully abandoned gold backing for the dollar under President Nixon, creating our current fiat currency system where money's value is based on government authority and public trust rather than physical commodities.

Today, money exists largely in digital form through credit cards, online banking, and mobile payments that have replaced physical cash for most transactions. Cryptocurrencies like Bitcoin, created in 2009, introduced decentralized digital money that operates without traditional banking institutions, though these systems remain volatile and energy-intensive.

This evolution toward increasingly abstract forms of money has enabled unprecedented wealth concentration because those who control financial systems can manipulate currencies, interest rates, and access to credit in ways that benefit themselves while imposing costs on ordinary people.

Today, money controls much of our daily lives in ways that previous generations could not have imagined. We see people fighting, stealing, and engaging in various forms of exploitation just to survive economically. Financial stress is breaking apart families, destroying communities, and creating social instability, yet we continue to treat these problems as individual failures rather than systemic issues that require collective solutions.

Instead of accepting this destructive system, we must say "enough is enough" and demand economic arrangements that serve human welfare rather than concentrating wealth among a small elite. We spend enormous amounts on goods that cost far less to produce than their selling prices, while corporations extract maximum profits from our labour and consumption.

Many people work multiple jobs just to afford basic necessities while shareholders and executives accumulate wealth far beyond any reasonable need. This system exploits workers' desperation and creates artificial scarcity for essential goods like housing, healthcare, and education that could be provided sustainably for everyone.

In my therapeutic practice, I work with many people who rely on credit cards just to afford food, housing, and medical care. This debt-based survival creates chronic stress that contributes to the mental health crisis we see throughout society. Then we wonder why depression rates are climbing, leading to increased medication use that primarily benefits pharmaceutical companies rather than addressing the underlying causes of people's distress.

When will this destructive cycle end? How long will we accept systems that prioritize profit maximization over human wellbeing and environmental sustainability?

My recommendation is to resist following others blindly when it comes to financial decisions. Live within your means as much as possible and pay attention to what is happening in the broader economic system. Make conscious choices about how you spend your money rather than being manipulated by advertising and media that encourage overconsumption.

Don't be influenced by marketing campaigns designed to create artificial desires for products you don't actually need. Decide for yourself what is truly necessary for you and your family's wellbeing, and resist the pressure to participate in consumption patterns that primarily serve corporate interests.

Support local businesses when possible, choose companies that treat workers fairly, and advocate for economic policies that prioritise human welfare and environmental sustainability over short-term profit maximisation.

The current economic system is not natural or inevitable—it is a human creation that can be changed through collective action and different choices about how we organise our societies. We have the knowledge and resources to create economic systems that serve everyone rather than concentrating wealth among a small elite while leaving millions in poverty and insecurity.

Learning Respect and Understanding

One morning, I woke to devastating news from a dear friend of mine who, though she now lives in another country, had become one of my closest companions during her time in Bournemouth. Our friendship demonstrates something important about human connection—sometimes we don't need many friends, just one or two genuine relationships that can sustain us across distance and time. With her, every conversation feels as if no time has passed, and our bond has only deepened through shared experiences and mutual support.

I want to dedicate these thoughts to her and to her partner, who recently passed away from cancer, that cruel and heartbreaking illness that takes so many of our loved ones too soon. Their relationship was a beautiful example of commitment, care, and love that transcended the narrow definitions some people try to impose on what relationships should look like.

I also want to extend this dedication to all the people who are suffering simply because they are trying to live authentically as who they truly are. Our world often demands that we behave and think like everyone else, conforming to rigid expectations about gender, sexuality, relationships, and personal expression. Tragically, many people do not respect ways of living and loving that differ from their own experiences or beliefs.

I want to be clear—I am not suggesting that everyone must agree with or personally understand every lifestyle choice or identity. But I am advocating for basic human respect and dignity for all people, regardless of whether their lives match our own experiences or comfort zones.

It is heartbreaking that after everything we have supposedly learned from history—the systematic persecution faced by Jewish people during the Holocaust, the centuries of violence and discrimination against Black communities, the ongoing persecution of LGBTQ+ individuals, and countless other examples of hatred based on difference—we still live in a world where people are bullied, rejected, or even killed simply for being different from the majority.

I don't claim to be perfect or to have always understood these issues clearly. Although I work with patients who identify as bisexual, lesbian, gay, transgender, and other identities, I admit that I don't always understand every aspect of their experiences. My own upbringing included certain stereotypes and prejudices that were passed down through generations, and I have had to consciously examine and challenge many of these inherited beliefs.

But what I try to do, and what I believe we all should strive for, is to treat every person with basic respect and dignity, regardless of whether their lives match our own experiences or expectations. This doesn't mean we must agree with every choice or lifestyle, but it does mean recognising the fundamental humanity in every person.

Like many people of my generation and background, I was raised with certain assumptions and stereotypes about sexuality and gender expression. These ideas were reinforced through religious teaching, cultural norms, and family attitudes that portrayed anything outside traditional heterosexual relationships as abnormal or wrong.

When I first encountered friends and colleagues in England and Spain who were gay or transgender, I felt conflicted and uncertain. I found myself torn between what I had been taught throughout my childhood and what I was beginning to learn through direct personal contact with people whose experiences differed from my own.

This internal conflict wasn't easy to navigate. Having been raised Catholic, topics related to sexuality and gender identity were often considered taboo or sinful. However, over time, through genuine conversations with people I came to respect and care about, I began to ask questions and listen to their experiences with curiosity rather than judgment.

Through these conversations, I learned that loving someone of the same gender involves the same emotions, commitment, and depth of feeling as any other loving relationship. The gender of the people involved doesn't change the fundamental human experience of connection, attraction, care, and partnership.

I may not fully understand every aspect of gender identity or sexual orientation that differs from my own experience, but I have consistently tried to respect people for who they are rather than judging them based on categories or assumptions. This approach has enriched my life immeasurably and has made me a more effective therapist and a more compassionate person.

Through my professional work, I have encountered many people whose stories have taught me about the tremendous pain they endure simply trying to be seen, heard, and validated for who they are. They are not asking for everyone to agree with their choices or to change their own beliefs—they are asking for basic dignity, respect, and the right to exist without constant fear of discrimination or violence.

It is still shocking to me that in some countries today, people are suffering, hiding, or being punished by legal systems simply because they cannot openly express their authentic selves or form relationships with the people they love. Laws that criminalise consensual adult relationships or gender expression represent a fundamental violation of human rights and dignity.

I have worked with transgender clients and heard their painful stories firsthand. Their suffering often comes not primarily from their own internal struggles with identity, but from the harsh judgment, rejection, and sometimes violence they experience from family members, communities, and institutions that should provide support and protection.

Many of these individuals have been rejected by their own families and excluded from communities simply for being honest about who they are. This kind of rejection from the people who are supposed to love us unconditionally is devastating and can lead to depression, anxiety, and in far too many cases, suicide.

I know that not everyone will share the same beliefs or comfort levels regarding different expressions of sexuality and gender identity. That is why I focus on encouraging respect and basic human decency rather than demanding that everyone change their personal beliefs or religious convictions.

However, I do believe it is important for people to examine where their attitudes come from and whether those attitudes contribute to harm or healing in the world. No one knows how their own life might unfold or what situations they might find themselves facing.

I often ask clients and friends to consider: Do you truly know yourself completely? Do you know what you are capable of feeling or experiencing throughout your lifetime? Life is unpredictable, and any of us might find ourselves in situations we never imagined—perhaps developing feelings for someone we didn't expect, or discovering aspects of our identity that we had never previously recognized.

Given this uncertainty about our own futures, who are we to judge others for their authentic expressions of love and identity? When we approach differences with curiosity rather than condemnation, we often find that what seemed strange or threatening is simply another way of being human.

I hope these reflections encourage people to examine their own attitudes and responses when they encounter individuals whose lives differ from their own. If you see a same-sex couple holding hands or expressing affection, consider responding with the same courtesy you would show to any couple. If you meet someone whose gender expression doesn't match your expectations, try treating them with the same respect you would want for yourself or your loved ones.

Think about how many people are struggling silently with rejection, discrimination, and fear simply because of who they are or whom they love. We live in a world of incredible technological advancement, yet we continue to face heartbreaking realities like suicide, bullying, and emotional violence that often stem from social rejection and lack of family or community support.

As parents and community members, we have the power to create environments where young people feel loved, safe, and supported, regardless of how their identities or relationships develop. Let's work toward raising children in communities that show them they are valued for who they are rather than requiring them to pretend to be someone else to earn acceptance.

No one should have to attend a funeral because someone was bullied or rejected into ending their own life. I have worked with people who remain in marriages not out of love or happiness, but out of fear of being rejected by family or society if they live authentically. This kind of fear-based living causes tremendous suffering and prevents people from experiencing genuine connection and fulfilment.

Please consider the impact your words and attitudes have on others, especially young people who may be struggling with identity questions or fear of rejection. Stop using derogatory labels or participating in bullying behaviour that contributes to the climate of fear many LGBTQ+ individuals navigate daily.

Some people have been completely rejected by their families and communities simply for being honest about who they are. This kind of abandonment by the people who are supposed to love us unconditionally is devastating and can have lifelong psychological consequences.

Imagine living with the knowledge that someone you loved was emotionally tortured, physically harmed, or even killed simply for being authentic about their identity or relationships. Unfortunately, in some countries and communities, this violence continues to occur with alarming frequency.

I want to be completely honest about my own journey in understanding these issues. When I was a child, I was taught many harmful and inaccurate things about LGBTQ+ individuals—that they were somehow "dirty" or that their relationships were purely sexual rather than involving the same range of emotions and commitment as any other relationships.

Later in life, when I met friends in England and Spain who were gay or transgender, I felt genuinely conflicted. I found myself torn between what I had been taught and what I was beginning to learn through direct personal relationships with people I came to respect and care about.

This internal conflict was challenging to navigate, especially given my Catholic upbringing where these topics were considered taboo or sinful. However, through genuine conversations and questions asked with curiosity rather than judgment, I began to understand that loving someone of the same gender involves the same depth of emotion, commitment, and care as any other loving relationship.

I had some confusing experiences in childhood that made me wary, such as uncomfortable interactions with a neighbor whose behavior was inappropriate. However, I learned that individual experiences should not be used to judge entire groups of people, just as negative experiences with any individual should not lead to prejudice against all people who share some characteristic with that person.

Through my professional work, I have met many individuals whose stories have taught me empathy and shown me the tremendous pain they endure simply trying to be seen, heard, and validated for who they are. They are not asking for everyone to personally understand or agree with their experiences—they are asking for basic dignity, respect, and the right to exist without constant fear.

I continue learning and growing in my understanding every day. My goal is to value people for who they are as complete human beings rather than focusing primarily on any single aspect of their identity or personal life.

I hope you will join me in approaching differences with curiosity rather than judgment, and in creating communities where every person can feel valued and respected for their authentic selves.

The Cost of Conflict

I wanted to write this reflection in honour of the men and women who, throughout history, have chosen to serve in military conflicts—whether motivated by power, control, financial necessity, or genuine belief in protecting others and defending important principles. The decision to serve in armed forces represents one of the most complex moral and personal choices humans face, involving sacrifice, courage, and often profound moral ambiguity.

Since the beginning of recorded history, there have been countless battles and wars. Many of these conflicts have been fought not for personal gain, but in service of protecting others, defending communities, or standing up for principles that transcend individual self-interest. The kind of courage required to leave your family behind to serve people you may never meet, to risk your life for abstract concepts like freedom or justice, represents something profound about human capacity for sacrifice and moral commitment.

Consider what it means to wake up every morning in a war zone without knowing if you'll see your family again. Imagine sharing what might be final moments with your fellow soldiers, wondering if you'll have one more conversation, one more laugh together, one more chance to tell the people you love how much they mean to you. The psychological weight of living with constant uncertainty about survival creates bonds and traumas that civilians can barely comprehend.

Meanwhile, back home, spouses give birth to children while their partners are deployed in dangerous locations, cleaning up conflicts often created by political decisions made by people who will never face the consequences of their choices. These family separations create their own forms of trauma and sacrifice that extend far beyond the individuals in uniform.

When we're young, many of us follow paths that seem predetermined by our environment and circumstances. Some people become doctors, lawyers, teachers, or engineers, sometimes following family traditions or pursuing higher education opportunities. Others choose not to pursue advanced education but instead decide to serve their country through military service. It is remarkable how many people choose this path of service, though it's important to remember that throughout history, many didn't have the luxury of choice.

I recall the era of Francisco Franco in Spain, when I was very young but old enough to remember that once young men turned eighteen, military service was mandatory for several years. Some people emerged from military service with valuable skills and discipline that served them well in civilian life. However, many others had no desire to serve and felt trapped by this requirement—some even injured themselves deliberately to avoid conscription. It was a difficult period when individual choice was subordinated to state demands.

Of course, there were also many who proudly served their country during that era and others, finding meaning and purpose in military service. From the outside, military service often appears honourable and noble, representing important values like duty, sacrifice, and commitment to something larger than oneself.

However, I've also heard stories—some heartbreaking—of soldiers who endured cruelty, humiliation, and systematic dehumanisation from their superiors during training and service. They might laugh now when recalling their experiences, using humour as a way to cope with difficult memories, but if you listen carefully, you can often hear the pain behind that laughter.

The psychological impact of military service, particularly combat deployment, can last for decades after service ends. Many veterans struggle with post-traumatic stress, survivor's guilt, difficulties adjusting to civilian life, and challenges maintaining relationships after experiencing the intensity and moral complexity of warfare.

Sometimes I watch videos of military families losing loved ones or welcoming them home after long deployments overseas. Those surprise reunion videos are incredibly emotional, filled with joy, relief, and sometimes unspoken grief for what has been lost during the separation. Behind those beautiful moments of reunion lie months or years of constant fear, uncertainty, and sacrifice by everyone involved.

Families left behind live in a state of chronic anxiety, wondering each day whether their loved one will return safely from war zones where civilians, children, and entire communities suffer from conflicts they did not create. The psychological burden on military families extends far beyond the service member to include spouses, children, parents, and communities that must cope with absence, uncertainty, and loss.

I cannot imagine what that experience is like, having never lived it myself. However, I've heard stories from people who served in various conflicts, and some of those accounts have stayed with me for years. My grandfather shared some tales from his military service—some were amusing anecdotes about camaraderie and adventures, but others were truly horrifying accounts of violence, loss, and moral compromise that war demands.

The experiences they endured and the choices they were forced to make in extreme circumstances are not for us to judge from our comfortable distance. Rather, our role is to listen with respect and compassion, and to understand that warfare represents one of humanity's most complex and tragic realities.

Many of these service members aren't thinking primarily of themselves when they deploy—they're focused on protecting innocent lives, defending their communities, or serving principles they believe are worth the risk. This selfless motivation makes their sacrifice even more poignant: to wake up each day wondering if you'll see your family again, or to return home with physical or emotional scars that will never fully heal, all in service of others.

Today, multiple regions of the world remain engulfed in active conflicts that cause tremendous suffering for both military personnel and civilian populations. These wars are devastating in their scope and complexity, involving not just professional soldiers but also affecting countless innocent people who become refugees, lose family members, or live under constant threat of violence.

We continue asking ourselves: When will these conflicts end? When will we finally achieve a world that is genuinely peaceful and secure for all people? How do we balance the need to defend against aggression with the moral imperative to seek nonviolent solutions to international disputes?

These questions become even more urgent when we consider that children continue being born into a world full of uncertainty, conflict, and violence. How do we raise them with hope and optimism while being honest about the serious challenges humanity faces? How do we teach them to value peace while preparing them for a world where conflict remains a persistent reality?

Perhaps this is where true courage lives—not just in the willingness to fight when necessary, but in the commitment to choose peace whenever possible, to continue loving and hoping despite evidence of human capacity for violence, and to work toward solutions that address the root causes of conflict rather than just managing their symptoms.

The courage shown by those who serve in military conflicts deserves our recognition and respect, but so does the courage required to pursue diplomatic solutions, to choose compassion over vengeance, and to work toward systems that make warfare less necessary and less likely.

This reflection is dedicated to all the men and women, past and present, who have served their countries with courage, integrity, and commitment to protecting others. To those who never returned home, to those who came back forever changed by their experiences, and to the families who carry the quiet weight of their absence and sacrifice, this recognition is offered with deep gratitude and respect.

May their stories be remembered honestly, their sacrifices be honoured meaningfully, and their humanity be recognized fully. As G.K. Chesterton wrote, "The true soldier fights not because he hates what is in front of him, but because he loves what is behind him." This love—for family, community, and principles worth defending—represents the highest motivation for service and the deepest reason to work toward a world where such sacrifice becomes less necessary.

Chapter 16: Cultural Observations and Celebrations

Throughout the years, we mark time through holidays, traditions, and seasonal celebrations that connect us to cultural heritage, spiritual beliefs, and shared human experiences. This chapter explores how these observances reveal deeper truths about belief, community, and what we choose to value. From ancient superstitions to modern holiday pressures, from solstice gatherings to New Year reflections, these cultural moments offer opportunities for both connection and critical examination of the traditions we inherit and pass along.

Superstitions Reflection

Inherited beliefs shape our daily choices in ways we rarely examine. The superstitions passed through generations often reveal more about human psychology and our need to find patterns in uncertainty than about any supernatural forces at work.

Superstitions stem from ancient beliefs, cultural traditions, and human attempts to explain the unknown. Many originated as ways to avoid bad luck or attract good fortune, often based on religious or mystical ideas that provided comfort in uncertain times.

Ancient religious beliefs form the foundation of many superstitions. The belief that breaking a mirror brings seven years of bad luck may have originated from ancient Roman ideas about reflections being connected to the soul. Before science could explain natural phenomena, people created superstitions to make sense of events like storms, disease, or accidents that seemed random and threatening.

Cultural traditions pass these beliefs down through generations until they become deeply ingrained. In many Western countries, Friday the 13th is considered unlucky, while in East Asian cultures, the number 4 is associated with death because it sounds similar to the word for death in several languages.

Humans naturally look for patterns, even when none exist. If someone wears a particular item and has a good day, they might attribute their fortune to that object, creating a personal superstition. Many superstitions originate from folktales meant to teach lessons or warn people about dangers. Black cats were linked to witches in medieval Europe, leading to the persistent belief that they bring bad luck.

Cats have been central to superstitions for centuries, with beliefs varying dramatically by culture. The most well-known superstition claims that a black cat crossing your path brings bad luck, but this isn't universally true.

In medieval Europe, black cats were associated with witchcraft and the devil. Many believed witches could transform into black cats, so encountering one was seen as a bad omen. During the Salem Witch Trials in 1692, black cats were considered witches' familiars, reinforcing their connection to evil. Even today, some people avoid black cats, especially around Halloween.

However, in ancient Egypt, cats, especially black ones, were considered sacred protectors. Killing a cat, even accidentally, was punishable by death. In Japan, black cats are believed to bring good fortune and love. In Scotland, if a black cat appears at your doorstep, it signifies prosperity. Sailors often kept black cats on ships, believing they brought good luck and protected crews from storms, while fishermen's wives kept black cats at home, hoping to safeguard their husbands at sea.

Despite many people no longer believing in these superstitions, black cats still face stigma. Animal shelters report that black cats are adopted less frequently than others, partly due to these old beliefs.

I recall an experience in England when someone told me about a superstition involving magpies. The belief was that seeing one magpie signified sorrow, two meant joy, and so on. They even said you had to salute the birds. Initially, I found myself copying this behaviour, but as I worked as a therapist, discussing old and new beliefs with clients, I began to reflect more deeply on superstition and the concept of luck.

How often have you heard someone say, "You are a lucky person"? In my opinion, we create our own luck through preparation, effort, and making good choices. I once had a patient who believed some people were simply lucky. We explored this idea, and I asked: If you study every section of a book, can you answer all the questions? Of course. But if you study only part of the book, your success becomes a gamble.

Similarly, a doctor should not rely on luck but on comprehensive knowledge of the human body. Would you feel secure seeing a doctor who relied on luck rather than expertise? What about winning the lottery? Is it luck, or did the winner buy more tickets, increasing their chances?

Some believe placing shoes on a table will lead to arguments, financial trouble, or general misfortune. Even if you're not superstitious, keeping shoes off the table is probably wise for hygiene reasons.

Ultimately, it's essential to question and reflect on our habits and cultural beliefs. I hope this information helps someone recognise superstition's role in their life and empowers them to form their own beliefs based on reason rather than inherited fear.

Easter 2025

Easter has both spiritual roots and seasonal associations, blending ancient traditions with Christian beliefs.

Easter is Christianity's most important celebration, commemorating the resurrection of Jesus Christ from the dead as described in the New Testament. It follows Good Friday, which marks Jesus' crucifixion, and culminates on Easter Sunday, celebrating His resurrection. The resurrection symbolises hope, renewal, and eternal life.

Long before Christianity, many cultures held spring festivals celebrating rebirth, fertility, and the return of life after winter. One key influence comes from Eostre or Ostara, a Germanic pagan goddess of spring and fertility. Her festival was celebrated around the spring equinox, and the name Easter is believed to have originated from her, particularly in English and German-speaking countries.

Modern symbols carry both ancient and Christian meanings. Eggs are ancient symbols of fertility and new life, but in Christianity, they also represent the empty tomb of Jesus. Bunnies and rabbits symbolise fertility and abundance. Lambs represent Jesus as "the Lamb of God." Flowers like lilies represent purity and rebirth.

The reality is that Easter was once a deeply religious occasion, but over time it has become more commercial. Today, for many, it's about sharing meals, giving chocolate eggs, or taking holidays. I'm not here to judge anyone—life changes and so do traditions. But it's interesting to notice how Easter has, in some ways, become similar to Christmas: a celebration focused on doing more, giving more, and eating better.

For some, Easter is also a time for redemption. Many turn to church, hoping to be forgiven for mistakes made during the year. I remember going to church every Sunday, listening to the priest say, "Pray and ask for forgiveness." I would find myself repeating the same behaviours week after week, thinking that as long as I confessed, I'd be forgiven.

This isn't criticism—just observation. What if, instead of only seeking forgiveness, we also looked inward and asked: "What do I want to change about how I live?" We are all imperfect in some way. But maybe Easter can be more than just a reset button—it could be a moment to ask: "What kind of life do I want to live going forward?"

I remember asking a priest once, "If I change my path at the end of my life, can I still go to heaven?" His answer was: "Yes, of course. God forgives all of us."

What does Easter mean to you—personally or spiritually? Whether it's a time for rest, reflection, or simply reconnecting with what matters most, I wish you a peaceful Easter.

April Fools' Day

Cultural traditions around humour reveal how differently societies mark time and create shared experiences. The varying dates for fool's days across countries highlight our need for collective release through laughter, even as these traditions sometimes expose our vulnerabilities to deception.

However, some friends in Spain got confused and started texting me about moving to Austria. I'm sorry for the confusion! It's funny how different countries have different days for everything—in Spain, April Fools' is celebrated on December 28th. Someone told me that in their country, it's celebrated in August! Can you imagine the mix-ups? It's fascinating how traditions vary.

Anyway, I hope this gave someone a good laugh. But just to clarify—if I were to move anywhere, it would definitely be to my beautiful Gran Canaria. I'll still be in England with my children, though. I love both places, but as I get older, I'm starting to think about which place suits me best.

April Fools' Day is celebrated with humour and fun, where people engage in light-hearted pranks and jokes. While the exact origins are unclear, there are several theories.

One popular explanation links the day to the switch from the Julian calendar to the Gregorian calendar in the 16th century. The new year was originally celebrated around April 1st in the Julian calendar, but when the Gregorian calendar was adopted, the new year moved to January 1st. Those who continued celebrating the new year on April 1st were called "April fools," and others would play pranks on them to mock their "old-fashioned" ways.

Some historians believe April Fools' Day could connect to the ancient Roman festival of Hilaria, which took place at the end of March. During Hilaria, people would dress in disguises and have fun together, which may have been a precursor to the playful spirit of April Fools' Day.

In France, the tradition of playing tricks dates back to the 16th century. One prank involved putting fish on people's backs, and this is still popular in France today, where it's called "Poisson d'Avril" (April Fish).

While the true origin may be uncertain, it has become a day for harmless pranks, jokes, and laughter. The essence is to have fun, not take things too seriously, and enjoy good humour.

I had a lot of fun today, especially seeing people's reactions and comments. Some fell for it, while others didn't, but it was great for a good laugh. Remember, doing something fun is fantastic for your mental health.

Stonehenge

Sleep eluded me the night before the Winter Solstice, anticipation building for an experience I had never allowed myself. When thousands gather to witness sunrise at ancient sites, they're participating in something that transcends individual belief—a collective acknowledgement of cycles, renewal, and our place in something larger than ourselves.

One of the most amazing aspects was the chance to go inside and touch the ancient stones. Words can hardly describe the experience. The atmosphere was electric—people were buzzing with excitement, some making noise and laughing, others deeply immersed in rituals. A group nearby seemed to be exercising, moving up and down in what looked like meditative practice. It was fascinating to see so many individuals, all dressed differently, expressing their beliefs and traditions in unique ways.

Around 15,000 people came together for this event. Stonehenge, the world's most famous Neolithic monument, serves as a stunning backdrop to mark the arrival of astronomical winter in the Northern Hemisphere.

For me, this felt like Christmas—a celebration filled with joy and connection. Despite freezing temperatures, I had an incredible time. I met so many people, exchanged phone numbers, and shared social media details. This was, without doubt, the best day I've had in Salisbury.

If you ever get the chance, you absolutely must experience this. Another item checked off my bucket list! There's something magical about spontaneous adventures—they often turn out to be the most memorable.

I felt so alive, and it was heartwarming to see so many people genuinely happy and engaged. Stonehenge is breathtaking, and the surrounding landscape is equally mesmerising. On days like this, it's easy to strike up conversations and connect with others.

As a bonus, entry was free, and you could even go inside to hug and touch the stones. This was truly an unforgettable day.

Trust Yourself This Christmas

You've faced countless challenges in your life, and many of them felt insurmountable at the time. Yet here you are, stronger and wiser. Trust in your ability to overcome whatever comes your way. You've survived before, and you'll survive again.

Think about those moments when you thought you couldn't handle a breakup, a strained friendship, family struggles, work pressures, or financial troubles. Despite the doubt and fear, you made it through. Those mornings when you woke up wondering how you'd afford a Christmas gift or provide your children with a little joy, you found a way. And even if it wasn't perfect, it was enough.

I understand the frustration you might be feeling. The pressure to please everyone, to meet expectations, to provide the best gifts, and to maintain a happy exterior can be overwhelming. And in the middle of it all, you might wonder: Who is taking care of me? Who is helping me handle my emotions and struggles?

I remember my own childhood—the nights before Christmas when I saw my mother feeling low because she couldn't afford fancy presents. Instead, she would sew clothes and knit jumpers to make sure we had something special to open. As a child, I didn't fully grasp the weight of her efforts. But as an adult, I look back with immense gratitude and admiration. Her creativity and love were the true gifts.

If you could change anything this Christmas, what would it be? Would you follow the crowd, or would you choose your own path? Remember, children often cherish the games you play with them, the hugs you give, and the memories you create far more than any expensive gift. Sure, material luxuries would be nice, but what truly stays with us are the simple joys—like the aroma of a home-cooked meal or the laughter shared around the table.

This year, trust in yourself and plan a Christmas filled with love and fun, not stress and expense. One year, I encouraged my children to pack small gifts and deliver them to people who had little. The gratitude and joy we witnessed were unforgettable. Little acts of kindness can transform lives, including your own.

Each year, the pressure seems to grow. By January, many families are struggling to pay bills, and tensions arise as couples face the financial aftermath of overspending. These challenges often strain relationships to the breaking point. So, pause and reflect: Do I need to keep up with others? Or can I create a Christmas that's meaningful and true to me and my family?

Your children and loved ones will remember the moments of connection—not the price tags on the gifts. And if someone is in your life only for the presents, perhaps it's time to reconsider their place in your heart. Think back to your favourite Christmas memories. Chances are, they're about laughter, love, and togetherness, not things.

Don't stress. Trust yourself. It's not about how many gifts you buy; it's about what you do with the people you love. Remember, you are enough, and what you do matters.

Happy New Year 2025!

A film about mean girls recently sparked deep reflection about the messages we internalise and pass on to others. The characters' behaviour patterns revealed truths about human nature that extend far beyond teenage dynamics, reminding me why writing serves as both personal therapy and a bridge to understanding others.

I've mentioned before that I lost both of my parents. As the year ends, many of you might be deciding how to celebrate and with whom. Wherever you are tonight, I hope you have the best evening and celebrate fully. Remember, not everyone made it this far. Life is precious, yet we often take it for granted, forgetting how fleeting time truly is.

For some, this evening will bring thoughts of loved ones who are no longer with us. Others might be spending these moments in hospitals, saying goodbye to someone they love. Meanwhile, some will be rejoicing—celebrating engagements, welcoming new babies, or cherishing the year's end with loved ones. Each of us will experience this evening differently, and it will hold unique meaning for everyone.

For some, this time might mark the end of a relationship, bringing feelings of despair or hopelessness. But let me remind you: life isn't over. If you're in a relationship that isn't working, staying for the wrong reasons will only hold you back. Wherever you are tonight, be kind to yourself and those around you.

Someone once told me, when you lose someone, you don't cry for them; you cry for yourself because you know you'll never see that person again. While our loved ones now rest free from struggle, we are left to process the pain. Don't avoid it—it's part of healing.

Two of my favourite songs are "Imagine" by John Lennon and "Time" by The Alan Parsons Project. Both have beautiful, meaningful lyrics. "Time" reminds us that life flows like a river, fast and unstoppable. "Imagine" envisions a world without hate, hunger, jealousy, or envy. My hope is to leave behind a legacy that inspires and supports others, even after I'm gone.

On a happier note, let's welcome the new year with positivity. What do you want to achieve in 2025? Set realistic and kind goals for yourself. Don't pressure yourself to overhaul everything on January 1st. Change takes time, and small, consistent steps can lead to big transformations. Be patient and allow yourself space to prepare for change.

Avoid setting extreme resolutions like losing excessive weight quickly or running a marathon overnight. Instead, focus on achievable goals, taking one step at a time. Be kind to yourself, and remember, progress is more important than perfection.

During 2024, I met many wonderful people, but I also encountered some relationships I need to let go of. One important lesson I've learned is that it's essential to walk away from things that hurt you. Holding onto something painful is like clutching a needle—why would you keep it? It hurts because you expected love or positivity from those people or situations, but after evaluating the relationship and observing their actions, it becomes clear that letting go is the best decision.

Perhaps this is something you might consider this year: Who brings you peace, and who takes it away? Who gives you their time, and who uses you? Watch, listen, and make the right choice. Even if you miss that person, believe me, in the long run, you'll realise you made the right decision. Eventually, you'll find the people who truly provide what you need.

Finally, whatever decisions you make for the new year, prioritise yourself. Remember, you are worthy, beautiful inside and out, and most importantly, believe in yourself.

Reflection on the New Year

A simple observation about love's true nature cuts through the elaborate stories we tell ourselves about relationships. When someone genuinely cares, their actions align with their words consistently, without excuses or explanations needed.

Let's be honest: if someone doesn't contact you, it's because they're not into you. It frustrates me when people say, "I'm too busy to talk." Trust me—if someone loves you and wants to reach out, they will make the effort. Don't let anyone use or mistreat you. Life is too short to waste another year of your precious time.

Life is valuable, and so are you. It's important to ask yourself: how much do you need to see or hear before you start valuing yourself? If someone isn't reaching out, it's not because they're too busy—it's because they don't feel the connection. When someone genuinely cares, they'll make the effort. If they don't, it's better to understand that now than to let them drain your time and energy.

The key question is: do you love yourself enough to know the difference? I've learned to set limits, and I won't allow someone to take more from me than I'm willing to give. Remember, sometimes it's not about you. Think of it like applying for a job—if you don't get a call back, it's not personal. It just means the organization had many candidates, and this wasn't your opportunity. But that doesn't mean you stop applying.

The same applies to love. You might not be the right fit for one person, but to someone else, you could be the most incredible person in the world. Rejection doesn't define you; it's a learning experience. I tell my patients all the time: love yourself first, and the right person will find you. After loving yourself, you'll understand that real love is about action. Love is when the other person takes time to contact you, cherishes you, and genuinely wants to spend time with you. There are no excuses—love is clear and unmistakable, and you don't need anyone to convince you otherwise.

When someone truly loves you, they'll go out of their way to make you feel special. They'll open the car door for you, take you to exciting places, and make you feel like their presence with you is their greatest joy. They'll want to hear your voice, to be near you, and time will never be an obstacle.

Yes, this is love. If you're experiencing anything less, it's a sign to focus on yourself, to grow, and to understand your worth. When you work on yourself and fully embrace your value, you'll recognise what real love looks and feels like.

I apologise if this sounds cynical, but if I were to call and say I have money to give you, I bet they would get back to you immediately. Just be kind to yourself and move on. Life is too short.

With Gratitude, Love and Care.

Chapter 17: Life Philosophy and Final Thoughts

As we reach the conclusion of this journey together, it feels important to examine some of the fundamental questions about how we relate to ourselves and others. This final chapter explores the delicate balance between necessary discernment and harmful judgment, the profound awakening that comes when we finally prioritize our own well-being, and the truth that genuine connection is built on authenticity rather than appearance. These reflections represent not just observations about human behaviour, but invitations to live more consciously and courageously.

Judging Others and Judging Yourself

Judging others means forming opinions or conclusions about them, often based on their actions, appearance, choices, or beliefs. Judgment can be positive, negative, or neutral. Sometimes it is necessary—such as when assessing someone's trustworthiness or safety—but it can also be unfair when based on assumptions, stereotypes, or incomplete information.

There is a crucial difference between discernment, which involves making thoughtful evaluations based on evidence and experience, and criticism, which often involves condemning or looking down on others from a position of assumed superiority. Healthy judgment helps us make better decisions about relationships and situations, while harmful judgment can lead to misunderstanding, division, and genuine harm to others.

I often hear people say, "I don't like to judge," and I completely understand this sentiment. No one enjoys being judged, especially when that judgment feels unfair or based on limited information. However, as I've learned through years of therapeutic work, judgment can be valuable as long as it is not used to destroy someone's character, identity, behaviour, or way of thinking.

Many people have suffered deeply—or even ended their lives—because of the way others have judged them. Some are judged simply because they think differently, behave differently, or are more open and honest than what society considers acceptable. This kind of destructive judgment often says more about the insecurities and limitations of the person making the judgment than about the person being judged.

If we never exercise any judgment at all, we may unknowingly welcome people into our lives who have harmful intentions or who are incompatible with our values and well-being. The key is understanding how to use discernment constructively rather than destructively.

Envy, jealousy, and a lack of courage to express our own authentic thoughts often lead people to judge others unfairly. Rather than examining their own lives and choices, they focus on criticising others as a way to avoid looking inward. I do not seek to judge anyone harshly, but rather to understand human behaviour and why people act the way they do.

We often speak about freedom of speech and expression, but when someone is genuinely different from us—when they think independently, make unconventional choices, or live authentically—they are quickly labelled as weird, strange, or problematic. This reveals our own discomfort with differences rather than any real problem with the other person.

Judging others is a natural human tendency that often happens instinctively. Our brains are wired to quickly assess people to determine if they are a threat or an ally—this survival mechanism leads to snap judgments that may have been useful in more dangerous times but can be counterproductive in modern relationships.

Society, culture, and upbringing shape our beliefs about what is "right" or "wrong," influencing how we judge others often without conscious awareness. People sometimes judge others to feel better about themselves, especially when they are feeling insecure about their own choices or circumstances.

When people do not fully understand someone's situation, choices, or lifestyle, they might judge rather than ask questions or try to empathize. Some judge others to feel superior or reinforce their own self-worth, using criticism as a way to elevate themselves rather than doing the inner work required for genuine self-improvement.

Humans naturally compare themselves to others, which can lead to judgment, especially in competitive environments like work, school, or social media. People often judge what they do not understand or what feels different from their own beliefs or experiences, particularly when those differences challenge their worldview.

While judging others is natural, it can also be limiting and unfair both to others and to ourselves. Practising empathy and open-mindedness helps us avoid unnecessary judgment while still maintaining healthy boundaries and discernment.

There is a huge stigma around judgment and what we should or should not say about others. Just because I work as a therapist does not mean my life is perfect or that I have all the answers. I ask you—do you truly know yourself? Do you know what you are capable of experiencing in life? These are questions worth considering deeply.

We are often taught to keep our struggles hidden because of what others might think. But why should this be necessary? Even doctors, nurses, lawyers, and public figures have personal struggles. No one's life is perfect, yet we are conditioned to present ourselves as flawless while hiding our real selves and authentic experiences.

As a therapist with extensive experience, I have worked continuously on understanding myself. When I share my experiences, it is not for sympathy but to help others see that behind my professional role, I am a human being with my own challenges and growth areas. I believe in being open because we all struggle at times, and pretending otherwise helps no one.

Years ago, I told some judgmental friends, "When you start paying my bills and handling my responsibilities, then you can have an opinion about my life. Until then, focus on your own self-growth." People often judge without realising the impact their words can have on others. If someone wants to express themselves authentically, let them. You do not have to listen or engage if you disagree, but harsh judgment can deeply hurt others and create unnecessary division.

Before you judge someone, take a moment to consider their perspective and circumstances. Instead of talking negatively about them, consider ways to be supportive or at least neutral. If we practised this more consistently, we might create a much better world for everyone.

Many mental health issues arise because we have been taught to stay silent, keep everything inside, and always appear strong and successful. I'm not suggesting we should share every detail of our personal lives with everyone, but we should feel free to be ourselves and express our authentic experiences when appropriate.

Many therapists and professionals prefer not to share their personal struggles, and I respect that choice. However, we are all different in our approaches to helping others. Even the most intelligent and well-educated individuals who have shared their challenges honestly often face criticism and condemnation. Is this fair? Should anyone's life have to be perfect in order to deserve basic respect and understanding?

Let's choose understanding over criticism, empathy over judgment, and kindness over condemnation whenever possible.

When You Finally Wake Up

They say the most important relationship you'll ever have is the one you have with yourself. You've heard this before—from self-help resources, wise friends, people who seem to have figured out how to live authentically. But hearing it and truly living it are two very different experiences.

Because what do most of us do instead? We give. We give and give and give. Our time, our energy, our care, our hearts. We show up consistently for others, hoping that if we demonstrate enough loyalty, enough support, enough love, they'll stay. They'll value us. They'll see us as we truly are.

But one morning—and it always comes like this—you wake up. And you realise they're not there. The friends, the family members, the colleagues, the romantic partners you gave so much of yourself to. Gone, silent, nowhere to be found when it matters most.

And you start to ask: How did I get here? How many years did I spend waiting for someone else to change? Hoping for situations to improve? Making myself smaller just to avoid being alone?

You think back to all the times you swallowed your truth, blurred your boundaries, smiled when it hurt inside, said "I'm fine" when you were breaking. All because you were afraid that without these people, you'd have no one. That if you said what you really felt, you'd be abandoned.

But here's what experience teaches: Being alone is not the worst thing that can happen to you. Being used is worse. Being lied to consistently is worse. Being surrounded by people who only care when it's convenient for them—that is the loneliest place of all.

I've observed people who say they love you, but their actions communicate something entirely different. They're curious about your struggles, not because they genuinely care about your well-being, but because it gives them something to discuss or makes them feel better about their own lives.

That's not love. That's not friendship. That's performance based on convenience rather than authentic connection.

So I stopped waiting. I stopped hoping that people would become what I needed them to be. And I started becoming that source of support and understanding for myself.

Because eventually you realise: You didn't lose them—they lost you. They lost your loyalty, your kindness, your energy, and your consistent presence in their lives.

Moving forward, I choose who gets access to my time and emotional energy. I set the terms of engagement. I protect my peace as the precious resource it is.

Real love doesn't feel like a game where you're constantly guessing about someone's intentions. Real friends don't disappear when life becomes challenging or when you actually need support.

So let me ask you: Do you choose your relationships consciously, or do you simply accept whoever shows interest in you? Are you receiving the respect and care you deserve, or are you just accepting what feels familiar, even when it's inadequate?

If you could go back and make different choices about how you invest your time and energy, what would you do differently? And more importantly, what's stopping you from making those changes now?

Because when you finally wake up to your own worth, you realise that the most important relationship—the only one you can count on to last your entire lifetime—is the one you have with yourself.

This awakening doesn't mean becoming selfish or uncaring toward others. It means recognising that you cannot pour from an empty cup, and that taking care of your own needs enables you to be truly present and helpful to others when appropriate.

It means understanding that some people are in your life for a season, some for a reason, and very few for a lifetime. Learning to distinguish between these categories can save you years of disappointment and wasted energy.

When you finally wake up, you stop making excuses for people who consistently show you through their actions that you're not a priority. You stop believing that if you just try harder, give more, or change yourself somehow, they'll suddenly become the person you need them to be.

You start investing in relationships that are reciprocal, where both people contribute to each other's well-being and growth. You seek connections based on mutual respect, shared values, and genuine care rather than convenience or habit.

This wake-up call often comes after loss, betrayal, or simply the accumulation of many small disappointments. While painful, it's also liberating. It's the beginning of living consciously rather than reactively.

The Truth About Love and Appearance

I watched "The Mirror Has Two Faces" recently, a film starring Barbra Streisand that offers profound insights about love, self-worth, and the difference between attraction based on appearance versus genuine connection. If you haven't seen it, I highly recommend it, especially if you struggle with self-esteem or believe you need to be physically attractive for someone to love you authentically.

This film reminded me that everyone has the capacity to experience real love, regardless of what they've been through—divorce, relationship endings, periods of low self-esteem, or simply not feeling satisfied with their physical appearance. The story powerfully demonstrates that love often begins with friendship and intellectual connection, and that lasting relationships are built on understanding rather than physical attraction alone.

Many people, particularly women, exhaust themselves trying to be liked and loved through their appearance. No matter how much money they spend on their bodies, cosmetic procedures, or beauty routines, it often still feels insufficient. When you look in the mirror and still feel unloved or unattractive despite all these efforts, it can be deeply discouraging.

It's painful to observe how many people spend hours in gyms, constantly checking mirrors, seeking validation from others about their appearance. It's equally disheartening when someone is spending time with their partner but remains constantly distracted—checking out other people or engaging with others on their phone instead of being present.

If you find yourself doing this in a relationship, understand that it's deeply disrespectful to your partner. Jealousy often stems not from inherent character flaws but from experiencing lack of respect and consideration in relationships. If you feel the need to look elsewhere for attention or validation, do that on your own time, not in front of someone you claim to care about.

To both men and women: if you want your partner to look like a celebrity or model, be prepared to invest the time, money, and effort that maintaining such an appearance requires. But more importantly, ask yourself whether you're valuing the person for who they are as a complete human being, or primarily for how they look.

What I loved about the film was that the male character wasn't seeking someone obsessed with beauty, hair, or physical perfection. He wanted someone he could talk to, someone with whom he could feel comfortable and intellectually connected. This reflects what many people actually want in long-term relationships, despite what popular culture might suggest.

I think many people, especially women, would agree that we want to be loved for who we are rather than how we look. Constantly trying to achieve and maintain physical perfection is exhausting and ultimately unsustainable as we age and our bodies naturally change.

The beautiful irony in the film is that when the female character transformed her appearance dramatically, it turned out that he had fallen in love with who she was before the transformation, when she was simply being herself. Their emotional connection and comfort with each other represented the foundation of genuine attraction.

Sexual intimacy is important in relationships for several reasons, but it's not the most important element—it's one component of a much larger picture. Sex can deepen intimacy and emotional bonding between partners through physical affection that communicates connection beyond words. A healthy sexual relationship often involves communication, trust, and vulnerability that strengthens mutual understanding.

Physical intimacy releases endorphins and hormones like oxytocin that reduce stress and increase feelings of happiness and bonding. Feeling desired by your partner is powerful—sexual intimacy can communicate "I choose you" and reinforce that attraction and connection remain alive.

Sometimes, lack of sexual connection can indicate that something else isn't working emotionally or relationally. It's not always about physical desire—it could reflect unresolved conflict, stress, or emotional distance that needs attention.

However, sexual compatibility alone doesn't create strong or lasting relationships. Trust, respect, communication, emotional support, and shared values are equally important, if not more so. Some couples have infrequent physical intimacy but maintain deeply loving, fulfilling relationships, while others with active sex lives may feel emotionally disconnected.

The film beautifully illustrates how the male character sought someone who wasn't focused on superficial appearances but rather someone with whom he could genuinely communicate and connect. He wanted authentic relationship, not a perfect image.

Physical intimacy can be an important part of partnership when both people are satisfied with the level and type of connection they share. But what's even more crucial is how well you understand each other, how deeply you connect intellectually and emotionally, and whether you genuinely enjoy spending time together in various circumstances.

That foundation of friendship, respect, and genuine compatibility is what makes relationships last through the inevitable changes that life brings to all of us.

Final Thoughts

As I bring this collection of reflections to a close, I find myself thinking about what I hope readers will take from these pages. This book began as a way to process my own grief and healing after losing my father, but it became something larger—a exploration of what it means to live authentically, love genuinely, and find meaning in both our struggles and our growth.

Through these chapters, we've examined the complexities of relationships, the importance of mental health, the challenges of ageing and loss, and the ongoing work of understanding ourselves and others. We've looked at how childhood experiences shape our adult patterns, how communication can heal or harm, and how setting boundaries becomes an act of self-respect rather than selfishness.

Perhaps most importantly, we've explored the truth that healing is not a destination but a continuous process. There is no perfect version of ourselves waiting at the end of enough therapy, enough self-reflection, or enough good choices. Instead, there is the ongoing practice of showing up honestly to our own lives, making course corrections when needed, and treating ourselves and others with the compassion that makes growth possible.

I've shared my own mistakes and insights not because I believe I have all the answers, but because I've learned that our struggles are often more universal than we imagine. The shame that keeps us isolated frequently dissolves when we realise that others have walked similar paths and found ways forward.

The work of living consciously—of building healthy relationships, processing loss, confronting our own patterns, and creating meaning from our experiences—is perhaps the most important work any of us can do. It affects not only our own well-being but ripples out to touch everyone we encounter.

As you close this book, I encourage you to be gentle with yourself as you continue your own journey. Change takes time. Healing happens in layers. Growth requires both courage and patience. You don't have to transform everything at once, but you do have the power to take the next small step toward the life and relationships you truly want.

Remember that seeking help is a sign of strength, not weakness. Whether through therapy, trusted friends, spiritual practices, or simple self-reflection, continuing to grow and understand yourself is one of the most valuable investments you can make.

Most of all, remember that you deserve relationships built on mutual respect, authentic communication, and genuine care. You deserve to feel safe, valued, and free to be yourself. If your current circumstances don't reflect these truths, know that change is possible, even when it feels impossible.

Thank you for taking this journey with me. May you find the courage to live authentically, the wisdom to choose relationships that nourish rather than drain you, and the peace that comes from accepting yourself as worthy of love exactly as you are.

The work continues, one day at a time, one choice at a time, one relationship at a time. And that work—the work of becoming more fully yourself while remaining open to growth and connection—is perhaps the most meaningful work any of us can do.

With Gratitude, Love and Care.

www.ingramcontent.com/pod-product-compliance
Lightning Source LLC
Chambersburg PA
CBHW061214070526
44584CB00029B/3834